Self-Study Research Methodologies for Teacher Educators

MW00783610

Professional Learning
Volume 7

Series editor:

J. John Loughran, *Monash University, Clayton, Australia*

Editorial board:

Renee Clift - *University of Illinois, Urbana-Champaign, USA*

Ruth Kane - *Massey University, New Zealand*

Mieke Lunenberg - *Free University, The Netherlands*

Anthony Clarke - *University of British Columbia, Canada*

Donald Freeman - *School for International Training, Vermont, USA*

MOK, Mo Ching Magdalena - *Hong Kong Institute of Education, Hong Kong*

Max van Manen - *University of Alberta, Canada*

Rationale:

This series purposely sets out to illustrate a range of approaches to Professional Learning and to highlight the importance of teachers and teacher educators taking the lead in reframing and responding to their practice, not just to illuminate the field but to foster genuine educational change.

Audience:

The series will be of interest to teachers, teacher educators and others in fields of professional practice as the context and practice of the pedagogue is the prime focus of such work. Professional Learning is closely aligned to much of the ideas associated with reflective practice, action research, practitioner inquiry and teacher as researcher.

Self-Study Research Methodologies for Teacher Educators

Cynthia A. Lassonde
State University of New York College at Oneonta

Sally Galman
University of Massachusetts at Amherst

Clare Kosnik
Ontario Institute for Studies in Education - University of Toronto

SENSE PUBLISHERS
ROTTERDAM/BOSTON/TAIPEI

A C.I.P. record for this book is available from the Library of Congress.

ISBN 978-90-8790-688-7 (paperback)
ISBN 978-90-8790-689-4 (hardback)
ISBN 978-90-8790-690-0 (e-book)

Published by: Sense Publishers,
P.O. Box 21858, 3001 AW
Rotterdam, The Netherlands
http://www.sensepublishers.com

Printed on acid-free paper

We dedicate this book to the self-study community and all teacher educators seeking to improve their practice through self-study.

Cindy, Sally, and Clare

TABLE OF CONTENTS

SERIES EDITOR'S FOREWORD

The editors have assembled a strong list of authors in order to bring together a fine project through this book *Self-Study Research Methodologies for Teacher Educators*. This book offers a wonderful way of introducing the work of Self-study to the world of Professional Learning. The book offers explicit examples of self-study methodologies by leaders in the field and in so doing, Professional Learning is now given easy and immediate access to interesting and exciting ways of documenting, researching and analysing practice.

As the editors note themselves, the last two decades have "witnessed a dramatic increase in research on teacher education." As this research has grown, so too has the realisation that Professional Learning is a distinct and different way of thinking about learning about teaching and learning from that of more traditional models of Professional Development. The research in teacher education over the last two decades has helped to make clear that simply telling prospective teachers what to do and how to do it, is not the same as creating real and meaningful learning experiences. Hence, it is no surprise that just as teacher education has begun to explicitly respond to this realisation, so too Education systems have begun to recognise the importance of creating opportunities for teachers to learn more about practice in ways that better embrace the essence of the notion of Professional Learning.

Self-study of Teacher Education Practices (S-STEP, Hamilton, 1998) emerged in the early 1990s as teacher educators began to take control of their profession by placing greater emphasis on the knowledge and learning derived from researching their own practice. The allure of self-study has been strong for many teacher educators and so it is only natural that eventually the ideas that created such a strong and now flourishing community would eventually flow over to other fields. This has been recognized by the fact the many members of the S-STEP community now explicitly incorporate teaching (beyond teacher education alone) as signified by the title of the *International Handbook of Teaching and Teacher Education Practices* (Loughran, Hamilton, LaBoskey, & Russell, 2004). Now this book by Lassonde, Galman and Kosnik extends that view by situating the methodologies of self-study within this series of Professional Learning.

One clear and strong aspect of this book is its concern to create new ways of strengthening the field of self-study by further making ways of researching practice open to public scrutiny and debate. However, as the editors make clear, one of their intentions in so doing has grown out of their concern "that the term self-study is being applied to a variety of practices, some of which bear little resemblance to the quality and systematic methodology [that the] S-STEP community values." Therefore, as you read the chapters that so nicely combine to make up this very good book, it is important to recognize that the methodological descriptions are designed to make clear not only what self-study is but also how it might be pursued in a scholarly manner.

This book builds on the work of many in the S-STEP community that have been (and continue to be) concerned to see the field develop in ways that demonstrate rigorous and systematic approaches to examining practice. And, as you will soon discover, it does that very well indeed.

The editors have assembled this book in the hope that it will not only offer insights into a variety of self-study methods but so that it might also help make clear some of the important methodological imperatives associated with conducting a self-study. They have brought together authors who have a great deal to offer those interested in Professional Learning as a consequence of their vast experience as teachers and researchers.

The book is organised in a thoughtful way. It brings together an array of very well regarded authors who outline a diversity of approaches to self-study. The structure works very well for the reader as the ideas and approaches of each chapter are grouped in complementary and informing ways. This book makes very clear how self-study can be characterised, understood and conducted. It is a wonderful addition to this series on Professional Learning as it invites the reader to seriously consider not only the value of researching practice, but also offers concrete, useable ways of doing so in a scholarly manner.

The editors are to be congratulated on a fine project that has been well conceptualised and carefully completed through a text that is easy to access, helpful and informing. I trust you find this to be an engaging and challenging book; it has certainly done that for me.

J. John Loughran
Series Editor

INTRODUCTION

The last two decades have witnessed a dramatic increase in research on teacher education: Ohio Project (Lasely et al., 2006), New York City Pathways Project (Boyd et al., 2006), Teachers for a New Era (http://www.teachersforanewera.org/), Blue Ribbon Commission for Educational Excellence Louisiana (Noell & Burns, 2006), and The National Commission on Excellence in Elementary Teacher Preparation for Reading Instruction (Hoffman et al., 2005). Accompanying this research has been a steady stream of publications on teacher education: *Studying Teacher Education: The Report of the AERA Panel on Research and Teacher Education* (2005) edited by Cochran-Smith and Zeichner, *Preparing Teachers for a Changing World: What Teachers Should Learn and be Able to Do* (2005) edited by Darling-Hammond and Bransford, *Innovations in Preservice Teacher Education: A Social Constructivist Approach* (2006) by Beck and Kosnik, *Developing a Pedagogy of Teacher Education: Understanding Teaching and Learning about Teaching* (2006) by Loughran, and *Current Issues in Teacher Education: History, Perspectives, and Implications* (2008) edited by Lassonde, Michael, and Rivera-Wilson. These texts have greatly contributed to our understanding of the challenges of preparing teachers, provided models of exemplary programs, underscored the need for induction programs, outlined the type of professional development new teachers need, examined the role of teacher educators, and so on.

During this period, a complementary strand of research emerged that further enhanced our understanding of teacher education – self-study research. Historically validated forms of research often do not allow researchers opportunities to closely examine their own work thus limiting its value for improving practice. Many teacher educators believe that studying their own practice is essential. As Samaras and Freese note, "Improving one's practice benefits the larger broader purpose of the advancement of knowledge about teaching and the educational system" (2006, p. 14). From this interest in studying their own work was born the self-study movement. The "official" home of self-study is widely considered to be the Self-Study of Teacher Education Practices (S-STEP) Special Interest Group of the American Educational Research Association. The group has become a flourishing community. Since its "birth" in 1992 there has been a steady increase in membership. The members have been highly active publishing a plethora of texts: *Enacting a Pedagogy of Teacher Education: Values, Relationships and Practices* (2007) edited by Russell and Loughran; *The Missing Links in Teacher Education: Innovative Approaches to Designing Teacher Education Programs* (2005) edited by Hoban; and *Making a Difference in Teacher Education through Self-study: Personal, Professional, and Program Renewal* (2005) edited by Kosnik, Freese, Samaras, and Beck. Discussion of the place of self-study research has extended beyond S-STEP. For example, key articles have been published in the *Journal of Teacher Education* (Loughran, 2007; Zeichner, 2007) and the establishment of local communities of self-study practitioners (e.g. Canadian Society for Studies in

Education, Self-Study of Teacher Education Practices, Special Interest Group). These varied activities have strengthened and extended the scholarship of self-study.

With any organization, movement, or community, there is an evolution. In the early days of S-STEP there was concern about the place of the individual within the research; this inward focus gave way to a broader range of topics. For example, at the 2008 Castle Conference topics such as the impact on identity when running for local school board (Muchmore, 2008) and the impact of external accreditation reviews on a faculty member (Craig, 2008) arose. From our perspective, the self-study field is maturing and diversifying. The publication of the *International Handbook of Self-study of Teaching and Teacher Education Practices* (2004) brought together many aspects of self-study research into one scholarly text. The publication of the handbook in a way formalized self-study research as an accepted form of research and S-STEP into a recognized community of scholars.

Not wanting to be naïve, we believe that we must be realistic about the field of educational research. Although we are proud that self-study research has become more accepted, we are concerned that the term self-study is being applied to a variety of practices, some of which bear little resemblance to the quality and systematic methodology our S-STEP community values. Each of us has overheard a colleague proudly declare, "Oh, I am doing a self-study" when we know that the work being done is only tangentially related to true self-study research. This use of the term self-study to describe dubious practices concerns us. A more troubling development has been the shift in the rhetoric on research that has elevated research that is "scientifically-based" to the pinnacle (Slavin, 2002). These two trends have influenced the development of the work of the S-STEP members. As a research community, S-STEP could not ignore the push in the United States to pay more attention to methodology. One of the turning points for the S-STEP was a keynote address given by Vicki LaBoskey at the 2004 Castle Conference where she argued that self-study research must be systematic. In her chapter in the *International Handbook of Self-study of Teaching and Teacher Education Practices* (2004) she expands her position saying that for self-study work to be accepted by the education community it needed to be less idiosyncratic and more rigorous.

The members of the self-study community responded to LaBoskey's challenge. For example, the conference proposals for the *International Conference on Self-Study of Teacher Education Practices* (also known as the Castle Conference) are now reviewed more rigorously (e.g., double blind reviews) than previously with great attention to the methodology used. This increased focus on methodology has led to more systematic studies but it has also revealed a gap in the literature on self-study – examination of the various methods that can be used for self-study research. The self-study community has begun to address this gap in the literature. Samaras and Freese recently published *Self-Study of Teaching Practices* (2006). Fitzgerald, Heston, and Tidwell are editing a text, *Research Methods for the Self-Study of Practice* (2009); and Pinnegar and Hamilton (2009) have co-authored the text, *Self-Study of Practice as a Genre of Qualitative Research: Theory,*

Methodology, and Practice. Each of these texts in its own way is expanding the discussion on methodologies for self-study. Yet, we felt there was the need for another text, one that systematically addressed many of the methodologies that could be used for self-study research. Hence, the publication of *Self-Study Research Methodologies for Teacher Educators.*

Self-Study Research Methodologies for Teacher Educators is a comprehensive text that delineates a range of research methodologies. This edited volume, with many chapters written by self-study scholars who are noted in the field for particular methodological and epistemological perspectives, helps fill the gap in the literature on self-study research methods. It provides readers with an opportunity to examine various methodologies that not only helps them deepen their understanding of research but also allows them to select one that best suits their needs. Both new and experienced researchers will find this text valuable.

THE ORGANIZATION OF THIS BOOK

In Part One, the general *Overview,* the reader is introduced to self-study. Chapter One by Samaras and Freese provides an historical perspective on self-study while showing its position in relation to other research paradigms; Craig in Chapter Two considers standards of quality in self-study research; Feldman's views on data analysis and interpretation in self-study research follow in Chapter Three.

Part Two, *Specific Methodologies,* affords the reader a chance to explore detailed accounts of specific methodologies that have been used successfully in self-study research. Chapter Four by Kosnik, Cleovoulou, and Fletcher discusses interviewing; Chapter Five by Russell is on personal-experience methods, such as re-experiencing K-12 teaching; Chapter Six by Paugh and Robinson considers participatory research methods; Chapter Seven by Kitchen and Ciuffetelli Parker presents issues around the formation of critical communities of practice; Chapter Eight by Galman addresses arts-based inquiry; Chapter Nine by Pinnegar and Erickson shows how to embed self-study practices in teacher education credentialing processes; Chapter Ten by Taylor and Coia examines co/autoethnography; and Chapter Eleven by Davey and Ham deals with self-study across sites.

To assist readers, all of the chapters in Part Two are organized in parallel fashion. Each chapter includes
- a description of the methodology with a working definition, basic concepts and distinctive features, and its relevance to self-study in teacher education;
- procedures connected to the methodology, including designs, data collection, and analysis;
- dissemination of findings;
- the standards for quality (i.e., validity, reliability, rigor);
- the analytic strength and limitation of the methodology; plus
- examples of each authors' experiences with the methodology, describing its advantages and challenges.

Each chapter concludes with the authors describing how their practices changed in light of their research. This inclusion of personal experiences is a hallmark of self-study work.

This consistent chapter format, we believe, will guide readers; however, it is not so rigid that the unique flavor of each methodology is lost. Each chapter provides sufficient information for educational researchers to select and use a particular and appropriate method thus allowing them to align their research questions with a particular and appropriate methodology.

In the final section of the book, Part Three, *Moving Forward*, the authors take a step back to reflect upon and consider what these self-study methodologies mean to teacher educators and teacher education. In Chapter Twelve, Lassonde and Strub reflect on the importance of promoting preservice teachers' use of self-study and present their work in this area. Finally, in Chapter Thirteen, the co-editors close with a brief discussion of possible personal and institutional meaning(s) of self-study work in teacher education and list several valuable resources.

Written in an inviting yet scholarly style, *Self-Study Research Methodologies for Teacher Educators* is readily accessible to teacher educators and administrators. Readers with varying levels of knowledge and experience with self-study research will find the book easy to follow and full of practical advice for rigorous application. Teacher educators and administrators at the university level could use the text in numerous ways: to study individual practice, to study work at an institutional level, or as a text in courses. The book will be of use to

- University faculty who are interested in studying their own practice on their own or with a group of colleagues
- University faculty who teach courses in general research methodologies or in self-study research specifically
- University faculty involved in either formal recertification processes (e.g., the National Council for Accreditation of Teacher Education) or in a self-study of their institution (e.g., following graduates to see the effectiveness of their programs)
- Graduate students who want to include a self-study component in their thesis work
- Teachers or groups of teachers who want to study their practice (e.g., ways to improve the effectiveness of their literacy programs)
- School-district personnel who want to study the impact of a curriculum development initiative on their teachers, pupils, or schools.

We consider *Self-Study Research Methodologies for Teacher Educators* a valuable contribution to the field of teacher education. We believe it will strengthen research both on teacher education and teacher education programs. Through self-study it is possible to extend the dialogue around effective, high-quality teacher education to include a wide array of personal and professional experiences, cultures, contexts, and practices. Samaras and Freese note in the first chapter of this text that self-study research is developing, and we believe this text will contribute to its evolution.

Like any new field of research, self-study has gone through growing pains and stages of development marked by a need for a shared understanding and shared language around the field of self-study. Self-study scholars have thought deeply about the nature of self-study, what it involves, and what distinguishes it from other types of research. (p. 5)

REFERENCES

Beck, C., & Kosnik, C. (2006). *Innovations in preservice teacher education: A social constructivist approach.* Albany, NY: SUNY Press.

Boyd, D., Grossman, P., Lankford, J., Loeb, S., & Michelli, N. (2006). Complex by design: Investigating pathways into teaching in New York City Schools. *Journal of Teacher Education, 2*(57), 239–250.

Cochran-Smith, M., & Zeichner, K. (Eds.). (2005). *Studying teacher education: The report of the AERA panel on research and teacher education.* Mahwah, NJ: Lawrence Erlbaum Associates.

Craig, C. (2008). Change, changing, and being changed: A study of self in the throes of multiple accountability demands. In M. L. Heston, D. L. Tidwell, K. K. East, & L. M. Fitzgerald (Eds.), *Pathways to change in teacher education: Dialogue, diversity, and self-study. Proceedings of the seventh international conference on the self-study of teacher education practices, Herstmonceux Castle, East Sussex, England* (pp. 87–90). Cedar Falls, IA: University of Northern Iowa.

Darling-Hammond, L., & Bransford, J. (Eds.). (2005). *Preparing teachers for a changing world: What teachers should learn and be able to do.* San Francisco: Jossey-Bass.

Hoban, G. (Ed.). (2005). *The missing links in teacher education: Innovative approaches to designing teacher education programs.* Dordecht: Kluwer Academic Publishers.

Hoffman, J., Roller, C., Maloch, B., Sailors, M., Duffy, G., & Beretvas, S. N. (2005). Teachers' preparation to teach reading and their experiences and practices in the first three years of teaching. *Elementary School Journal, 105*(3), 1–24.

Kosnik, C., Freese, A., Samaras, A., &. Beck, C. (Eds.). (2006). *Making a difference in teacher education through self-study: Studies of personal, professional, and program renewal.* Dordrecht: Springer Academic Publishers.

LaBoskey, V. (2004). The methodology of self-study and its theoretical underpinnings. In J. Loughran, M. L. Hamilton, V. LaBoskey, & T. Russell (Eds.), *International handbook of self-study of teaching and teacher education practices* (pp. 817–869). Dordrecht: Kluwer.

Lasely, T., Siedentop, D., & Yinger, R. (2006). A systemic approach to enhancing teacher quality: The Ohio model. *Journal of Teacher Education, 57*(1), 13–21.

Lassonde, C., Michaels, R., & Rivera-Wilson, J. (Eds.). (2008). *Current issues in teacher education: History, perspectives, and implications.* Springfield, IL: Charles C. Thomas Publishers.

Loughran, J. (2006). *Developing a pedagogy of teacher education: Understanding teaching and learning about teaching.* London: Routledge.

Loughran, J. (2007). Researching teacher education practices: Responding to the challenges, demands, and expectations of self-study. *Journal of Teacher Education, 58*(1), 12–20.

Loughran, J., Hamilton, M. L., LaBoskey, V., & Russell, T. (Eds.). (2004). *International handbook of self-study of teaching and teacher education practices.* Dordrecht: Kluwer.

Muchmore, J. (2008). Running for the local school board—and finishing last: A story of opposing narratives. In M. L. Heston, D. L. Tidwell, K. K. East, & L. M. Fitzgerald (Eds.), *Pathways to change in teacher education: Dialogue, diversity, and self-study. Proceedings of the seventh international conference on the self-study of teacher education practices, Herstmonceux Castle, East Sussex, England* (pp. 243–247). Cedar Falls, IA: University of Northern Iowa.

Noell, G., & Burns, J. (2006). Value-added assessment of teacher preparation: An illustration of emerging technology. *Journal of Teacher Education, 57*(1), 37–50.

Pinnegar, S., & Hamilton, M. L. (2009). *Self-study of practice as a genre of qualitative research: Theory, methodology, and practice*. Dordrecht, the Netherlands: Springer.

Russell, T., & Loughran, J. (Eds.). *Enacting a pedagogy of teacher education: Values, relationships and practices*. London: Routledge.

Samaras, A., & Freese, A. (2006). *Self-study of teaching practices: A primer*. New York: Peter Lang.

Slavin, R. (2002). Evidence-based education policies: Transforming educational practice and research. *Educational Researcher, 31*(7), 15–21.

Teachers for a New Era. Retrieved from http://www.teachersforanewera.org/

Zeichner, K. (2007). Accumulating knowledge across self-studies in teacher education. *Journal of Teacher Education, 58*(1), 36–46.

PART ONE: OVERVIEW

ANASTASIA P. SAMARAS AND ANNE R. FREESE

1. LOOKING BACK AND LOOKING FORWARD

An Historical Overview of the Self-Study School

The White Rabbit put on his spectacles.
"Where shall I begin, please your Majesty?" he asked.
"Begin at the beginning" the King said, very gravely,
"and go on till you come to the end: then stop."

(Carroll, 1998, p. 105)

As educational researchers and reformers, in our ongoing search for ways to improve teaching and learning, it is important to look backward to take stock of our beginnings, where we have been, what we have accomplished, and what we have learned. This chapter provides a retrospective look at the field of self-study by tracing its roots, including how and when it started, as well as discussing how it has developed and grown into a large field of research. We discuss the nature of self-study, definitions of self-study and its purposes, as well as the role the community of self-study researchers has played in its development. In addition, we offer suggestions for the future of self-study and the possibilities ahead.

ROOTS OF SELF-STUDY

To gain a deeper understanding of the background and development of self-study, it is helpful to trace its roots from its inception to the formal field of study. In the following section we will give a brief overview of how self-study has evolved over time. We begin with a discussion of the key research paradigms that have directly influenced the outgrowth, process, and focus of self-study of teaching. These areas are teacher inquiry, reflective practice, and action research.

Teacher Inquiry

Prior to the late 1980s, teachers' practical and everyday theories of how to improve teaching and learning were not considered particularly important, nor were they considered as areas of research (Cochran-Smith, 1991). Classroom teachers viewed educational research as academic-oriented, something generally conducted by university researchers from various disciplines (Dana & Yendal-Silva, 2003). Teachers primarily saw their responsibility as implementing what researchers told them was valid in their classrooms. They did not think about problematizing their experiences or classroom observations to learn more about their students, their

C. A. Lassonde, S. Galman and C. Kosnik (eds.), Self-Study Research Methodologies
for Teacher Educators, 3–19.

context, and their teaching practices. However, in the late 1980s, teachers began to inquire into and explore their teaching and their students' learning. Questioning one's practice became an integral aspect of teacher research (Duckworth, 1987; Richardson, 1989). Prior to the formalization of self-study research, a number of teacher educators began to question their teaching and conducted systematic research of their practice (LaBoskey, 1994; Russell & Munby, 1992; Zeichner & Liston, 1987).

Reflective Practice

Research in the area of reflection and reflective practice has had a strong influence on self-study. The movement towards developing reflective practitioners led to a body of research that focused on the teacher as researcher of his or her own practice (Cochran-Smith & Lytle, 1993). Researchers found that teachers could examine and problematize their teaching by reflecting on their practice and by becoming reflective practitioners (Schön, 1987; Zeichner & Liston, 1996). Teachers studying their teaching spurred research that used a number of qualitative research approaches. By the late 1980s, university researchers began to use biographical forms of inquiry as well as personal histories, life history approach, and narrative inquiry to better understand their practice (Bullough & Gitlin, 1995; Connelly & Clandinin, 1990). These research approaches provided a foundation for teachers and teacher educators to incorporate similar methods to systematically study their practice. As teachers critically reflect on their practice, they strive to make sense of their teaching and participate consciously and creatively in their growth and development (Zeichner, 1999). Many self-study researchers were influenced by the area of reflective practice, particularly Schön's (1983, 1987) and Dewey's (1933) work in reflection.

Action Research

Action research has also had a strong influence on self-study research and has been referred to as a "useful tool for self-study" because it provides a method to conduct systematic inquiry into one's teaching practices (Feldman, Paugh, & Mills, 2004, p. 970). Introduced by Carr and Kemmis (1986), action research involves a systematic approach to problem solving. Teachers and teacher educators engage in action research (McNiff, 1988; Mills, 2000) to examine their teaching and their students' learning as a basis for making changes.

Although teacher educators had written about, discussed, and promoted the use of reflection and action research in their education courses in the 1980s, it wasn't until the early 1990s that teacher educators began doing what they encouraged preservice and inservice teachers to do: that is, reflect on, inquire into, and study their practice (Cochran-Smith & Lytle, 1993; Loughran, 2004a; Mills, 2000). The shift in the focus of educational research was characterized by research questions that delved into the complexities of teaching and learning. An important result of this shift in research focus was that the role of teachers and teacher educators changed as they began to investigate and question their practice. Teaching was viewed as highly contextualized, and the research began to focus on the complex and dynamic interactions between the teacher and the students. Research on teaching and schooling became more inclusive, and the knowledge generated about teaching came from the teachers' questions and wonderings.

DISTINGUISHING SELF-STUDY FROM ACTION RESEARCH

Like many self-study researchers before us, we moved into the area of self-study through our involvement in action research. Although we found self-study to be familiar because of its close relationship to action research, we also found ourselves asking one another "How does self-study differ from action research?" In both methodologies, the researcher inquires into problems situated in practice, engages in cycles of research, and systematically collects and analyzes data to improve practice. Nonetheless, self-study may incorporate other methods, such as personal history, narrative inquiry, reflective portfolios, memory work, or arts-based methods (LaBoskey, 2004a; Samaras & Freese, 2006).

Feldman, Paugh, and Mills (2004) argue that a critical way to differentiate the two research genres is to focus on the relationship between *action* and *research*, and *self* and *study*. When the accent is on action, there is an assumption that the primary purpose of conducting action research is

> to modify or transform one's practice or situation, or those of the community or institution. This means that the collection and analysis of data are used to guide the development of a plan of action or to articulate a critical analysis of the individual and institutional barriers that are shaping their lives (p. 953).

However, when the accent is on the word *self*, then the self becomes the focus of the study and this is a "distinguishing characteristic of self-study as a variety of practitioner research" (p. 953).

Feldman, Paugh, and Mills further explain "action research provides the methods for the self-studies, but what made these *self-studies* (italics in original) were the methodological features" (p. 974). Self-study researchers use their experiences as a resource for their research and "problematize their selves in their practice situations" with the goal of reframing their beliefs and/or practice (Feldman, 2002, p. 971). Action research is more about what the teacher does, and not so much about who the teacher is.

Another important difference is that self-study focuses on improvement on both the personal and professional levels. Self-study builds on the personal processes of reflection and inquiry, and takes these processes and makes them open to public critique. Self-study is not done in isolation, but rather requires collaboration for building new understandings through dialogue and validation of findings. Self-study research requires openness and vulnerability since the focus is on the self. And finally, self-study is designed to lead to the reframing and reconceptualizing of the role of the teacher.

FORMALIZATION OF SELF-STUDY

Self-study emerged as a recognizable area of research in the early 1990s (Loughran, 2004a). The first step in the development of self-study research occurred in a 1992 American Educational Research Association (AERA) session on self-study that included the collaborative work of some of the self-study leaders, such as the Arizona Group (Guilfoyle, 1992; Hamilton, 1992; Pinnegar, 1992; Placier, 1992). It was also at this session that Russell (1992) presented his work entitled "Holding up the mirror: Teacher educators reflect on their own teaching." The presenters raised issues and questions about teacher education, such as the personal and professional struggles of teachers, the unspoken rules of tenure in the academy, aligning one's beliefs with one's teaching practices, and the nature of learning to teach about teaching (Loughran, 2004b). This 1992 AERA session attracted researchers from related areas such as teacher inquiry, reflective practice, and action research. In 1993, the AERA Special Interest Group (SIG), called the Self-Study of Teaching and Teacher Education Practices (S-STEP), was created. This was a critical step towards formalizing the area of self-study (Hamilton et al., 1998). The establishment of S-STEP proved to be a significant turning point in creating a community of self-study researchers. Valuable opportunities for professional networking and collaboration among researchers resulted from the SIG's creation, thus contributing to the further development of self-study (Loughran, 2004a).

   Another significant influence on the development of self-study was the First Castle Conference held in East Sussex, England in 1996. The four-day conference, sponsored by Queen's University in Canada and the S-STEP SIG, drew eighty participants from four continents (Australia, Europe, North America, and South America). The Castle Conference served as a valuable forum for bringing researchers together to dialogue, to ask probing questions, to make their knowledge public and open for critique, and to contribute to the evolving nature of the field. The educational researchers in attendance presented papers, created and displayed alternative representations, and explored the philosophy, methodology, and practice of self-study (Hamilton & Pinnegar, 1998, p. viii). The Castle Conference was significant in terms of the emerging understandings of self-study that grew out of the discussions and debate, culminating in the publication of *Reconceptualizing Teaching Practice: Self-Study in Teacher Education* (Hamilton et al., 1998).

EVOLUTION OF SELF-STUDY AS SCHOLARSHIP

Looking back we can see that the First Castle Conference held in 1996 (Richards & Russell, 1996) was fundamental in establishing a forum for exploring and expanding the conversations about self-study. The first conference was followed by six subsequent biannual conferences: Cole & Finley, 1998; Loughran & Russell, 2000; Kosnik, Freese, & Samaras, 2002; Tidwell, Fitzgerald, & Heston, 2004; Fitzgerald, Heston, & Tidwell, 2006; and Heston, Tidwell, East, & Fitzgerald, 2008, respectively. The conferences have provided a safe space for creating a learning community of self-study researchers who are willing to ask questions, clarify terms, take risks experimenting with innovative approaches, and examine and reframe their views about teaching and teacher education practices.

The Castle Conferences, the extensive contributions to the literature over the last 15 years, and *The International Handbook of Self-Study of Teaching and Teacher Education Practices* (Loughran, Hamilton, LaBoskey, & Russell, 2004) have shaped the field and document how self-study has evolved and grown since the early 1990s. The Handbook is the most definitive and comprehensive collection of self-study research written to date. In 2005, *Studying Teacher Education*, a peer-reviewed, international journal of self-study of teacher education practices, was launched and contributed to the formalization of the self-study of teaching research. The publication of this journal and the Handbook has brought much attention and interest to the increasingly popular movement of the self-study of teaching, and marked turning points in the coming of age of what we call the *Self-Study School* (Samaras & Freese, 2006). The self-study movement came out of a desire to "combine the best of both worlds: the world of scientific research on education and the world of practice" (Korthagen, 1995, p. 100). Although self-study is a relatively new field of research, it has been growing quickly and, at the same time, evolving. As the self-study field has matured, it has made great strides in gaining legitimacy in academia and among educational researchers due to the extensive amount and quality of research conducted by self-study researchers. Only seven years after the AERA session where self-study began, Zeichner asserted that "the birth of the self-study in teacher education movement around 1990 has been probably the single most significant development ever in the field of teacher education research" (Zeichner, 1999, p. 8).

THE NATURE OF SELF-STUDY

Like any new field of research, self-study has gone through growing pains and stages of development marked by a need for a shared understanding and shared language around the field of self-study. Self-study scholars have thought deeply about the nature of self-study, what it involves, and what distinguishes it from other types of research. In this section we chronologically present the development of the language and terms used in the literature to describe the nature or characteristics as noted by self-study scholars.

Open, Collaborative, and Reframed Practice

Beginning in the mid 1990s, and particularly at the First Castle Conference, questions were raised about the nature of self-study. Participants asked, "What is self-study and what constitutes self-study research?" An important step towards clarifying these questions took place after the First Castle Conference. Barnes (1998) conducted a content analysis of the conference papers and the results of the analysis were helpful in moving the field towards a shared understanding of how self-study scholars were characterizing self-study. He identified three characteristics based on his analysis. These characteristics include: 1) openness; 2) collaboration; and 3) reframing. Barnes explained how self-study researchers must have a disposition that is open to ideas from others, and how collaboration plays a critical role in self-study. Through dialogue and collaboration with other teacher educators and students, the researcher can frame and reframe a problem or situation from different perspectives. Reframing is important in self-study because it provides an opportunity for the researcher to think about things differently, change how he/she looks at what's going on in classrooms, and ultimately change one's practice (Hamilton et al., 1998, p. xii). As we continued to review the self-study literature, we identified additional characteristics that distinguish self-study from other forms of research, i.e., its nature is paradoxical, postmodern, and multiple and multifaceted.

Paradoxical

An intriguing characteristic that we discovered in our research was that self-study seems paradoxical. For example, the term *self-study* suggests that the study is about the individual, and yet self-study researchers assert that it must involve collaboration and "critical friends" or trusted colleagues who provide alternative perspectives for reframing, support, and validation (LaBoskey, 2004a; Loughran, 2007). McNiff and Whitehead (2006) have worked to emphasize the need for critical friends and validation groups. Bullough and Pinnegar (2001) and Whitehead (2004) argue that self-study scholars must have a deep commitment to checking data and inter-pretations with colleagues to broaden possibilities and challenge perspectives to increase the credibility and self-study validity. Whereas validity in conventional research involves empirical evidence, generalizability, and professional critique, self-study is validated through collaboration including testing, sharing, and challenging exemplars of teaching practices (LaBoskey, 2006, p. 252). Multiple perspectives provide ways of validating the findings (Loughran & Northfield, 1998). We found that although self-study involves an intrapersonal quest to understand one's practice, it is the interpersonal mediation that allows individuals to work within "learning zones" or "communities of expertise where learners co-mediate, negotiate, and socially construct an understanding of a shared task" (Samaras & Freese, 2006, p. 51). This revealed yet another paradox: although self-study involves a private and personal exploration, it is also public.

Postmodern

Self-study is often noted as having a postmodern nature because of its non-linear and unpredictable outcomes (Wilcox, Watson, & Paterson, 2004). According to Cochran-Smith and Lytle (2004), self-study scholars have demonstrated that "self-study works from the postmodernist assumption that it is never possible to divorce the 'self' from either the research process or from education practice" (p. 607). Self-study doesn't claim to know a truth but rather seeks to understand what is. Pinnegar and Hamilton (2007) explore using an ontological, rather than an epistemological, lens for analysis and state that by comparing opposing views, one's analysis is open to alternative views. Postmodern researchers understand that knowledge production has a cultural component and, therefore, they contend that researchers should take a reflective and analytical stance and seek to identify the cultural, interpretive, and ideological basis built into their conceptions of knowledge. Accordingly, Pinnegar (1998) explained that "self-study is methodologically unique" (p. 31) and that in self-study, researchers operate from and embrace the premise of subjectivity and "present evidence of meaning and relationships among phenomenon from the authority of their own experience" (p. 32). Self-study serves a common purpose of "finding power in practice" (Allender & Allender, 2008, p. 145) because its inclusive nature encourages practitioners to be researchers and constructors of knowledge.

Multiple and Multifaceted

Another characteristic of self-study research that we discovered is that it is multiple and multifaceted (Samaras & Freese, 2006). Self-study scholars come from various theoretical orientations and conceptually frame their studies accordingly. Also, self-study scholars conduct their research with multiple and diverse qualitative methods (LaBoskey, 2004b). Some choose to employ autobiographical and personal history self-study, narratives, memory work, and multiple artistic modes such as visual representations, theater, drama, and poetry (LaBoskey, 2004a; Lighthall, 2004). Loughran (2007) explains "there is no one way, or correct way, of doing self-study. Rather, how a self-study might be done depends on what is sought to be better understood" (p. 15). LaBoskey emphasizes the multiple characteristics of self-study as follows: "it is self-initiated and focused; it is improvement-aimed; it is interactive; it includes multiple, mainly qualitative, methods; and it defines validity as a validation process based in trustworthiness" (LaBoskey, 2004a, p. 817). A variety of methods that self-study scholars have incorporated into their work are included in our *Invitations to Practice* (Samaras & Freese, 2006). Self-study scholars continue to discuss the nature of self-study while also working to clarify its definition.

DEFINING SELF-STUDY

Looking back, we recall that we first met in 1998 where we found ourselves both intrigued and yet somewhat confused by the notion of self-study as we listened to conference presentations. At that time, we were both sharing our work (Freese, 1999; Samaras, 1998) and openly discussed some of our questions and concerns about a lack of a clear definition. We later discovered that many self-study members raised their own questions about how to define self-study according to their role, practice, and/or purpose.

Self-Study Defined by Role

Self-study involves a strong personal reference in that it involves study *of* the self and study *by* the self although there are variations of that theme. Baird (2004) brought attention to the possible interpretations of self in self-study when he analyzed types of studies and distinguished the foci of self-study research, i.e., a focus on "the self in teaching"; "the self as teacher"; "the self as researcher of my teaching"; "the self as researcher of teacher education"; and "the self as researcher of self-study" (p. 1445). Hamilton and colleagues (1998) define self-study as "the study of one's self, one's actions, one's ideas, as well as the 'not self'… Self-study also involves a thoughtful look at texts read, experiences had, people known, and ideas considered" (p. 236). Hamilton and colleagues conclude "a critical examination of the self's involvement both in aspects of the study and in the phenomenon under study" is central to self-study (p. 240).

Self-Study Defined by Situated Practice

We also found that self-study scholars have presented definitions that were situated within their personal and professional experiences. For example, Pinnegar (1998) defined self-study as "a methodology for studying professional practice settings" (p. 33). Clarke and Erickson (2004) claim that "For teaching to occur, there must be a *some how* (bold and italics in original), a way for an educator to know, recognize, explore, and act upon his or her practice" (p. 59). After studying her integration of Vygotskian (1981) theory in her teaching, Samaras (2002) designed a self-study model for teacher educators and wrote "I use the words self-study to mean critical examination of one's actions and the context of those actions in order to achieve a more conscious mode of professional activity, in contrast to action based on habit, tradition, or impulse" (p. xiii). Similarly, describing self-study from their teacher education program contexts, Beck, Freese, and Kosnik (2004), described self-study as "a personal-constructivist-collaborative approach" to empha-size important components of self-study. Self-study is constructivist because it includes elements of ongoing inquiry, respects personal experience, and empha-sizes the role of knowledge construction. The collaborative component of self-study acknowledges the important role of the social construction of knowledge.

Self-Study Defined by Purpose

Cole and Knowles (1998) argue that there are multiple reasons why people practice self-study and those purposes are typically integrated and not mutually exclusive. Although the purposes may be layered and multifaceted, researchers often focus on one aspect of professional practice. At the same time, the purpose may extend beyond the self towards educational reform. Kosnik, Beck, Freese, and Samaras (2006) identified three purposes for practicing self-study: 1) personal renewal, 2) professional renewal, and 3) program renewal.

Furthermore, there are a number of different methods of self-study that can serve to focus one's lens on a particular issue. An example of this is personal history self-study where teachers explore and begin to identify who they are as teachers for self-knowing, forming, and reforming a professional identity (Samaras, Hicks, & Garvey Berger, 2004). Another example is self-study action research whereby classroom teachers conduct a manageable professional inquiry that enables them to study their classroom strategies and actions for change, and also who they are as teacher professionals (Samaras, Beck, Freese, & Kosnik, 2005). Regardless of purpose or method, the self-study scholar questions practice with the support of colleagues, and frames, assesses, and reframes his/her practice within the context of broader educational aims.

LaBoskey's work (2004a) emphasizes the important moral, ethical, and political purposes of self-study when she defines self-study work as moral and value-laden. In addition, teacher educators have employed self-study to question the status quo of education programs and their role within teacher education pedagogy (Samaras, 2002; Loughran, 2006). They have questioned the assertions of their practice (Loughran & Northfield, 1996), the tensions in their practice (Berry, 2007), and the taken for granted assumptions of their practice (Brandenburg, 2008). Whitehead (1988) also calls upon teachers to consider the possible alignment or disparities between what they say, and what they believe, and what they actually do in practice. He referred to this gap between one's teaching philosophy and actual practice as a "living contradiction," although LaBoskey (2004b) notes that our inquiries do not have to derive from problematic situations.

As we strive to clarify and provide a shared understanding of what self-study includes, it is wise to keep in mind the following caveat.

> Despite the development, refinement and clarification that has occurred...it is clear that the 'one true way,' the template for a self-study method, has not emerged. Rather self-study tends to be methodologically framed through the question/issue/concern under consideration so that it invokes the use of a method(s) that is most appropriate for uncovering the evidence in accord with the purpose/intent of the study (Loughran, 2004a, p. 17).

Perhaps it isn't possible to come up with a fixed definition, and perhaps it isn't desirable. Bullough and Pinnegar (2004) assert that the inclusive nature of self-study and its multiple definitions provoke a continuous and communal conversation about its characteristics.

THE SELF-STUDY COMMUNITY

Self-study scholars include a dynamic group of teachers, teacher educators, and administrators committed to studying their practice through self-study in an effort to make their teaching and programs more effective for students' learning. Many hold membership in the Self-Study of Teacher Education Practices (S-STEP) Special Interest Group (SIG) of the American Educational Research Association (AERA). Allender and Allender (2008) recall, "A small notice in the *Educational Researcher*, ... with the help of some word of mouth brought together a group of over 200 members at the 1993 [AERA] annual meeting—to explore the value of studying their own practices as teacher educators" (p. 129). The S-STEP SIG, now with nearly 300 members, has fostered a sense of intellectual safety in a collaborative and highly supportive culture, much like what we encourage teachers to do in their classrooms.

The S-STEP membership is diverse and unified by its use of the self-study methodology rather than by a discipline, theory, or educational issue. Although self-study grew out of the work of teacher educators, it has expanded to include practitioners such as administrators, librarians, occupational therapists, psycho-therapists, counselors, and community educators working for social justice and educational reform (e.g., Allender, 2004; Manke, 2004; Wilcox, Watson, & Paterson, 2004). We refer to this extension from self-study of teaching practices to other fields as self-studyship (Samaras & Freese, 2006).

The Castle Conferences have proven to be an important forum in the develop-ment of the self-study community, attracting self-study teacher practitioners from a wide range of countries from both research-intensive and teaching-focused universities. People from many different disciplines gather to gain feedback and insights from colleagues as they share their applications of doing self-study in their contexts.

THE *DOING* OF SELF-STUDY

As we looked back, we recognized that it was in the *doing* of self-study that we were better able to understand it. Applying the methodology of self-study research, actually immersing ourselves in doing self-study, helped us understand its nature and purposes. We initially had a fear of sharing our work and making ourselves vulnerable—but as we moved to a feeling of openness and learning together, we found ourselves framing and reframing our understandings of self-study through our teaching and our application of self-study to our practice. We recall that when we engaged in action research, the focus was on our students and what they learned. However, through our dialoguing we realized that by focusing on the students we left out a very important aspect of the study—the self, the role we played in the research, and what we learned and how we subsequently changed. Self-study and our work with students reinforced our belief that teaching needs to be purposeful. And we found that by studying and systematically examining our teaching, we became more focused on our purposes and whether we were aligning our beliefs with our practice.

Engaging in conducting self-studies, serving as co-editors of the *Castle Proceedings* (Kosnik, Freese, & Samaras, 2002), developing the primer (Samaras & Freese, 2006), and working with our doctoral students (Freese & Strong, 2008; Mittapalli & Samaras, 2008; Samaras et al., 2007), helped us come to a rich understanding of its multiplicity. Our understandings of self-study deepened through our ongoing discussions and collaboration with our self-study colleagues and students. Just as we tried to pin down self-study definitions and the research methodology, we have seen how our graduate students wrestle with the multiple definitions and methods of conducting self-study. We realized that our students learned about self-study best through doing it. By initiating a research question they were passionate about, they were able to move to a better understanding of the process of self-study research. Like us, they gained an enhanced understanding and appreciation for the impact self-study had on their practice and to the field at large. We have found there is a self-discovery aspect of self-study that necessitates inquiring and engaging with others. The result is that we socially construct our understandings and gain new insights through others' perspectives.

Looking back, we realize that we were drawn to self-study because it was a way for us to ask the deep questions about our practice that we dared not ask alone. Together we were able to negotiate our beliefs, understandings, and misunderstandings through reading texts and articles, e-mails, conversations, and through joint writing. We value the supportive self-study community and the way the Castle Conferences have enhanced inquiry and scholarship. Although we had different questions and we worked in different contexts, we became part of a community in which teacher educators could and were asking the taken-for-granted questions about their practice and the impact of their work. We still have many questions, but we are constantly intrigued at the possibilities that only self-study research provides.

LOOKING FORWARD

As important as it is to look backward, we also see the value in looking forward. Like Alice, looking back can be useful in providing direction to guide us to where we want to go. In this final section, we offer suggestions informed by our work and that of our colleagues. They are not meant to be inclusive or definitive because the road ahead is uncertain, and at the same time full of new possibilities.

"Would you tell me, please, which way I ought to go from here?"
"That depends a good deal on where you want to get to," said the Cat.
(Carroll, 1998, p. 56)

The Need for Brighter Guideposts

As we gained more experience engaging in self-study, we have come to understand that there is not one road, not one direct path to conducting self-study. The purpose of this book is to explore some of the many paths with which self-study scholars have been experimenting. However, at the same time, we argue that for our fellow self-study travelers there needs to be better research guideposts. We see the value of having a shared understanding about how studying our practice can lead us "to where we want to get to" and can help in guiding our decision making. We see the need for some agreed upon methodological components. We encourage continued efforts to provide some standardization for applying the self-study methods with exemplars of practitioners conducting their self-studies such as those shared in this book. We offered some beginning work in providing a structure for informal and formal self-study research as a starting point (Samaras & Freese, 2006). But the self-study community needs to go further.

Clearer Connections with Validation of the Impact of Our Work

LaBoskey (2006) argues that self-studies need to be validated over time with continued work that helps us understand and contribute to a body of knowledge and a specific domain. Bullough and Pinnegar (2001) offer guidelines for quality in autobiographical forms of self-study research. Self-study scholars are continuing to address issues of validity and quality in self-study (Feldman, 2003; LaBoskey, 2006; Loughran, 2007). Although much progress has been made in this area, AERA program chairs, editors of the *Castle Proceedings*, and those teaching about self-study research need to continue to provide clearer requirements for quality papers that include descriptions of the research process, how colleagues contributed to the validity of the research, and what knowledge has been generated from the study.

Accumulating Knowledge across Self-Study

Zeichner (2007) suggests that self-study could be strengthened by "situating individual studies within coherent research programs on particular substantive issues" (p. 36). He says this is "a logical next step for this movement, one that would begin to infuse the insights of practicing teacher educators into the broader knowledge-base of the field and to affect the policy-making process" (p. 40). As the field continues to grow and develop, a number of recent publications have emerged in a variety of topic areas, such as self-study and diversity (Tidwell & Fitzgerald, 2006), teacher education reform (Loughran & Russell, 2002), and self-study and the arts (Mitchell & Weber, 1999). Samaras and Freese (2006) offered a collection of self-study publications organized by topic (pp. 132–53). Zeichner (2007) now recommends that a discussion is needed on "how a study builds on the work of others" (p. 39). Zeichner, who has conducted his own self-study research with a focus on social change (Zeichner, 1995), suggests a next step for self-study scholars is a focus on analyzing connections across issues such as fostering social justice, science education reform, leadership, preservice teacher preparation, and technology.

Loughran (2004b) emphasizes that we need to state our assertions more clearly and boldly. LaBoskey (2006) adds, "Only in that way can the ideas be employed, applied, and re-tested by the teacher education community in ways that will help us embrace, discard, or transform those assertions; that is the essence of the validation process for the field" (p. 258). It is ultimately the self-study community that has shaped, and will continue to shape, the future of self-study research (Dalmau & Guðjónsdóttir, 2008). These recommendations warrant our attention as we maintain our uniqueness as a methodology, while also bringing our work into the mainstream of teacher education. In that manner, our voices can be heard by our teacher education colleagues outside the field of self-study. They too are fellow travelers, all working for the common purpose of improving teaching and learning and contributing to the knowledge base of education and research.

REFERENCES

Allender, D. (2004). What happens to the self in self-study? In D. Tidwell, L. Fitzgerald, & M. Heston (Eds.), *Journeys of hope: Risking self-study in a diverse world. Proceedings of the fifth international conference on self-study of teacher education practices, Herstmonceux Castle, East Sussex, England* (pp. 17–19). Cedar Falls, IA: University of Northern Iowa.

Allender, J. S., & Allender, D. S. (2008). *The humanistic teacher*. Boulder, CO: Paradigm Publishers.

Baird, J. (2004). Interpreting the what, why, and how of self-study in teaching and teacher education. In J. J. Loughran, M. L. Hamilton, V. K. LaBoskey, & T. Russell (Eds.), *International handbook of self-study of teaching and teacher education practices* (Vol. 2, pp. 1442–1481). Dordrecht: Kluwer Academic Publishers.

Barnes, D. (1998). Forward: Looking forward: The concluding remarks at the Castle conference. In M. L. Hamilton, with S. Pinnegar, T. Russell, J. Loughran, & V. LaBoskey (Eds.), *Reconceptualizing teaching practice: Self-study in teacher education* (pp. ix–xiv). London: Falmer Press.

Beck, C., Freese, A. R., & Kosnik, C. (2004). The preservice practicum: Learning through self-study in a professional setting. In J. J. Loughran, M. L. Hamilton, V. K. LaBoskey, & T. Russell (Eds.), *International handbook of self-study of teaching and teacher education practices* (Vol. 2, pp. 1259–1293). Dordrecht: Kluwer Academic Publishers.

Berry, A. (2007). *Tensions in teaching about teaching: Understanding practice as a teacher educator*. Dordrecht, The Netherlands: Springer Press.

Brandenburg, R. (2008). *Powerful pedagogy: Self-study of a teacher educator's practice*. Dordrecht: Springer Press.

Bullough, R. V., Jr., & Gitlin, A. (1995). *Becoming a student of teaching: Methodologies for exploring self and school context*. New York: Garland Publishing.

Bullough, R. V., Jr., & Pinnegar, S. (2001). Guidelines for quality in autobiographical forms of self-study research. *Educational Researcher, 30*(3), 13–21.

Bullough, R. V., Jr., & Pinnegar, S. (2004). Thinking about the thinking about self-study: An analysis of eight chapters. In J. J. Loughran, M. L. Hamilton, V. K. LaBoskey, & T. Russell (Eds.), *International handbook of self-study of teaching and teacher education practices* (Vol. 1, pp. 313–342). Dordrecht: Kluwer Academic Publishers.

Carr, W., & Kemmis, S. (1986). *Becoming critical: Education, knowledge and action research*. London: Falmer Press.

Carroll, L. (1998). *Alice's adventures in Wonderland*. London: Penguin Books.

Clarke, A., & Erickson, G. (2004). The nature of teaching and learning in self-study. In J. J. Loughran, M. L. Hamilton, V. K. LaBoskey, & T. Russell (Eds.), *International handbook of self-study of teaching and teacher education practices* (Vol. 1, pp. 41–67). Dordrecht: Kluwer Academic Publishers.

Cochran-Smith, M. (1991). Learning to teach against the grain. *Harvard Educational Review, 61*(3), 279–310.

Cochran-Smith, M., & Lytle, S. L. (1993). *Inside/Outside: Teacher research and knowledge*. New York: Teachers College Press.

Cochran-Smith, M., & Lytle, S. L. (2004). Practitioner inquiry, knowledge, and university culture. In J. J. Loughran, M. L. Hamilton, V. K. LaBoskey, & T. Russell (Eds.), *International handbook of self-study of teaching and teacher education practices* (Vol. 1, pp. 601–649). Dordrecht: Kluwer Academic Publishers.

Cole, A. L., & Finley, S. (Eds.). (1998). *Conversations in community. Proceedings of the second international conference on self-study of teacher education practices, Herstmonceux Castle, East Sussex, England.* Kingston, ON: Queen's University.

Cole, A. L., & Knowles, J. G. (1998). The self-study of teacher education practices and the reform of teacher education. In M. L. Hamilton, with S. Pinnegar, T. Russell, J. Loughran, & V. LaBoskey (Eds.), *Reconceptualizing teaching practice: Self-study in teacher education* (pp. 224–234). London: Falmer Press.

Connelly, F., & Clandinin, D. J. (1990). Stories of experience and narrative inquiry. *Educational Researcher, 19*(5), 2–11.

Dalmau, M., & Guðjónsdóttir, H. (2008). *Learning to find the future together: Distilling public educational knowledge through focused self-study.* A conference inquiry project presented at the Seventh International Conference on the Self-Study of Teacher Education Practices, Herstmonceux Castle, East Sussex, England.

Dana, N. F., & Yendal-Silva, D. (2003). *The reflective educator's guide to classroom research.* Thousand Oaks, CA: Corwin.

Dewey, J. (1933). *How we think: A restatement of the relation of reflective thinking to the reflective process.* New York: Heath and Company.

Duckworth, J. (1987). *The having of wonderful ideas and other essays on teaching and learning.* New York: Teachers College Press.

Feldman, A. (2002). Bec(o/a)ming a teacher educator. In C. Kosnik, A. R. Freese, & A. P. Samaras (Eds.), *Making a difference in teacher education through self-study. Proceedings of the fourth international conference on self-study of teacher education practices, Herstmonceux Castle, East Sussex, England* (Vol. 1, pp. 66–70). Toronto, ON: OISE, University of Toronto.

Feldman, A. (2003). Validity and quality in self-study. *Educational Researcher, 32*(3), 26–28.

Feldman, A., Paugh, P., & Mills, G. (2004). Self-study through action research. In J. Loughran, M. L. Hamilton, V. K. LaBoskey, & J. Russell (Eds.), *International handbook of self-study of teaching and teacher education practices* (Vol. 2, pp. 943–977). Dordrecht: Kluwer Academic Publishers.

Fitzgerald, L. M., Heston, M., & Tidwell, D. (Eds.). (2006). *Collaboration and community: Pushing boundaries through self-study. Proceedings of the sixth international conference on self-study of teacher education practices, Herstmonceux Castle, East Sussex, England.* Cedar Falls, IA: University of Northern Iowa.

Freese, A. R. (1999). The role of reflection on preservice teachers' development in the context of a professional development school. *Teaching and Teacher Education, 15*(8), 895–910.

Freese, A. R., & Strong, A. P. (2008). Establishing a learning community as a site to explore our multicultural selves. In A. P. Samaras, A. R. Freese, C. Kosnik, & C. Beck (Eds.), *Learning communities In practice* (pp. 103–116). Dordrecht: Springer Press.

Guilfoyle, K. (1992, April). *Communicating with students: The impact of interactive dialogue journals on the thinking and teaching of a teacher educator.* Paper presented at the annual meeting of the American Education Research Association, San Francisco.

Hamilton, M. L. (1992, April). *Making public the private voice of a teacher educator.* Paper presented at the annual meeting of the American Education Research Association, San Francisco.

Hamilton, M. L., & Pinnegar, S. (1998). Preface. In M. L. Hamilton, S. Pinnegar, T. Russell, J. Loughran, & V. K. LaBoskey (Eds.), *Reconceptualizing teaching practice: Self-study in teacher education* (p. viii). London: Falmer Press.

Hamilton, M. L., Pinnegar, S., Russell, T., Loughran, J., & LaBoskey, V. K. (Eds.), (1998). *Reconceptualizing teaching practice: Self-study in teacher education.* London: Falmer Press.

Heston, M., Tidwell, D., East, K., & Fitzgerald, L. (Eds.). (2008). *Pathways to change in teacher education: Dialogue, diversity and self-study. Proceedings of the seventh international conference on the self-study of teacher education practices, Herstmonceux Castle, East Sussex, England.* Cedar Falls, IA: University of Northern Iowa.

Korthagen, F. A. J. (1995). A reflection on five reflective accounts. Theme issue self study and living educational theory. *Teacher Educational Quarterly, 22*(3), 99–105.

Kosnik, C., Beck, C., Freese, A. R., & Samaras, A. P. (Eds.). (2006). *Making a difference in teacher education through self-study: Studies of personal, professional, and program renewal.* Dordrecht: Springer.

Kosnik, C., Freese, A. R., & Samaras, A. P. (Eds.). (2002). *Making a difference in teacher education through self-study. Proceedings of the fourth international conference on self-study of teacher education practices, Herstmonceux Castle, East Sussex, England* (Vols. 1 & 2). Toronto, ON: OISE, University of Toronto.

LaBoskey, V. K. (1994). *Development of reflective practice*. New York: Teachers College Press.

LaBoskey, V. K. (2004a). The methodology of self-study and its theoretical underpinnings. In J. J. Loughran, M. L. Hamilton, V. K. LaBoskey, & T. Russell (Eds.), *International handbook of self-study of teaching and teacher education practices* (Vol. 1, pp. 817–869). Dordrecht: Kluwer Academic Publishers.

LaBoskey, V. K. (2004b). Afterword: Moving the methods of self-study research and practice forward: Challenges and opportunities. In J. J. Loughran, M. L. Hamilton, V. K. LaBoskey, & T. Russell (Eds.), *International handbook of self-study of teaching and teacher education practices* (Vol. 2, pp. 1169–1184). Dordrecht: Kluwer Academic Publishers.

LaBoskey, V. K. (2006). The fragile strengths of self-study: Making bold claims and clear connections. In P. Aubusson & S. Schuck (Eds.), *Teaching learning and development: The mirror maze* (pp. 251–262). Dordrecht: Springer.

Lighthall, F. F. (2004). Fundamental features and approaches of the s-step enterprise. In J. J. Loughran, M. L. Hamilton, V. K. LaBoskey, & T. Russell (Eds.), *International handbook of self-study of teaching and teacher education practices* (Vol. 1, pp. 193–245). Dordrecht: Kluwer Academic Publishers.

Loughran, J. (2004a). A history and context of self-study of teaching and teacher education practices. In J. J. Loughran, M. L. Hamilton, V. K. LaBoskey, & T. Russell (Eds.), *International handbook of self-study of teaching and teacher education practices* (Vol. 1, pp. 7–39). Dordrecht: Kluwer Academic Publishers.

Loughran, J. (2004b). Informing practice. Developing knowledge of teaching about teaching. In D. L. Tidwell, L. M. Fitzgerald, & M. L. Heston (Eds.), *Journeys of hope: Risking self-study in a diverse world. Proceedings of the fifth international conference of the self-study of teacher education practices, Herstmonceux Castle, East Sussex, England* (pp. 186–189). Cedar Falls, IA: University of Northern Iowa.

Loughran, J. (2006). *Developing a pedagogy of teacher education*. London: Routledge.

Loughran, J. (2007). Researching teacher education practices: Responding to the challenges, demands, and expectations of self-study. *Journal of Teacher Education, 58*(1), 12–20.

Loughran, J. J., Hamilton, M. L., LaBoskey, V. K., & Russell, T. (Eds.). (2004). *International handbook of self-study of teaching and teacher education practices*. Dordrecht: Kluwer Academic Publishers.

Loughran, J. J., & Northfield, J. (1996). *Opening the classroom door: Teacher, researcher, learner*. London: Falmer.

Loughran, J. J., & Northfield, J. (1998). A framework for the development of self-study practice. In M. L. Hamilton, with S. Pinnegar, T. Russell, J. Loughran, & V. K. LaBoskey (Eds.), *Reconceptualizing teaching practice: Self-study in teacher education* (pp. 7–18). London: Falmer Press.

Loughran, J. J., & Russell, T. (Eds.). (2000). *Exploring myths and legends of teacher education. Proceedings of the third international conference on the self-study of teacher education practices, Herstmonceux Castle, East Sussex, England*. Kingston, ON: Queen's University.

Loughran, J. J., & Russell, T. (2002). *Improving teacher education practices through self-study*. London: Routledge/Falmer.

Manke, M. P. (2004). Administrators also do self-study: Issues of power and community, social justice, and teacher education reform. In J. J. Loughran, M. L. Hamilton, V. K. LaBoskey, & T. Russell (Eds.), *International handbook of self-study of teaching and teacher education practices* (Vol. 2, pp. 1367–1391). Dordrecht: Kluwer Academic Publishers.

McNiff, J. (1988). *Action research: Principles and practice*. London: Routledge Press.

McNiff, J., & Whitehead, J. (2006). *All you need to know about action research*. London: Sage.

Mills, G. (2000). *Action research: A guide for the teacher researchers*. Upper Saddle River, NJ: Merrill.

Mitchell, C., & Weber, S. (1999). *Reinventing ourselves as teachers: Beyond nostalgia*. London: Falmer Press.

Mittapalli, K., & Samaras, A. P. (2008). Madhubani art: A journey of an education researcher seeking self-development answers through art and self-study. *The Qualitative Report, 13*(2), 244–261.

Pinnegar, S. (1992, April). *Student teaching as a teacher educator.* Paper presented at the annual meeting of the American Education Research Association, San Francisco.

Pinnegar, S. (1998). Introduction: Methodological perspectives. In M. L. Hamilton, S. Pinnegar, T. Russell, J. Loughran, & V. LaBoskey (Eds.), *Reconceptualizing teaching practice: Self-study in teacher education.* London: Falmer Press.

Pinnegar, S., & Hamilton, M. L. (2007, April). *Exploring ontology in self-study methodology.* Paper presented at the annual meeting of the American Educational Research Association, Chicago.

Placier, P. (1992, April). *Maintaining practice: a struggle of too little time.* Paper presented at the annual meeting of the American Education Research Association, San Francisco.

Richards, J., & Russell, T. (Eds.). (1996). *Empowering our future in teacher education. Proceedings of the first international conference on self-study of teacher education practices, Herstmonceux Castle, East Sussex, England.* Kingston, ON: Queen's University.

Richardson, V. (1989). The evolution of reflective teaching and teacher education. In R. Clift, W. R. Houston, & M. Pugach (Eds.), *Encouraging reflective practice: An examination of issues and exemplars* (pp. 3–19). New York: Teachers College Press.

Russell, T. (1992, April). *Holding up the mirror: Teacher educators reflect on their own teaching.* Paper presented at the annual meeting of the American Education Research Association, San Francisco.

Russell, T., & Munby, H. (Eds.). (1992). *Teachers and teaching: From classroom to reflection.* London: Falmer Press.

Samaras, A. P. (1998). Finding my way: Teaching methods courses from a sociocultural perspective. In A. L. Cole, R. Elijah, & J. G. Knowles (Eds.), *The heart of the matter: Teacher educators and teacher education reform* (pp. 55–79). San Francisco: Caddo Gap Press.

Samaras, A. P. (2002). *Self-study for teacher educators: Crafting a pedagogy for educational change.* New York: Peter Lang Publishers.

Samaras, A. P., Adams-Legge, M., Breslin, D., Mittapalli, K., Magaha O'Looney, J., & Wilcox, D. R. (2007). Building a plane while flying it: Reflections of teaching and learning self-study. *Reflective Practice, 8*(4), 467–481.

Samaras, A. P., Beck, A., Freese, A. R., & Kosnik, C. (2005). Self-study supports new teachers' professional development. *Focus on Teacher Education Quarterly, 6*(1), 3–5, & 7.

Samaras, A. P., & Freese, A. R. (2006). *Self-study of teaching practices.* New York: Peter Lang.

Samaras, A. P., Hicks, M. A., & Garvey Berger, J. (2004). Self-study through personal history. In J. Loughran, M. L. Hamilton, V. K. LaBoskey, & T. Russell (Eds.), *The international handbook of self-study of teaching and teacher education practices* (pp. 905–942). Dordrecht: Kluwer Academic Publishers.

Schön, D. A. (1983). *The reflective practitioner: How professionals think in action.* New York: Basic Books.

Schön, D. A. (1987). *Education the reflective practitioner: Toward a new design for teaching and learning in the profession.* San Francisco: Jossey-Bass.

Tidwell, D., & Fitzgerald, L. M. (Eds.). (2006). *Self-study and diversity.* Rotterdam: Sense Publishers.

Tidwell, D., Fitzgerald, L., & Heston, M. (Eds.). (2004). *Journeys of hope: Risking the journey of self-study in a diverse world. Proceedings of the fifth international conference on self-study of teacher education practices, Herstmonceux Castle, East Sussex, England.* Cedar Falls, IA: University of Northern Iowa.

Vygotsky, L. S. (1981). The genesis of higher mental functions. In J. V. Wertsch (Ed.), *The concept of activity in Soviet psychology* (pp. 144–188). Armonk, NY: Sharpe. (Original work published 1960)

Whitehead, J. (1988). Creating a living educational theory from questions of the kind, 'How do I improve my practice? *Cambridge Journal of Education, 19*(1), 41–52.

Whitehead, J. (2004). What counts as evidence in self-studies of teacher education practices? In J. J. Loughran, M. L. Hamilton, V. K. LaBoskey, & T. Russell (Eds.), *International handbook of self-study of teaching and teacher education practices* (Vol. 2, pp. 871–903). Dordrecht: Kluwer Academic Publishers.

Wilcox, S., Watson, J., & Paterson, M. (2004). Self-study in professional practice. In J. J. Loughran, M. L. Hamilton, V. K. LaBoskey, & T. Russell (Eds.), *International handbook of self-study of teaching and teacher education practices* (Vol. 1, pp. 273–312). Dordrecht: Kluwer Academic Publishers.

Zeichner, K. (1995). Reflections of a teacher educator working for social change. In T. Russell & F. Korthagen (Eds.), *Teachers who teach teachers: Reflections on teacher education* (pp. 11–24). London: Falmer Press.

Zeichner, K. (1999). The new scholarship in teacher education. *Educational Researcher, 28*(9), 4–15.

Zeichner, K. (2007). Accumulating knowledge across self-studies in teacher education. *Journal of Teacher Education, 58*(1), 36–46.

Zeichner, K. M., & Liston, D. P. (1987). Teaching student teachers to reflect. *Harvard Educational Review, 57*(1), 23–48.

Zeichner, K. M., & Liston, D. P. (1996). *Reflective teaching: An introduction.* Mahway, NJ: Lawrence Erlbaum.

CHERYL J. CRAIG

2. TRUSTWORTHINESS IN SELF-STUDY RESEARCH

> The fact that a story is credible tells us nothing—*absolutely* nothing—about whether or not it is true or false.
>
> (Phillips, 1993, p. 21, italics in original)

Like many other kinds of inquiry, the self-study of teaching and teacher education genre of research employs narrative as an expression of practical knowledge and/or a research methodology and/or a form of representation. Hence, critiques such as the aforementioned one have been leveled at it and similar kinds of research. On one hand, the claim can be made—with sufficient evidence (human initiation and ongoing intervention)—that no research genre achieves its results from brute data and that criticisms directed at personal inquiries apply to all forms of investigation, albeit to varying degrees. On the other hand, it also can be argued that self-study research is part of a movement toward a "new epistemology of practice" (Schön, 1995) and that it is being held accountable to misplaced demands for verification (Bruner, 1986). In other words, new approaches are being "grafted on" (Schön, 1991) to conventional ways of warranting knowledge and are not passing muster (Fenstermacher, 1994). Hence, pressure has built in the field and the "new paradigm wars" (Anderson & Herr, 1999) have waged. In fact, Fenstermacher (Personal Communication in Munby, Russell & Martin, 2001) has noted that it remains unclear whether conventional criteria will continue to hold sway or whether an "epistemologically humble" (Barone, 2008) way to verify human knowledge—already at work in so many practice-oriented inquiries, will be officially recognized as something other than an aberration or anomaly indicative of the swampy lowland of practice (Schön, 1983) and its perceived lack of rigor. In the meantime, signs of struggle abound in the field. One prime example is *Studying teacher education: The report of the AERA panel on research and teacher education* (Cochran-Smith & Zeichner, 2005). In that report, the hegemony of the dominant research paradigm rendered invalid self-study research contributions, despite self-study researchers constituting the largest Special Interest Group of the American Educational Research Association. Another prominent example is the *Report of the National Reading Panel: Teaching children to read: An evidence-based assessment of the scientific research literature on reading and its implications for reading instruction* (NICHD, 2000), which managed to nullify the contributions of all qualitative researchers, including those involved in the self-study of teaching and teacher education practices.

C. A. Lassonde, S. Galman and C. Kosnik (eds.), Self-Study Research Methodologies for Teacher Educators, 21–34.

In this chapter, I steer clear of the cantankerous "what constitutes truth" debate, which has become increasingly politicized due to the U.S. government's privileging of medical model research in the educational arena. Instead, I accept at face value trustworthiness as a way to ground self-study researchers' claims to knowing and doing in the Deweyan (1938) sense of the terms. My interest is not in abstract discourse—talk about "deathless shadow[s] of once living act[s]" (Carse, 1986, p. 77). Rather, my concern is with what comprises trustworthiness when one practically engages in, and makes sense of, self-study inquiries. I focus my attention on the kinds of obvious and not-so-obvious decisions self-study researchers make as they conduct, represent, and communicate their inquiries in public forums. Like Schön (1983), I respect the value of practitioner research and the contributions of the study of teaching and teacher education to the production of knowledge (Bullough & Gitlin, 2001). However, I also understand that such knowledge would have to be, in Schön's words, "valid, according to criteria of appropriate rigor,... susceptible to critical review and evaluation, and accessible for exchange and use by other members of one's scholarly community" (Lyons & LaBoskey, p. vii). Before I continue this discussion, I need to share my understanding of self-study research and the way I see it positioned on the educational research landscape.

THEORETICAL BACKDROP

In my work, I adopt Hamilton and Pinnegar's (1998) definition of self-study as "the study of one's self, one's actions, one's ideas, as well as the 'not self'" (p. 238). In that view, self-study is "autobiographical, historical, cultural, and political and takes a thoughtful look at texts read, experiences had, people known and ideas considered" (Hamilton & Pinnegar, 1998, p. 236) and their connections to teachers' and teacher educators' practices. As can be seen, matters of context, process, and relationship are foundational to the self-study study of teaching and teacher education (Bullough & Pinnegar, 2001). Also, self-study research differs from reflective practice in that it is "an extension of reflection on practice, with aspirations that go beyond professional development" to the "wider communication and consideration of ideas, i.e., the generation and communication of new knowledge and understandings" (Loughran & Northfield, 1998, p. 15).

The self-study research genre employs a broad range of qualitative methods, all of which employ narrative in one form or another—for example, narrative inquiry (i.e., Kitchen, 2005; Pinnegar, Dulude Lay, Bigham & Dulude, 2005), case study research (i.e., Dinkelman, 2003; Gipe, 1998), action research (i.e., Feldman, Paugh, & Mills, 2004; Whitehead, 2000), teacher research (i.e., Cochran-Smith & Lytle, 2004; Senese, 2005) and arts-based approaches (i.e., Weber & Mitchell, 2004). As is evident, self-study's intellectual roots are intimately tied to the development of the qualitative research paradigm (Bullough & Pinnegar, 2004; Pinnegar & Daynes, 2006). Hence, interpretation and meaning-making, rather than explanation, sit at its core. As with other qualitative research approaches (see Lincoln & Guba, 1985), the idea of the trustworthiness of research findings—as opposed to their validity—is a generally accepted rule of thumb. In this view, trustworthiness is defined as "the degree to which other practitioners or researchers turn to, rely or will rely on, and *use* the concepts, methods, and inferences of a practice as the basis of their own theorizing, research, or practice" (Mishler, 1990, p. 419 in Lyons & LaBoskey, 2002, p. 6). Thus, instead of capital 'T' Truth, studies trustworthy in nature demonstrate a "true for now" (Bruner, 1986) quality since studies involving narrative—indeed life—are inevitably "unfinished and unfinishable business" (Elbaz-Luwisch, 2006).

Thomas Kuhn's (1962/1996) concept of a "'paradigm shift'" greatly aided the development of qualitative research methodologies in education. Kuhn asserted that new paradigm researchers "think with exemplars" (Schön, 1983, pp. 183–184) rather than communicating certainties as "rhetoric of conclusions" (Schwab, 1961/1978), which is the prevailing approach. These exemplars, in Kuhn's words, are "the concrete problem-solutions" encountered "in laboratories, on examinations, or at the ends of chapters in...texts...that...show...by example how the job is to be done" (Kuhn, 1962/1970, p. 187). As for Schwab, one of the first with whom Kuhn shared his groundbreaking manuscript (Ian Westbury, Personal Communication, 2006), such exemplars would necessarily be "narratives of enquiry" that communicate tentative formulations—not facts, but *interpretations* of facts" (p. 242; italics in original). Furthermore, these interpretations would "end in doubt or in alternative views of what the evidence shows" (p. 270). This is because scientists, in Schwab's (1967) view, do not prove truths as the rhetoric of the dominant research paradigm would have us believe, but tell "likely stories" (pp. 14–15) until such time new discoveries are made.

Further building on the available research in the field, Lyons and LaBoskey (2002) maintained that "validity in the [exemplar] approach...*depends on concrete examples of actual practices, fully elaborated so that members of a relevant research community can judge for themselves their 'trustworthiness' and the validity of observations, interpretations...*" (p. 20, italics in original). In this scenario, validation rather than validity forms the impetus for action. As Mishler (1990) further explained:

> focusing on trustworthiness rather than truth, displaces validation from its traditional location in a presumably objective and neutral reality, and moves it to the social world—a world constructed in and through our discourse and actions, through praxis" (p. 420).

Having introduced self-study research and pertinent background concerning trustworthiness and validation, I now launch into a fine-point discussion of trustworthiness as evidenced in the self-study of teaching and teacher education.

THE NATURE OF NARRATIVE EXEMPLARS IN SELF-STUDY RESEARCH

Following in the scholarly footsteps of Kuhn in the nature of science and Mishler in social psychology, Lyons and LaBoskey (2002) made a case for the use of narrative exemplars to instantiate the trustworthiness of teaching and research practices involving narrative. Because self-studies interrogate practice and often use narrative in a variety of ways, it makes sense to filter representative self-studies through the criteria Lyons and LaBoskey proposed. Such an approach would add to the body of knowledge concerning what is known about the trustworthiness of self-study of teaching and teacher education practices research in two important ways: one, rather than taking narrative in self-study for granted, as often is the case in both qualitative and quantitative types of research, narrative would be placed at the forefront of discussion; and two, the approach would offer a productive response to Zeichner's (2008) recent critique of self-study inquiries. In Zeichner's professional opinion, those researchers involved in the self-study of teaching and teacher practices have too frequently focused on asking whether particular pieces of research fit the self-study genre (i.e., bounding the field) and too little time "accumulating knowledge across self-studies" (i.e., building the knowledge base). Hence, this chapter follows the lead of researchers already pushing the self-study of teaching and teacher education practices in that direction. For example, Korthagen, Loughran, and Russell (2006), writing in the year preceding Zeichner's criticism, discussed fundamental principles that transcended their sustained research on teacher education programs in The Netherlands, Australia and Canada, research that curiously went unreported in the U.S.-dominated AERA report on research and teacher education (see Brower & Korthagen, 2005; Loughran, Korthagen, & Russell, 2008). Also, Hamilton, Smith, and Worthington (2008) have probed narrative, self-study, and auto-ethnography and have connected the overall intent of the studies with the most appropriate methodologies. With this additional background in place, Lyons and LaBoskey's characteristics of narrative exemplars will now be elucidated, with the understanding that exemplars are "candidate" ones until they are accepted by rigorous review by the field.

QUALITIES OF NARRATIVE EXEMPLARS

In Lyons and LaBoskey's view, narrative exemplars share five characteristics that traverse studies, regardless of the content of the inquiries. Narrative exemplars:
- capture intentional human actions that not only tell a story, but convey the developing knowledge of those involved;
- are lodged in socially and contextually embedded situations; hence, readers come to know pertinent background, the subtle nuances of how the self-study unfurled, and the inner thinking of main characters;
- draw other people into the mix as the narrative exemplar is unpacked and experiential storying and restorying (Connelly & Clandinin, 1990) ensues;
- implicate people's identities as a consequence of the inquiry;
- focus on interpretation, frequently taking different perspectives into account.

With these characteristics in mind, the four self-studies I have selected to analyze as narrative exemplars will now be identified.

By way of general introduction, each of my four choices is conducted by a different researcher/different research team; each takes up a topic illustrative of the broad spectrum of themes self-study addresses; and each has been published in a reputable venue, elevating it from a candidate exemplar to narrative exemplar status. Vicky Anderson-Patton and Elizabeth Bass's (2002) work, *Using narrative teaching portfolios for self-study*, is a collaborative research study involving two investigators and includes both student and faculty participation in the creation of narrative teaching portfolios. This chapter, by the way, is in some ways a doubly recognized exemplar; it is found in Lyons and LaBoskey's (2002) edited volume. Located in the *Teacher Education Yearbook XVI* (Craig & Deretchin, 2008), the second study, Helen Freidus's *Small steps: Moving toward a renaissance in teacher education*, centers on an innovation made to a graduate literacy course that then became part of Bank Street College's teacher education program. As for the third study, Clare Kosnik's (2005) *No teacher educator left behind: The impact of U.S. policies and trends on my work as a researcher and teacher educator*, it is situated at the intersection where U.S. educational policy and teacher educators' and researchers' practices meet and involves Kosnik's transition from a Canadian teacher education landscape to an American teacher education milieu. Finally, my essay (Craig, 2006), *Change, changing and being changed: A self-study of a teacher educator's becoming real in the throes of urban school reform*, addresses the theme of school reform, a topic largely on the edge of mainstream self-study literature. Referred to as the Craig article from here on in, the latter self-study has been chosen because it provides insider insights into trustworthiness, but also because it holds me accountable to the same criteria to which the other researchers are being held, which is in keeping with the spirit of self-study. Both the Kosnik and Craig articles are carried in *Studying Teacher Education*, the flagship journal of the Special Interest Group of the Self-Study of Teaching and Teacher Education Practices.

QUALITY 1: INTENTIONAL HUMAN ACTION LINKED TO HUMAN KNOWLEDGE GROWTH

In the first exemplar, Anderson-Patton and Bass (2002) recognized that "reading research on teaching is not effective in transforming practice" (p. 101). Their collaborative action introduced narrative teaching portfolios to their creativity and writing classes: Anderson-Patton, in an elementary school context, and Bass, in a practicum setting. As a result, interactions took place in a layered sort of way, as did the reflections that accompanied the narrative portfolio development. The inquiry question, 'Do we teach according to our values?', borrowed from Whitehead's (1993) action research-driven self-studies, propelled the multi-dimensional inquiry.

Freidus, in the second self-study, recognized that the teaching preservice candidates had observed in New York schools had radically changed due to the No Child Left Behind Act and the manner in which local implementation had taken place. In order to provide prospective teachers with more robust literacy experiences, Freidus intentionally revised a graduate course as a way of responding appropriately to the teacher candidate's needs and those of future students with whom they would interact. Along the way, Freidus documented her own and others' responses in order to trace their knowledge growth.

As for Kosnik, in the third narrative exemplar, she purposefully moved from a premier public research university in Canada (University of Toronto) to a premier private institution in California (Stanford University). She temporarily changed contexts to learn about teacher education in the U.S. and to carry lessons back with her to Canada when she resumed her work at the University of Toronto.

In the fourth self-study, Craig centered on a reform initiative where she worked alongside teachers on five school campuses as a planning and evaluation consultant and on a sixth campus as a formal evaluator. Craig's dual role-taking afforded her multiple insights by virtue of the different perspectives to which she was privy. In the investigation, she centered on four dilemmas with the intent of arriving at overarching understandings.

QUALITY 2: SOCIALLY AND CONTEXTUALLY SITUATED

As foreshadowed, Anderson-Patton and Bass's study involved different ages of students, different content areas, different contexts, and different instructional responsibilities for the two self-study researchers as well as Jerry Allender, another self-study researcher, who questioned their assumptions and helped them to sharpen their thinking. As for Freidus, she worked closely with an American Museum of Natural History collaborator and her students additionally participated as learners and as prospective teachers. Also, the workshop took place in the museum setting, which was in the local community, although outside Freidus and her students' educational milieu. In Kosnik's case, she was situated in the context of teacher education reform in one of the most diverse, populated states in the U.S., working alongside preeminent researcher, Linda Darling-Hammond. Craig was also located in the midst of reform, albeit a K-12 initiative. In Craig's diverse, urban backdrop, interactions occurred with teachers, principals, reform movement personnel, students and other evaluators as well as university detractors.

QUALITY 3: ENGAGING SELVES AND OTHERS IN INTERROGATING ASPECTS OF TEACHING AND LEARNING BY "STORYING" EXPERIENCE

In the first narrative exemplar, Anderson-Patton and Bass provided longer reflective passages excerpted from their portfolio project as well as pithy examples of exchanges among their students. What follows is an example of the latter:

THEME 1: PROCESS ANXIETY

A: What does she want?

B: What's a teaching portfolio?

A: She said we could do anything we want.

B: But we need artifacts, and it has to be about our teaching.

A: What's an artifact? This is too loose for me. I need more structure. Tell me how many words, and I'll do a research paper. I'm good at that.

B: I just want to learn some new tricks to be more creative in my classroom.

A: Self-study—what's that?

B: She's not clear. She said it is a process and will emerge.

A: I guess it has to do about self. That's no different than research.

B: I just don't get it. (Anderson-Patton & Bass, 2002, p. 104).

Like Anderson-Patton and Bass's exemplar, Freidus's (2008) chapter was chock-full of reflective passages about what the Bank Street College teacher candidates said about the revised course—i.e., "It inspired me to include not only factual texts in my work with students, but also objects, manipulatives, and other items, students can interact with and research" (p. 323), but also of how they applied what they learned in classroom settings, as the following representative passage written by one of Freidus's students suggests:

In context, Emma [one of the student's students] was able to understand and use new vocabulary to describe objects. Her vocabulary includes limited descriptive language. Still, since she is younger than six and speaks Spanish at home, it seems obvious that she simply needs more exposure, appropriate modeling and more opportunities to use more specific vocabulary (in order to learn)... Walking back from the museum, I realized how important the pumpkin was to Emma...Children with no prior knowledge of pumpkins as plants assume that they come from the market, and the men in the market make them. No wonder Emma had trouble making sense of the story we read about pumpkins last week. (Freidus, 2008, p. 325)

Moving on to the Kosnik exemplar, much of the interrogation in her work is necessarily centered on self. In the essay, Kosnik framed her discussion around 'Working as Teacher in Canada,' 'Working in the U.S. Context', and finally, 'Balancing My Integrity and Not Being Left Behind.' After reviewing her accumulated evidence, Kosnik frankly declared:

It has become strikingly apparent that I must continue to modify my practices, or I will be left behind. The challenge will be to remain true to my values while living and working in a highly politicized world. This will require a high level of ingenuity and the identification of strategies to achieve this balancing act. (Kosnik, 2005, pp. 218–219)

As for Craig, she made sense of her school reform work alongside teachers from several campuses and other evaluators involved in the effort. Her evidence included journal entries, meeting notes, and audio-taped discussions. The following exchange is with teachers from three schools and is illustrative of the tenor of the work:

Craig: When we first started, the group at one of the schools sometimes met before I came and decided "this is what we are going to share with her today."

Shannon: Oh, my word.

Mari: That is so funny because that was my initial reaction to you—with us too it was like, she is 'the man' and we need to be perfect for her (because she comes from the university).

Shannon: That is because you did not have her living in your school...like we did...We never had that issue.

Annette: As for (my school)...we came to know Cheryl Craig before the...retreat. And we already knew we didn't have to do that.

Craig: So this is what makes relationships interesting for all of us.

Mari: Well...We're teachers, we're pleasers. You know, somebody who is above us, we want to show them that we are wonderful...and what is wonderful makes us interesting...but it is not the full picture.

Craig: Point of clarification, Mari. I don't consider myself above you. I think we have knowledge of different kinds.

Sandi: But being at the university does that to you...

Craig: I guess it does.

Annette: Yes, it does.

Shannon: That is how you were chosen to work with us. (Craig, 2005, 109–110)

QUALITY 4: IMPLICATING IDENTITIES

The short passages highlighted in the previous section set the stage for the fourth characteristic of narrative exemplars: implicating identities. Anderson-Patton and Bass, for instance, frequently spoke of the vulnerability of their identities and learning to work with that vulnerability. Anderson-Patton, for example, reflected:

> I was caught between my belief that the self is intrinsic to transformation and my aversion to narcissism. My three-part graphic—Who am I? What and how do I teach? And what did I learn? forced me to articulate my living contradictions. I felt exposed through this process; however, the work reminded me how central personal voice, risk taking, and diversity, are in my teaching. Wrestling with how to articulate my teaching helped me stay more authentic with students. (Anderson-Patton & Bass, 2002, p. 112).

The Freidus chapter also implicated identities, most especially the identities of the teacher candidates Freidus taught. The following lengthy excerpt captures how deeply student identities were confronted and positively shaped:

Working with Ann [a particular young child] has been an inspiring experience for me. I went into this practicum thinking it was my job to fill a child with new knowledge. I now see that teaching is a far more complicated and interesting task. It is the teacher's job to inspire a student to motivate him/herself to deepen and expand the knowledge. Simply sitting at a desk and having children write and observe may enable some children to absorb the facts, but I see now that the goal of a good teacher is first to engage the student...I have read these ideas over and over. It took the hands-on experience at the museum [and my second trip] with Ann to make this real for me... (Freidus, 2008, p. 326).

As for the Kosnik work, the 'Balancing My Integrity and not Being Left Behind' section captured the identity of a more internationally-informed teacher educator and researcher. In her essay, Kosnik asserted:

Over the past 5 years, some of my perspectives and practices have changed. I now give greater attention to the global context and am acutely aware of how difficult it can be to gain a true understanding of another culture when working outside of it. Shared research agendas, collaboration across countries, joint publications, exchange programs, and on-going conversations may be strategies to help acquire insider knowledge. (Kosnik, 2005, p. 222)

Among the specific commitments Kosnik made—without putting her integrity at risk—was a minded decision to advance the knowledge base for teaching and teacher education, to become more involved in cross-site research, and to urge her Self-Study of Teaching and Teacher Educator Practice (S-STEP) colleagues to play a greater role in policy discussions through voicing their interests and concerns "forcefully and convincingly" in public audiences (p. 223).

The Craig essay came next. She took up the identity topic as well. She wrote: "I developed my identity as a teacher educator further in my new setting, rather than claiming a "high ground of theory" position or evaluator plotline, other opportunities that were readily available to me." And she concluded: "In the process, I found my teacher educator self to be vulnerable yet resistant, tentative yet knowing, hurt but not destroyed, in the making but never made..." (Craig, 2005, p. 114).

QUALITY 5: TOWARD CONSTRUCTION OF MEANING AND KNOWLEDGE

After presenting four of Lyons and LaBoskey's criteria and a plethora of evidence drawn from each of the exemplars, we have now reached the fifth quality of narrative exemplars: the knowledge contributions they make. Anderson-Patton and Bass (2002) vividly showed how flaccid "force-fed best practices" are and how "working with what is real is a great palliative" (p. 101). More than that, they provided the field with a roadmap of how two teacher educators worked productively together and with their students and a more distant colleague. Stated differently, they shone the spotlight on the process of "trying something different, being vulnerable, exposing one's self, articulating one's teaching, and interacting with a wider world," (p. 112) all experiences that they found engaging and valuable.

Moving on to the second narrative exemplar, Freidus illustrated how teacher educators might creatively resist the test-driven culture underway in schools, which inherently spills over to teacher education programs. Pulling on her institution's long and distinguished history, Freidus found both instruction and ammunition in the words of Lucy Sprague Mitchell, Bank Street's founder, who maintained that "We are not interested in perpetuation of any special 'school of thought.' Rather, we are interested in imbuing teachers with an experimental, critical and ardent approach to their work" (Mitchell, in Antler, 1987, p. 309, cited in Freidus, 2008, p. 316). Freidus not only defended and held the revamped course open to public scrutiny, but she also clearly articulated that her teacher education practice was anchored in the history of the field and broader visions of what constitutes science-based research.

Where Kosnik was concerned, in her work, she showed teacher educators how to wrestle incessantly with educational policy, while keeping their integrity intact. Kosnik especially demonstrated an inquiry stance, even with a topic she found confounding and disagreeable at times. Perhaps more than this, Kosnik illustrated how teacher educators can strengthen their research repertoires in order to respond to, and more fully participate in, the politicized teacher education debates.

Lastly, Craig added conceptual heft to existing understandings. While Clandinin and Connelly (1996) conceptualized stories of school—school stories and stories of teachers—teachers stories on the professional knowledge landscape of schools and Craig (2001) added stories of reform—and reform stories and stories of communities—communities stories (2004), the idea of stories of teacher educators—teacher educators' stories had not yet been included as part of the story constellation. Hence, Craig's exemplar made this knowledge contribution. Also, it demonstrated how deeply embedded faculty members are in the conduit (Clandinin & Connelly, 1995). To this point in time, the conduit has mostly been associated with individuals outside of classrooms, such as those in administrative and school district positions. But, in Craig's work, the role that teacher educators play in the conduit rises to the fore.

All in all, the four selected candidate exemplars resonated well with the five characteristics Lyons and LaBoskey associated with narrative exemplars and their trustworthiness. In short, each of the self-studies fit the proposed criteria, despite at least three of them not being written with the particular characteristics foremost in mind. This suggests that those who conduct research in the self-study of teaching and teacher education arena are well-versed in Kuhn's idea of "thinking with exemplars," in Schwab's commitment to "*interpreting* facts" and in Mishler's challenge to validate practice "through discourse and action, through praxis." At the same time, the representative self-study researchers appear to have intuitively embraced Lyons and LaBoskey's characteristics of narrative exemplars. Yet, the selected narrative exemplars made no claims to Truth. Rather, they conveyed "likely stories" that were "true for now."

CONCLUDING REFLECTIONS

Working closely with the aforementioned exemplars, the idea of how the trustworthiness of self-study research might be increased crossed my mind, particularly since all four had undergone critical blind review and were no longer of the candidate variety. Hence, I conclude with some friendly suggestions that are meant as much for me as for anyone else in the self-study community. One of the first things that struck me was that the first two narrative exemplars—the Anderson-Patton and Bass one and the Freidus one —were in many ways a response to "the literacy wars" and the results of the National Reading Panel I mentioned in passing earlier in this chapter. It occurred to me that those authors— and Craig (me) as well with the organized school reform topic—could have been much more explicit about their policy connections. If we are writing around the debates—rather than in them, we are apt to be excluded, as Kosnik compellingly argued. Hence, for me, this became one important way the narrative exemplars could have been more deeply embedded in ways that would add to their trustworthiness and fuel their usefulness in the action arena. At the bare minimum, the studies would at least show up in the relevant literature searches.

A second idea would be to pay more attention to history. Freidus beautifully demonstrated how history could be used to her and her students' advantage but also to the advantage of her self-study. This caused me to wonder why Kosnik had not been more explicit about the differing histories in Canadian and U.S. educational policy and why Anderson-Patton and Bass and Craig (me) spoke about creativity, portfolios and school reform as if they were devoid of history. Here, I suspect word length prohibited what the authors wrote. Nevertheless, a few lines appropriately placed in the narrative exemplars would have captured the historical connections and rendered the exemplars more believable and actionable to other teacher educators and researchers.

Finally, I would like to address conceptualization. Self-study is a relatively new field and "a mongrel" at that (Stefinee Pinnegar, Personal Communication, 2007). But its eclectic nature does not preclude it from having its own language and terms. Here, I am not advocating for taxonomies or anything of that nature. But I am thinking of "conceptual containers" that could hold big ideas central to the field. As I read the Anderson-Patton and Bass work, for example, I became intrigued by the rigor and the complexity expressed in an elegant and compact way. The same thought came to mind as I became immersed in the Freidus chapter and the Kosnik essay and I know that other people have responded in similar ways to my own work. At the same time, I intuitively knew that there was something more in the works than what the authors had written. Perhaps the something more intentional is the linking of clusters of self-studies as a way to enhance and draw additional attention to them as Zeichner has advised. However, for me, more explicit naming of their knowledge contributions also has a major role to play in increasing the trustworthiness of studies as defined and described in this chapter. Taking up Zeichner's suggestion as well as the three I have offered would help expand the trustworthiness of exemplars in the self-study of teaching and teacher education enterprise, augmenting their utility and potential outcomes when acted upon. While

J. C. Phillips, author of the opening quotation, may still not be satisfied, thinking across self-study exemplars as I have done in this chapter helps to move the deliberations along and to fortify the ground on which the self-study community has chosen to stand.

REFERENCES

Anderson, G., & Herr, K. (1999). The new paradigm wars: Is there room for rigorous practitioner knowledge in schools and universities? *Educational Researcher, 28*(5), 12–21.

Anderson-Patton, V., & Bass, E. (2002). Using narrative teaching portfolios for self-study. In N. Lyons & V. LaBoskey (Eds.), *Narrative inquiry in practice: Advancing the knowledge of teaching* (pp. 101–114). New York: Teachers College Press.

Barone, T. (2008). *Business meeting.* Narrative and Research in Education Special Interest Group. Annual meeting of the American Educational Research Association, New York.

Brower, N., & Korthagen, F. (2005). Can teacher education make a difference? *American Educational Research Journal, 42*(1), 153–224.

Bullough, R., & Gitlin, A. (2001). *Becoming a student of teaching: Linking knowledge production and practice.* London: RoutledgeFalmer.

Bullough, R., & Pinnegar, S. (2001). Guidelines for quality in autobiographical forms of self-study research. *Educational Researcher, 30*(3), 13–21.

Bruner, J. (1986). *Actual minds, possible worlds.* Boston: Harvard University Press.

Carse, J. (1986). *Finite and infinite games.* New York: Free Press.

Clandinin, D. J., & Connelly, F. M. (1996). Teachers' professional knowledge landscapes: Teachers stories—stories of teachers, School stories—stories of school. *Educational Researcher, 25*(3), 24–30.

Cochran-Smith, M., & Lytle, S. (2004). Practitioner inquiry, knowledge, and university culture. In J. Loughran, M. Hamilton, V. LaBoskey, & T. Russell (Eds.), *International handbook of self-study of teaching and teacher education practices* (pp. 601–649). Dordrecht, The Netherlands: Kluwer Academic.

Cochran-Smith, M., & Zeichner, K. (Eds.). (2005). *Studying teacher education: The report of the AERA panel on research and teacher education.* Washington, DC: American Educational Research Association.

Connelly, F. M., & Clandinin, D. J. (1990). Stories of experience and narratives of inquiry. *Educational Researcher, 19*(5), 2–14.

Craig, C. (2001). The relationships between and among teacher knowledge, communities of knowing, and top down school reform: A case of "The Monkey's Paw". *Curriculum Inquiry, 31*(3), 303–331.

Craig, C. (2004). The dragon in school backyards: The influence of mandated testing on school contexts and educators' narrative knowing. *Teachers College Record, 106*(6), 1229–1257.

Craig, C. (2006). Change, changing, and being changed: A self-study of a teacher educator's becoming real in the throes of urban school reform. *Studying Teacher Education, 2*(1), 105–116.

Dewey, J. (1938). *Education and experience.* New York: Collier Books.

Dinkelman, T. (2003). Self-study in teacher education: A means and ends tool for promoting reflective thinking. *Journal of Teacher Education, 54*(1), 6–18.

Elbaz-Luwisch, F. (2006). Studying teachers' lives and experience. In D. J. Clandinin (Ed.), *Handbook of narrative inquiry: Mapping a methodology* (pp. 357–382). Thousand Oaks, CA: Sage Publications.

Feldman, A., Paugh, P., & Mills, G. (2004). Self-study through action research. *International handbook of self-study of teaching and teacher education practices* (pp. 943–978). Dordrecht, The Netherlands: Kluwer Academic Publishers.

Fenstermacher, G. (1994). The knower and the known: The nature of knowledge in research on teaching. *Review of Research in Education, 20*, 3–56.

Gipe, J. (1998). Case studies of collaborative self-study. In M. L. Hamilton (Ed.), *Reconceptualizing teaching practice: Self-study in teacher education* (pp. 75–76). London: Falmer Press.

Hamilton, M. L., & Pinnegar, S. (1998). Conclusion: The value and the promise of self-study. In M. L. Hamilton (Ed.), *Reconceptualizing teaching practice: Self-study in teacher education* (pp. 235–246). London: Falmer Press.

Hamilton, M. L., Smith, L., & Worthington, K. (2006). Fitting the methodology with the research: An exploration of narrative, self-study and auto-ethnography. *Studying Teacher Education, 4*(1), 17–28.

Kitchen, J. (2005). Looking backwards, moving forward: Understanding my narrative as a teacher. *Studying Teacher Education, 1*(1), 17–30.

Korthagen, F., Loughran, J., & Russell, T. (2006). Developing fundamental principles for teacher education programs and practices. *Teaching and Teacher Education, 22*(8), 1021–1041.

Kosnik, C. (2005). No teacher educator left behind: The impact of U.S. policies and trends on my work as a researcher and teacher educator. *Studying Teacher Education, 1*(2), 209–223.

Kuhn, T. (1962/1996). *The structure of the scientific revolution* (3rd ed.). Chicago: University of Chicago Press.

Lincoln, Y., & Guba, E. (1985). *Naturalistic inquiry*. Thousand Oaks, CA: Sage Publications.

Loughran, J., & Northfield, J. (1998). A framework for the development of self-study practice. In M. L. Hamilton (Ed.), *Reconceptualizing teacher practice: Self-study for teacher education* (pp. 7–18). London: Falmer Press.

Loughran, J., Korthagen, F., & Russell, T. (2008). Teacher education that makes a difference: Developing foundational principles of practice. In C. Craig & L. Deretchin (Eds.), *Imagining a renaissance in teacher education* (pp. 405–423). Lanham, MD: Roman & Littlefield.

Lyons, N., & LaBoskey, V. (Eds.). (2002). *Narrative inquiry in practice: Advancing the knowledge of teaching*. New York: Teachers College Press.

Mishler, E. (1990). Validity in inquiry-guided research: The role of exemplars in narrative studies. *Harvard Educational Review, 60*(4), 415–442.

Munby, H., Russell, T., & Martin, A. (2001). Teachers' knowledge and how they develop it. In V. Richardson (Ed.), *Handbook of research on teaching* (4th ed., pp. 877–904). Washington, DC: American Educational Research Association.

National Institute of Child Health and Human Development (NICHD). (2000). *Report of the National Reading Panel: Teaching children to read: An evidence-based assessment of the scientific research literature on reading and its implications for reading instruction* (NIH Publication No. 00-4769). Washington, DC: U.S. Department of Health and Human Services.

Phillips, D. C. (1993, April). *Telling it straight: Issues in assessing narrative research*. Paper presented at the annual conference of the Philosophy of Education Society of Great Britain, Oxford, England.

Pinnegar, S., & Bullough, R., Jr. (2004). Thinking about the thinking about self-study: An analysis of eight chapters. In J. Loughran, M. Hamilton, V. LaBoskey, & T. Russell (Eds.), *International handbook of self-study of teaching and teacher education practices* (pp. 313–342). Dordrecht, The Netherlands: Kluwer Academic Publishers.

Pinnegar, S., & Daynes, J. G. (2006). Locating narrative inquiry historically: Thematics in the turn to narrative. In D. J. Clandinin (Ed.), *Handbook of narrative inquiry: Mapping a methodology* (pp. 3–34). Thousand Oaks, CA: Sage Publications, Inc.

Pinnegar, S., Dulude Lay, C., Bigham, S., & Dulude, C. (2005). Teaching as highlighted by mothering: A narrative inquiry. *Studying Teacher Education, 1*(1), 55–67.

Schön, D. (1983). *The reflective practitioner: How professionals think in action*. New York: Basic Books.

Schön, D. (1995). The new scholarship requires a new epistemology. *Change, 27*(6), 26–34.

Schön, D. (1991). *The reflective turn: Case studies in and on educational practice*. New York: Teachers College Press.

Schwab, J. (1961/1978). Education and the structure of the disciplines. In I. Westbury & N. Wilkoff (Eds.), *Science, curriculum and liberal education: Selected essays* (pp. 229–272). Chicago: University of Chicago Press.

Schwab, J. (1967). Joseph J. Schwab: On scientific inquiry. In C. Madden (Ed.), *Talks with scientists* (pp. 3–24). Carbondale and Edwardsville: Southern Illinois University Press.

Senese, J. (2005). Teach to learn. *Studying Teacher Education, 1*(1), 43–54.

Weber, S., & Mitchell, C. (2004). Visual artistic modes of representation in self-study. In J. Loughran, M. Hamilton, V. LaBoskey, & T. Russell (Eds.), *International handbook of self-study of teaching and teacher education practices* (pp. 979–1038). Dordrecht, The Netherlands: Kluwer Academic Publishers.

Whitehead, J. (1993). *The growth of educational knowledge: Creating your own living educational theory*. Bournemouth, UK: Hyde Publications.

Whitehead, J. (2000). How do I improve my practice? Creating and legitimating an epistemology of practice. *Reflective Practice, 1*(1), 91–104.

Zeichner, K. (2008). Accumulating knowledge across self-studies in teacher education. *Journal of Teacher Education, 58*(1), 36–46.

ALLAN FELDMAN

3. MAKING THE SELF PROBLEMATIC

Data Analysis and Interpretation in Self-Study Research

...the self must bother itself

(Britzman, 1998, p. 2)

DEFINING SELF-STUDY

My purpose in writing this chapter is to examine how the nature of self-study research affects the way in which data are analyzed and interpreted. This will also lead me to questions about what constitutes evidence when engaged in self-study. To do this, I make problematic what we mean by *self* in self-study, and examine the nature of the self through the lenses of psychoanalysis and existentialism. First, because self-study is a new form of scholarship and its practitioners have multiple conceptions of it, it is necessary for me to provide readers with some idea of what I mean by the self-study of teacher education practices. I begin by looking at two descriptions of self-study. The first is the one given by John Loughran:

> ...quality self-study requires that it is a disciplined and systematic inquiry; values professional learning as a research outcome for students of teaching as well as teacher educators; and, aims to develop and better articulate a knowledge of practice. (Loughran, 2008, p. 9)

Loughran's characteristics of quality self-study tell us about the doing of self-study – it is a form of inquiry in which the researcher pays attention to the research process; what it values – professional learning of the researcher's practice; and its product – knowledge of practice.

The second characterization of self-study that I draw on comes from Vicki LaBoskey's chapter in the *International handbook of self-study of teaching and teacher education practices* (LaBoskey, 2004). In it she argues that self-study is improvement-aimed; interactive; employs multiple methods; and it is reported to the professional community for deliberation, testing, and evaluation (LaBoskey, 2004). Loughran's and LaBoskey's lists contain similar elements. They tell us that self-study researchers use a variety of accepted research methods, which are for the most part qualitative, and do so collaboratively and interactively with colleagues, students and texts. These methods and interactions are what make self-study disciplined and structured. To LaBoskey one of the values of self-study is in its improvement-aimed nature. Self-study "aims to improve teaching and teacher education and the institutional contexts in which they take place" (2004, p. 844).

C. A. Lassonde, S. Galman and C. Kosnik (eds.), Self-Study Research Methodologies for Teacher Educators, 35–49.

The purpose for doing this is "to better understand, facilitate, and articulate the teaching-learning process" (2004, p. 857) in order to maximize the benefits for preservice and inservice teachers, and their students (2004)). A second value is that knowledge of teaching is a product of self-study. It is for this reason that the trustworthiness of self-studies must be demonstrated through the use of multiple methods and by having the studies scrutinized by the professional community.

Reviews of the self-study literature in this volume and elsewhere indicate that there is good consensus around the characteristics described by Loughran, LaBoskey, and others (Bullough & Pinnegar, 2001; Feldman, Paugh, & Mills, 2004; Hamilton & Pinnegar, 1998; Zeichner & Noffke, 2001). Self-study research is usually done by teacher educators who have as their aim the improvement of their practice and the production of new knowledge about teaching and the relationship between teaching and learning. In general, self-study research is done using qualitative methods, and in particular, narrative and autobiographical methods, and is reported to others through a variety of media and forms of representation for the purposes of dissemination and critique.

The Methodology of Self-Study

While this set of characteristics can serve the purpose of distinguishing self-study from other forms of research, it really does not tell us what is special about self-study as a form of inquiry. Pat Paugh, Geoff Mills and I have explored its similarity to action research (Feldman, Paugh, & Mills, 2004), and on the surface there appears to be little difference between self-study and Lee Shulman's scholarship of teaching (Shulman, 2000). It, too, is done by researchers who teach, its aim is to improve teaching and learning, and to produce knowledge about teaching and learning, and, according to Shulman, has these features: "… being public, open to critique and evaluation, and in a form that others can build on" (Hutchings & Shulman, 1999, p. 13). In addition, the scholarship of teaching, "involves question-asking, inquiry and investigations, particularly around the issues of student learning" (1999, 13). It is important to note that Shulman does not see the investigation of student learning as an end unto itself; rather, it is a way to gain information and develop understanding about teaching. Given that, it is clear that the scholarship of teaching shares the features of self-study research.

So while there is consensus among self-study researchers about the features of self-study, this set of features does not serve to distinguish self-study from other forms of practitioner research. I argued elsewhere (Feldman, 2006; Feldman, Paugh, & Mills, 2004) that to understand the nature of self-study scholarship, it is important to treat it as a methodology rather than a set of methods. I used Sandra Harding's work on the methodology of feminist scholarship (Harding, 1989) as a to understand what it would mean for self-study to be a methodology. To Harding, a methodology is the theoretical basis for a field of research, which can be seen in what the field makes problematic in its inquiries. In feminist methodology, gender is made problematic, which leads Harding to posit three features that distinguish feminist scholarship from other methodologies. They are:

- The discovery of gender and its consequences.
- Women's experience as a scientific resource.
- The reflexivity of feminist research (Harding, 1989).

In self-study, it is the self that is made problematic, and Harding's list becomes transformed into the following:

- A self-study methodology brings to the forefront the importance of the self;
- It makes the experience of the teacher educators a resource for research; and
- It urges those who engage in self-study to be critical of themselves and their roles as researchers and teacher educators (Feldman, Paugh, & Mills, 2004, p. 959).

It should be clear from my review of Loughran's and LaBoskey's characteristics of self-study that there is consonance between how they see self-study and the second and third features of a self-study methodology. What is not so clear is how self-study spotlights the importance of the self and how it makes it problematic in the same way that gender serves feminist studies. To do so we must first look at what Harding means by the "discovery of gender and its consequences." The idea that "gender" was "discovered" is inconceivable to many people who came of age after the women's liberation movement of the 1960s and 1970s. Before then people generally saw maleness and femaleness as products of biology and were referred to as *sex* rather than *gender*. What feminist scholars discovered was "the idea of a systematic social construction of masculinity and femininity" (Harding, 1989, p. 26). Once gender was identified as a social construct, it allowed for investigations, for example, of how gender is constructed, what influences its construction, and how gender relates to social, political, and economic power structures. In other words, the discovery/illumination/invention of gender made possible and defines feminist research.

At this time, little has been done in the field of self-study of teacher education practices that makes the self problematic in the same way that feminist studies use gender. We certainly find the experiences of teacher educators being used as a resource for research in the sense that it is the practices or the life histories of teacher educators that are being investigated. We can also find many examples of self-study researchers being critical of their roles as researchers and teacher educators. One way to understand this is to use the typology developed by Pat Paugh, Geoff Mills and me in our *Handbook* chapter (Feldman, Paugh, & Mills, 2004). We divided self-studies into three types:

- Research on the self.
- Research on the self in practice.
- Research on how one understands oneself in practice (Feldman, Paugh, & Mills, 2004, p. 950).

Although there is not a one-to-one correspondence, types 2 and 3 are related to features 2 and 3 of the characteristics of a self-study methodology. That is, when teacher educators research themselves in practice, they rely on their experiences as data and other resources for research. And, when they attempt to understand themselves in practice, they critique their roles as researchers and teacher educators.

I believe that the reason that we see so little of the first type of self-study research is because the field is still being developed and we are in the process of discovering/inventing/illuminating what we mean by *self*. It is important to note that questions about men's and women's roles and their effects on people's lives were explored extensively before the "discovery" of gender. However, feminist theory makes those roles, how they are related to maleness and femaleness, and so on, problematic. In the same way, self-study researchers are not the first to use self-perspective in the examination of teaching and teacher education. Stories or narratives and autobiographies of teachers have existed for millennia in religious writing, novels, and plays, and teachers have been represented in painting, sculpture and music. In fact, that may be why these forms of representation predominate in self-study scholarship.

I see the main difference between types 1 and 2 of self-study research in the following way. In Type 2, the researcher is investigating her practice in the same way that she would be investigating another teacher educator's practice, with the main difference being that she herself is the teacher educator whose practice is being studied. In Type 1, the researcher is studying her *way of being* a teacher educator. A person's way of being is the result of his or her experience, and the set of intentional states – dispositions, talents, interests, fears, and visions –that locate the person and point him or her in one direction or another (Stengel, 1996). The human being who is a teacher educator has a way of being that is uniquely his or hers as a teacher educator. In addition, he or she has other ways of being that include his or her relation to family, community, vocations, and avocations (Stengel, 1996).

I also believe that if we are to succeed in our project to discover/invent/illuminate what we mean by self, we need to draw upon scholarly traditions that make our ways of being teacher educators problematic. This is something that I have begun to do by looking at existentialism and psychoanalysis. In the next section of this chapter, I look at aspects of these traditions to see what they can tell us about researching ourselves *as* teacher educators.

EXISTENTIALISM AND SELF-STUDY

In this section I revisit my argument that existentialism can serve as a theoretical basis for self-study research (Feldman, 2003, 2006, 2007). To me, existentialism is one of many possible ways of looking at the world, and is distinguished by making *existence* problematic. Therefore, it is possible to have an existential research methodology in which the central problematic concept is existence, and questions are asked such as, "What is existence?" "What does it mean to be?" "What is it to human beings that we are beings who are aware of our own being?" and, "What does it mean that we are aware that we will eventually cease to exist?" During much of my time as an educational researcher, I have used an existential methodology to seek answers to the question, "What does it mean to teach and to be a teacher?" The importance of this question to my work is that it allows me to distinguish the *act of teaching* from *being a teacher*. This has led me to ask questions like, "Who am I as a teacher educator?" "How does the way I am a teacher educator affect how I teach?" And, "How do I change who I am as a teacher educator to improve my educational situation for myself and my students?" (See Feldman (2006) for an existential analysis of my being a teacher educator.)

From my study of the literature of existentialism and its relation to action research and self-study, I have identified three characteristics of personhood: situatedness, the emergence of the self, and freedom. Human existence is situated. That is, we exist in a web of relationships that spreads through time and space (Greene, 1973) and is constituted by the milieu of "traditions, institutions and customs, and the purposes and beliefs that carry and inspire" (Dewey, 1938, p. 43). Educational situations are ones that involve educators and students, and therefore all that occurs in those situations is affected by the educators' past and present, moods and gestures, expectations and intentions, and, of course, the students with which they are engaged. Because human existence is situated, and because a basic aspect of being human is that we continuously learn, as we go about our lives we construct who we are and our selves emerge through our experiences (Greene, 1973). Or, as Sartre said, existence precedes essence (Sartre, 1956). As we live our situated existences and construct ourselves, we have an existential freedom to make choices about what we do, even when our ability to act is constrained. To Maxine Greene human freedom "is the capacity to surpass the given and look at things as if they could be otherwise" (Greene, 1988, p. 3) and to be able "to name alternatives, imagine a better state of things, [and] share with others a project of change" (Greene, 1988, p. 9).

These existential characteristics of personhood help us to understand how we construct ourselves through our choices and our actions. For people to gain this understanding, they must become aware of their situatedness, their construction of their selves, and their freedom to choose how to act. Most people not only find this awareness difficult to achieve, there is also a tendency to flee from it, because if we are aware that we construct ourselves, then we must accept the responsibility for who we are. This is, as Van Cleve Morris put it, a "mountainous" responsibility (Morris, 1966). These existential characteristics also make it clear that it is not enough to acknowledge our own becoming – we must also be aware of and acknowledge the humanness of other people. In schools, colleges, and universities, educators and students, as well as administrators, parents, and others, need to recognize that every person is a human being who is situated, whose self emerges through experience, and has freedom to choose. This awareness and acknowledgement is needed for the establishment and sustaining of what Martin Buber called "I-Thou" relationships (1937) rather than the "I-It" relationships that result in the objectification of the other.

Existentialism can serve as a theoretical basis for self-study research (Feldman, Paugh, & Mills, 2004). It puts the self as a person becoming as its focus, and therefore brings to forefront of any existential inquiry the importance of the self. It also makes an explicit connection between the experiences that we have and who we are as a person. Because of this it would not be possible to make the self problematic in inquiries without using personal and professional experiences as resources for research. Finally, a self-study guided by existentialist theory would need to be reflexive and critical because of the requirement to acknowledge one's responsibility to oneself and to others (Feldman, 2006). But it also tells us about the way in which the self can be made problematic in self-studies of the first type. To do so we need to uncover the ways in which we are responsible to ourselves and for others. We need to examine the web of relationships that constitute the responsibilities. If we are seeking ways to improve the ways we can act responsibly as teacher educators, then we also need to identify the choices that we make, and the decisions not to choose, and to distinguish between the real and the mythic constraints (Britzman, 1986) that prevent us from acting responsibly. However, to say that this is what ought to be done is not the same as saying how to do it. In the next section of this chapter I turn to the field of psychoanalysis, and in particular self-psychology, for some clues as to how to proceed.

PSYCHOANALYSIS AND SELF-STUDY

I begin by making clear that psychoanalysis is both a method of psychotherapy and a theory of the self. As a theory it has entered folk psychology, and Freudian terms like the ego and defense mechanism, both of which I will use below, have become part of everyday thinking about who we are. Therefore, I will make clear what I mean by these terms when I use them. Psychoanalysis as a theory can be used to understand educational experience, as demonstrated by Peter Taubman (2007). To Taubman, the methodology of psychoanalytic theory offers us a way to focus on how we are complicit in the creation of our perception of the external world, primarily through the interaction of the unconscious and conscious aspects of our mentality. As a result

Psychoanalysis leads us to question how unconscious forces affect our interactions with our students, the curriculum, and the meanings we give to our experiences. (Taubman, 2007, p. 3)

From this it can be seen that psychoanalysis is a methodology that makes problematic the self through its exploration of the interactions between the conscious and unconscious, and with the external world.

Deborah Britzman has explored the relationship between education and psychoanalysis in her book, *Lost subjects, contested objects: Toward a psychoanalytic inquiry of learning* (1998). Although her focus is on teaching and learning, and the relationship between teacher and learner, her analysis is useful for understanding the problematic nature of self in self-study. Drawing upon the work of Anna Freud (1936), Sigmund Freud (1923), Alice Balint (1945) and others, Britzman develops a way of seeing the self in educational experiences.

Britzman tells us that in psychoanalytic terms, learning cannot be seen as only a cognitive event, but also takes in the affective domain and its states, such as desire, conflict, joy, and unhappiness. As a result, to speak of learning from a psychoanalytic perspective, one must think in terms of changes in the self.

...learning is a psychic event, a moment when the difference between affect and cognition, between perception and interpretation, between desire and defense, and between being and having cannot be determined. (Britzman, 1998, p. 30)

Britzman also refers to the work of Alice Balint, and in particular, her use of the concept of "identificatory thinking." Identificatory thinking occurs when there is little separation between what is external and internal to the person. That is, the person sees the world only through his or her eyes, to the extent of shaping and reshaping understanding so that it conforms to one's conceptions of the world. The result is a kind of "mental mimicry". We do this because it is a way to console and defend ourselves against anxiety. However, learning is very different from identificatory thinking. When one learns, according to psychoanalytic theory, there is "a crafting of identification into understanding" (Britzman, 1998, p. 31).

Psychoanalysis also provides a way of looking at the educational enterprise. Anna Freud (1936), in her "Four Lectures on Psychoanalysis for Teachers and Parents," wrote about three ways in which psychoanalysis contributes to the understanding of pedagogy:
- As a means to critique educational methods;
- As means to help teachers gain knowledge and understanding of the complex social relations in classrooms; and
- As a way to help students who have suffered psychologically during their school experiences (Britzman, 1998).

Anna Freud also tells us that education must address two directions at the same time. They are "the turning of education back upon itself to view how its practices affect its structures, and the turning of education upon the learner to notice how its practices affect its subjects" (Britzman, 1998, p. 9). Both of these directions are addressed in the self-study of teacher education practices. Self-study research, as characterized by Loughran, LaBoskey, and others, focuses both on the effects that educational practice has on students, and the ways that the practices of education are dependent on and affect educational structures. However, both of these foci of inquiry can be done without making the self problematic. One reason for this is the process that Anna Freud refers to as "intellectualization," which is the way in which researchers become preoccupied and lose themselves in theoretical constructs (Britzman, 1998). Intellectualization, while cognitive, shifts our thoughts away from ourselves and therefore prevents the problematization of the self in self-study.

Intellectualization is usually classified as a "defense mechanism" – a psychological strategy that is used to protect oneself from negative feelings, such as guilt, anxiety, and inferiority. To Freudians the ego is that part of a person's mentality that is conscious and deals with the external world. In Freudian terms, the self is usually referred to as the ego – the part of a person's mentality that is conscious and deals with the external world. To Sigmund Freud, the ego is what could be called reason or common sense (S. Freud, 1923). But, as Britzman points out, the ego is continually mediating between its self and its perceptions of the external world. As a result, questions are raised such as

What belongs to the ego, and what belongs to the object? Is it me, or is it them? How do I know that what I think is happening is actually happening? What if I cannot believe what I see? How do my actions become puzzling to me? How do I recognize my self when my self is at the same time conflictive, ambivalent, and caught between my own demands and the demands of others? (Britzman, 1998, p. 12)

Questions about the self like these asked by Britzman are how psychoanalytic theory can help to make the self problematic in self-study. When the self-study researcher raises questions like, "What belongs to me, the teacher educator, and what belongs to the students?" and, "Where do my emotional ties become entangled in my pedagogy and in my inquiry?" the self is brought to the forefront in self-study. Or, as Britzman put it,

the self must bother itself. It must learn to obligate itself to notice the breaches and losses between acts and thoughts, between wishes and responsibilities, between dreams and waking life. (Britzman, 1998, p. 32)

Taubman (2007) suggests that the way to do this is with a form of reflection that is shaped by psychoanalytic theory. Before explaining what he means by that, it is important to note that the term reflection is associated with a variety of different stances in the world. One can engage in a technical form of reflection, in which one seeks straightforward solutions to problems of practice (Valli, 1990). Deliberative reflection, which is related to a practical orientation toward teaching (Grundy, 1987), involves "weighing competing claims or viewpoints," and its content may be "a range of teaching concerns" (Valli, 1990, p. 221). When teachers engage in critical reflection they consider the social and political complexities of teaching and schooling, and the ways in which these can be hidden causes of what happens in classrooms and schools.

Taubman gives the example of a teacher who is "ferociously committed to exposing racism in American society" (Taubman, 2007, p. 5). Technical reflection may lead the teacher to search for curriculum materials on racism. Deliberative reflection may entail weighing the pros and cons of different materials from an ethical perspective. A teacher reflecting critically may look at the ways in which racism affects his or her practice. The teacher engaging in a psychoanalytic form of reflection would instead be trying to understand what accounts for his or her "ferocious commitment." A psychoanalytic form of reflection is most similar to critical reflection, but rather than seek for hidden "causes" in the social world, one tries to understand oneself in relation to the educational situation, and therefore, teacher educators could engage in psychoanalytic reflection when the self is made problematic is self-studies.

METHODS OF SELF PSYCHOLOGY

Existentialism and psychoanalytic theory provide us with perspectives that allow us to recognize the problematic nature of self in self-study. Psychoanalysis also provides us with some ideas of how we can go about investigating our selves in practice. I draw upon the work of Heinz Kohut (1977) for some methods and caveats. Kohut's main contribution to psychoanalysis was the idea that there are psychological conditions that are related to the ways in which the self is constructed. He created the field of self psychology, which makes the development of the self the central problematic for understanding the psyche. In clinical self psychology therapists attempt to understand their clients' subjective experience through introspection and empathy. That is, the client engages in introspection, the examination of one's own thoughts, feeling, beliefs, etc., and the therapist engages in empathy to create a "concrete representation of another person's mental state, including the accompanying emotions" (de Mijolla, 2005).

Kohut was aware of the dangers that arise from an inquiry that relies on the subjective data that come from introspection and empathy. He saw at leas two problems inherent in this approach. The first is that because clinical inquiries are most often reported as cases, there is always the possibility that readers come to believe the report because of the quality of the writing, rather than the quality of the data and their interpretation (Kohut, 1977). The second is the possibility of the skewing of empathic data by the therapist's theoretical views. That is, data are always seen through a lens that is shaped by the viewer's theories and beliefs.

Kohut suggests several different ways to guard against these challenges to veracity. First, he refers to two principles: the "Emperor's New Clothes" and the "Rosetta-Stone." The former is the idea that it is possible that an untrained, naïve observer can see more accurately than one who is burdened by theories, social constructs, or complex cognitive structures. What this means is that therapists, when trying to understand data from introspection and empathy, should try to begin to do so by inferring as little as possible. Kohut described the Rosetta-Stone principle in this way:

> ... the validity of newly discovered meanings (or their significance) must be established in analogy to the validation procedure employed in the deciphering of hieroglyphics. If the observer-decipherer can demonstrate to himself that an increased number of phenomena can be combined to spell out a meaningful message when seen from a new point of view, that a broader range of data can now be understood and interpreted meaningfully, then one can indeed say that his conviction about the new mode of interpretation has become stronger. (Kohut, 1977, p. 144)

The Rosetta-Stone principle is similar to the idea of hermeneutic reading and re-reading, in which new meaning arises from seeing the text anew as a result of the understanding gained from the previous readings. It is also similar to what Posner and his colleagues (Posner, Strike, Hewson, & Gertzog, 1982) call the plausibility and fruitfulness of a new scientific theory. A theory is plausible when it is at least as successful in explaining phenomena as the theory that it is replacing. A theory is fruitful when it has the potential to be extended to new areas of research (Posner, Strike, Hewson, & Gertzog, 1982). That is, a theory gains in strength because of its usefulness in helping to understand new situations.

Second, Kohut suggests that the therapist pay attention to his or her stance toward the data. This is done by persistently examining the data from as many different viewpoints as possible, by attempting to identify which viewpoint results in seeing the data in the most meaningful way; and by removing obstacles to empathy. It is important to remember that Kohut uses empathy to refer to the data that one gains from observing and listening to the client, as well as interrogating the feelings that one has about the client. Therefore, obstacles to empathy include any barriers to accurately seeing and hearing, as well as interpreting what is seen, heard, and felt.

Finally, Kohut warns us against the power of "the comfortable certainty of the 'Aha-experience'" (Kohut, 1977, p. 168). It is easy to fall into the trap of believing a particular meaning or understanding is correct because it so well agrees with what we have expected. The therapist "should learn to mistrust explanations that suddenly surge up in him with unquestioned certainty" (Kohut, 1977, p. 169).

In summary, Kohut provides us with a variety of ways to analyze and interpret the data that comes introspection and empathy in self psychology. He suggests that we approach the data with the open-mind suggested by the Emperor's New Clothes principle, and that we test, modify, and retest interpretations with the existing data and new situations using the Rosetta-Stone principle. He also suggests that we examine the data from as many different perspectives as possible, and to question the accuracy of our data. Finally, he warns us about the power of face validity, the click of recognition that what is being described or explained rings true (Lather, 1991).

MAKING THE SELF PROBLEMATIC IN SELF-STUDY

Existentialism and psychoanalysis provide us with the frameworks that allow us to make the study of the self problematic in the self-study of teacher education practices. Kohut's self psychology provides us with two tools for investigating the self: introspection and empathy. However, self psychology as a form of inquiry is something that one person does in relation to another. The therapist gathers data from the client's introspections and from his or her empathic observations of the client. In self-study, the researcher-subject pair is collapsed into one person – the self-study researcher. What this means is that the person engaging in a self-study that makes his or her self problematic finds him or herself in the situation of being introspective and empathic of his or her own self. But, as Madeline Grumet reminds us,

> It seems natural to assume that the first person is closer to us than the third, an intimacy that Sartre repudiates emphatically in *The Transcendence of the Ego* (1972) arguing that we do not know ourselves better than we know others, and reminding ourselves not to confuse familiarity with knowledge (Grumet, 1991, p. 68).

Clearly this makes it even more difficult to ensure that as we analyze and interpret data we do so in a way that we and others can believe what we say.

This problem surfaces time and again in critiques of self-study research from those in and out of the self-study community. For example, Marilyn Cochran-Smith has written that

There is strong skepticism that self-study can make a useful contribution to the research literature because it is biased – it doesn't have the traditional distance between researcher and researched … (Cochran-Smith, 2005, p. 221).

John Loughran has acknowledged the problem by telling us that in self-study "there is a need to demonstrate scholarship by making clear that personal theories are challenged in ways that help the researcher (and the audience) to see beyond the personal alone" (Loughran, 2007, p. 13); and by reminding us that "…the closer we are to a situation, the more difficult it is to not only see alternative perspectives but more so, to even accept that they exist" (Loughran, 2008, p. 7).

These concerns, as well as those of Kohut, raise the question of the validity of self-study research. I use a definition of validity that comes from the work of Martyn Hammersley:

An account is valid or true if it represents accurately those features of the phenomena that it is intended to describe, explain, or theorise. (Hammersley, 1992, p. 69)

Because types 2 and 3 self-studies are similar to other varieties of research on teacher education, there are well-established methods that can be used to increase their validity (see for example Bullough and Pinnegar (2001) and Feldman (2003)). However, they fall short when the self is the subject of the self-study.

As I have already shown, Kohut developed a method for inquiry into the self of others, and provided us with warnings about bias and suggestions on how to minimize it. If the self becomes the subject of the self-study, then the dangers of misreading the data increase, and the self-study becomes what detractors of the methodology call "navel gazing". I believe, however, that there already exists in the self-study literature ways to solve the problem. To put it simply, the way to reduce the bias caused by the studier being studied is to involve others in the research process. This can be seen in how LaBoskey uses the characteristics of self-study scholarship to identify ways to reduce the inherent bias that arises from being both the researcher and the researched. Each of LaBoskey's four ways to reduce the bias inherent in self-studies involves other people. The first way is to seek evidence that there has been an improvement in the self-study researcher's practice and a positive effect on his or her practice. The practice of teacher educators involves other people, and the qualities of that practice have an effect on those others, for example, students and colleagues. It is not possible to determine whether or not the self-study has led to an improvement in practice without including the perspectives of these others. LaBoskey's second way depends on the interactivity of self-study. This extends the participation of others in the self-study to roles such as co-researcher, collaborator, critical friend, and so on. Their participation goes beyond the evaluation of the effects of the research to providing additional expertise and viewpoints for the collection and analysis of data.

LaBoskey also argues that the validity of self-study can be enhanced by the use of multiple research methods. For this to be the case, the research methods need to be those that have become, in Elliott Mishler's terms, ones that have been accepted by the research community to instill a sense of trustworthiness in the study (Mishler, 1990). Again, the participation of others is inherent in this call for use of reliable methods. For the methods to be deemed as such, there must be a research community that has come to some consensus that when a certain set of research methods is carried out in a certain way, then the results of the research are valid, or, as Mishler would put it, trustworthy. Finally, LaBoskey suggests that self-study researchers report their research in ways that make it accessible to the self-study professional community for deliberation, testing, and judgment.

These last two require the participation of others in a significantly different way than the first two. The latter two are required because self-study research has as its goal more than the improvement of practice; there is also the goal to produce knowledge about teacher education. The improvement of practice and the sharing of the skills and know-how that make up the improvement of practice can occur with others in a community of practice (Wenger, 1998). However, when the goal of producing knowledge is added, the community of practice must take on the characteristics of an epistemic community (Creplet, Dupouet, & Vaast, 2003; Knorr Cetina, 1999), which is a community engaged in the production of knowledge.

Peter Haas, who works in the area of environmental policy, defines an epistemic community as

> a network of professionals with recognized expertise and competence in a particular domain and an authoritative claim to policy-relevant knowledge within that domain or issue-area. (Haas, 1992, p. 3)

Although policy has major effects on the work of teacher educators, not all teacher educators do work in educational policy, and so I modify Haas' definition by removing the phrase "policy-relevant". Therefore, a group of self-study researchers is an epistemic community when its members have recognized expertise and competence in research on teacher education, and have an authoritative claim to knowledge within that domain. Given this definition, there are three characteristics of epistemic communities from Haas' work that apply to self-study groups. First, members of the groups agree on what the central problems are of their domain. Second, they share beliefs about what make responses to those problems valid. Third, they share a set of normative beliefs about how their work relates to a greater good (Haas, 1992).

The creation of new knowledge in science is tied to recognition of expertise and competence (Mishler, 1990). What this means is that members of an epistemic community must have the knowledge and skills needed to create and warrant new knowledge. These skills and knowledge are those that are accepted by the wider community as being trustworthy, and are established as exemplars. These exemplars are used as guidelines by implicit or explicit procedural authorities –

such as the review panels for conference papers, journal articles, and funding proposals – that publicly acknowledge one's expertise and authority

As I have shown above, an important way to reduce the problem of bias in self-study is to engage others in many, if not all, parts of the research study. However, in addition, those who engage in self-study of teacher education practices must be involved in an epistemic community if they are to "develop and better articulate a knowledge of practice" (Loughran, 2008, p. 9). I believe that what is happening now within the community of self-study researchers is the development of a broader epistemic community and the recognition of the types of guidelines that can help to determine the quality of self-studies. This is what Ken Zeichner is calling for when he urges self-study researchers to frame their work as part of programs of study. To Zeichner, a research program is one in which

> … researchers explicitly build on each other's work conceptually, theoretically, and methodologically. This would entail such things as defining concepts and terms in similar ways and using and adapting research methods and instruments from previous studies. (Zeichner, 2007, p. 40)

It should be clear from these characteristics that participation in a research program connects a self-study researcher to a wider community, and in doing so, increases the validity of the study.

CONCLUSION

I began this chapter by stating that my intention was to examine how the nature of self-study research affects the way in which data are analyzed and interpreted. I began by developing a definition of self-study from the literature. I argued that the consensus definition does not characterize what makes self-study a unique methodology, rather than a set of methods. Using the work of Sandra Harding I next demonstrated that what makes self-study a distinct methodology is that it brings to the forefront the importance of the self. Self-study researchers do this by doing research on the self, research on the self in practice, and by doing research to understand oneself in practice.

In the remainder of the chapter I attempted to show ways to think about the first type of self-study by referring first to existentialism and then to psychoanalysis. The self psychology of Heinz Kohut provided me with an example of how the self can be inquired into in the therapist-client relationship, possible validity problems in doing so, and suggestions for how to improve the way in which the therapist understands the client. When applied to self-study, an additional threat to validity arises because it is the researcher who is studying his or her self.

I end the chapter by arguing that an important way to increase the validity of self-studies is to include others in all facets of the research process. This includes the collection and analysis of data, as well as critique of the self-study report. However, in addition, if the self-study is to add to the knowledge of teacher education as well as improving the practice of individual teacher educators, the others must be involved as part of an epistemic community. What that means is that the validity of self-studies be established through the use of exemplars; that the working of the procedural authorities in the self-study community that review conference papers and journal articles be made explicit; and that as much as possible self-study researchers work together to develop research programs that build upon each others work.

REFERENCES

Balint, A. (1945). Identification. In *The yearbook of psychoanalysis* (Vol. 1, pp. 317–338). New York: International Universities Press.

Britzman, D. P. (1986). Cultural myths in the making of a teacher: Biography and social structure in teacher education. *Harvard Educational Review, 56*(4), 442–456.

Britzman, D. P. (1998). *Lost subjects, contested objects: Toward a psychoanalytic inquiry of learning.* Albany, NY: SUNY Press.

Buber, M. (1937). *I and thou* (R. G. Smith, Trans.). Edinburgh: T. & T. Clark.

Bullough, R. V., & Pinnegar, S. (2001). Guidelines for quality in autobiographical forms of self-study. *Educational Researcher, 30*(3), 13–22.

Cochran-Smith, M. (2005). Teacher educators as researchers: Multiple perspectives. *Teaching and Teacher Education, 21,* 219–225.

Creplet, F., Dupouet, O., & Vaast, E. (2003). Episteme or practice? Differentiated communitarian structures in a biology laboratory. In M. Huysman, E. Wenger, & V. Wulf (Eds.), *Communities and technologies: Proceedings of the first international conference on communities and technologies* (pp. 43–63). Dordrecht: Kluwer.

de Mijolla, A. (2005). *International dictionary of psychoanalysis.* Retrieved May 15, 2008, from www.enotes.com/psychoanalysis-encyclopedia/empathy

Dewey, J. (1938). *Logic: The theory of inquiry.* New York: Henry Holt and Company.

Feldman, A. (2003). Validity and quality in self-study. *Educational Researcher, 32*(3), 26–28.

Feldman, A. (2006). Using an existential form of reflection to understand my transformation as a teacher educator. In C. Kosnik, C. Beck, A. R. Freese, & A. P. Samaras (Eds.), *Making a difference in teacher education through self-study: Studies of personal, professional and program renewal* (pp. 35–50). Dordrecht, The Netherlands: Springer.

Feldman, A. (2007). Teachers, responsibility and action research. *Educational Action Research, 15*(2), 239–252.

Feldman, A., Paugh, P., & Mills, G. (2004). Self-study through action research. In J. Loughran, M. L. Hamilton, V. K. LaBoskey, & T. Russell (Eds.), *International handbook of self-study of teaching and teacher education practices.* Dordrecht, The Netherlands: Kluwer Academic Publishers.

Freud, A. (1936). Four lectures on psychoanalysis for teachers and parents. In *The writings of Anna Freud* (Vol. 1, pp. 73–133). New York: International Universities Press.

Freud, S. (1923). *The ego and the id* (J. Riviere, Trans.). New York: Norton.

Greene, M. (1973). *Teacher as stranger: Educational philosophy for the modern age.* Belmont, CA: Wadsworth Publishing Company.

Greene, M. (1988). *The dialectic of freedom.* New York: Teachers College Press.

Grumet, M. (1991). The politics of personal knowledge. In C. Witherell & N. Noddings (Eds.), *Stories lives tell: Narrative and dialogue in education* (pp. 67–77). New York: Teachers College Press.

Grundy, S. (1987). *Curriculum: Product or praxis.* New York: Falmer Press.

Haas, P. M. (1992). Introduction: Epistemic communities and international policy coordination. *International Organization, 46*(1), 1–35.

Hamilton, M. L., & Pinnegar, S. (1998). The value and promise of self-study. In M. L. Hamilton (Ed.), *Reconceptualizing teaching practice: Self-study in teacher education* (pp. 235–246). London: Falmer.

Harding, S. (1989). Is there a feminist method? In N. Tuana (Ed.), *Feminism and science* (pp. 18–32). Bloomington, IN: Indiana University Press.

Hutchings, P., & Shulman, L. (1999). The scholarship of teaching: New elaborations, new developments. *Change*.

Knorr Cetina, K. (1999). *Epistemic cultures: How the sciences make knowledge.* Cambridge, MA: Harvard University Press.

Kohut, H. (1977). *The restoration of the self.* Madison, CT: International Universities Press.

LaBoskey, V. K. (2004). The methodology of self-study and its theoretical underpinnings. In J. Loughran, M. L. Hamilton, V. LaBoskey, & T. Russell (Eds.), *International handbook of self-study of teaching and teacher education practices* (pp. 817–869). Dordrecht, The Netherlands: Kluwer Academic Publishers.

Lather, P. (1991). *Getting smart: Feminist research and pedagogy with/in the postmodern.* New York: Routledge.

Loughran, J. J. (2007). Researching teacher education practices: Responding to the challenges, demands, and expectations of self-study. *Journal of Teacher Education, 58*(1), 12–20.

Loughran, J. J. (2008, March 24–28). *The difficulties in "coaching" self-study research.* Paper presented at the annual meeting of the American Educational Research Association, New York.

Mishler, E. G. (1990). Validation in inquiry-guided research: The role of exemplars in narrative studies. *Harvard Educational Review, 60*(4), 415–442.

Morris, V. C. (1966). *Existentialism in education: What it means.* Prospect Heights, IL: Waveland Press.

Posner, G., Strike, K., Hewson, P., & Gertzog, W. (1982). Accommodation of a scientific conception: Toward a theory of conceptual change. *Science Education, 66*(2), 211–227.

Sartre, J.-P. (1956). *Being and nothingness* (H. Barnes, Trans.). New York: Philosophical Library.

Sartre, J.-P. (1972). *The transcendence of the ego* (F. Williams & R. Kirkpatrick, Trans.). New York: Octagon Books.

Shulman, L. (2000). From Minsk to Pinsk: Why a scholarship of teaching and learning? *Journal of Scholarship of Teaching and Learning, 1*(1), 48–52.

Stengel, B. (1996, April 18–22). *Teaching epistemology through cell reproduction: A narrative exploration.* Paper presented at the annual meeting of the American Educational Research Association, New York.

Taubman, P. M. (2007). The beautiful soul of teaching: The contribution of psychoanalytic thought to critical self reflection with reflective practice. In M. Gordon & T. V. O'Brien (Eds.), *Bridging theory and practice in teacher education* (pp. 1–16). Rotterdam, The Netherlands: Sense Publishers.

Valli, L. (Ed.). (1990). *Reflective teacher education: Cases and critiques.* Albany, NY: State University of New York Press.

Wenger, E. (1998). *Communities of practice: Learning, meaning, and identity.* Cambridge, UK: Cambridge University Press.

Zeichner, K. M. (2007). Accumulating knowledge across self-studies in teacher education. *Journal of Teacher Education, 58*(1), 36–46.

Zeichner, K. M., & Noffke, S. E. (2001). Practitioner research. In V. Richardson (Ed.), *Handbook of research on teaching* (pp. 298–332). Washington, DC: American Educational Research Association.

PART TWO: SPECIFIC METHODOLOGIES

CLARE KOSNIK, YIOLA CLEOVOULOU AND TIM FLETCHER

4. THE USE OF INTERVIEWS IN SELF-STUDY RESEARCH

> Human beings are complex, and their lives are ever changing; the more methods
> we use to study them, the better our chances to gain some understanding of
> how they construct their lives and the stories they tell us about them.
>
> (Fontana & Frey, 2000, p. 668)

Oh, the stories that we tell each other! In some cases we try to recount the story
faithfully, being careful to accurately present every fact. In other cases, our
emotions affect our story-telling. Aspects of the story may grow in prominence,
reflecting our heightened emotions. And then there are times when we stray from
the actual events, not intending to deceive others but the story takes on a life of its
own. Stories are not neutral and rarely are stories told in such a way that both the
teller and the listener "hear" the same version. Our stories are important because
they help us understand our world and assist others in appreciating us.

DEFINING INTERVIEWING

One of the ways that we can hear others' stories is through interviews. As Fontana
and Frey (2000) note, we have become an "interview society"; we may encounter
professors conducting research in the university but then we might just as easily
meet members of a special interest group interviewing shoppers in the local shopping
centre. "It seems that many, not just social researchers, rely on the interview as a
source of information, with the assumption that interviewing results in true and
accurate pictures of respondents' selves and lives" (2000, p. 646). The interview as
a tool to gather information is widely accepted and in this chapter we focus on the
use of the interview for self-study research.

Interviewing has been defined "simply as a conversation with a purpose.
Specifically, the purpose is to gather information" (Berg, 2007, p. 89). This concise
definition, although helpful, fails to recognize that information is not neutral or that
information can be interpreted differently between the interviewer and interviewee.
Jones (1985) has a much broader view of interviews and provides this perspective:

> In order to understand other persons' constructions of reality, we would do
> well to ask them .... And to ask them in such a way that they can tell us in
> their terms (rather than those imposed rigidly and *a priori* by ourselves) and
> in a depth which addresses the rich context that is the substance of their
> meanings" (p. 46).

*C. A. Lassonde, S. Galman and C. Kosnik (eds.), Self-Study Research Methodologies
for Teacher Educators, 53–69.*
© *2009 Sense Publishers. All rights reserved.*

Merriam (1998) adds, "Interviewing is necessary when we cannot observe behaviour, feelings, or how people interpret the world around them. It is also necessary to interview when we are interested in past events that are impossible to replicate" (p. 72). Glesne and Peshkin (1992) further elaborate, "You might also interview in search of an explanation for why something happened. Interviewing puts you on the trail of understandings that you may infer from what you observe, but not as the actors themselves construe their actions. You cannot, that is, except through interviewing get the actor's explanations" (p. 65).

The Interviewer In Self-Study Research

The interviewers' beliefs, intentions, methods, and values may play a significant role in the interview process. Kvale (1996) suggests two metaphors for interviewers. First, interviewers could be considered "miners": knowledge is understood as buried material to be unearthed, seeking of essential meaning. "The interviewer digs nuggets of data or meanings out of a subject's pure experiences, unpolluted by any leading questions" (p. 3). The second metaphor he offers is interviewers as "travelers": on a journey leading to a tale to be told upon returning home. "The interviewer asks questions that lead the subjects to tell their own stories of their lived world" (p. 4). Which of the two metaphors we gravitate towards is most likely consistent with our world-view and our conception of knowledge. The second metaphor may resonate more closely with those involved in self-study.

For self-study researchers, there is recognition that researchers bring to the enterprise their biases, histories, goals, interests, world-view, and so on. The first metaphor of the interviewer, one who uncovers nuggets of meaning which are "pure," is not consistent with self-study which recognizes (and values) the subjectivity of the interviewer and sees meaning-making as a process, often a collaborative one. LaBoskey (2004) argues that the "self" in self-study is not neutral: "A critical identifying feature of the methodology of self-study involves the question of 'Who?' – both who is doing the research and who is being studied. In self-study the self is necessarily included in the response to both queries. Thus the professional practices settings we study are our own" (p. 842).

Relevancy of Interviewing for Self-Study

A quick scan through the many texts and articles written by self-study researchers reveals that the interview is a commonly used tool. It might be helpful to consider LaBoskey's (2004) five principles for self-study research:
– Self-initiated and focused
– Improvement-aimed
– Interactive
– Multiple, primarily qualitative, methods
– Exemplar-based validation (pp. 842–852)
   One of the main pillars of self-study research is that it is conducted to gain understanding. In order to understand and improve one's own practice one needs

data: self-study researchers often generate data through reflective logs, video tapes of their teaching, autoethnography, and so on. Yet, the researcher's data only provides one perspective. To be improvement-oriented, there need to be the voices of other stakeholders - how is our work affecting them? What can we learn from their perspective? For example, in teacher education we might want to know if we are helping our students deepen or question their understanding of what it means to be a teacher. Does our teaching lead to an improvement in their practice? Are we giving them tools to study their practice? Interviewing our students can be a highly effective way to hear their views on teaching, for us to determine the impact of our work on them, and to give them an opportunity to offer suggestions for improvement to the course.

When we involve our student teachers in our research we are modeling for them an inquiry approach to teaching which is central to self-study. For example, one year Clare intended to interview a small number of student teachers three times during the course of the one-year program to track their evolving views of literacy teaching and determine which aspects of her courses were helpful or confusing. Initially about 10 students volunteered. As the year progressed she was inundated with requests from other students who wanted to be part of the research because they heard that she really wanted to know their views and the students who were involved recounted to others that the interview process was really interesting. Given limited funds and time, she could not interview all students who volunteered, so she developed a survey for all students who wished to share their views. She gained a tremendous amount of information from the students; an interesting spin-off from this work was her noticing that during their practice teaching placements a significant number of student teachers surveyed and/or interviewed their pupils. Many of the student teachers found the pupils' feedback very helpful – it not only validated them as teachers but it also helped them get to know their pupils better and allowed them to pinpoint ways to improve their teaching. Through her modeling, the students saw first-hand the value of studying their own practice and the power of interviews.

DESCRIPTION OF METHODOLOGY

Self-study research must conform to the basic elements of research design. These steps include: articulating the research questions, inviting participants, gathering data, analyzing the data, and drawing conclusions. Like all research, the data gathering methods in self-study research must match the goals of the study. Interviewing has a strong appeal to self-study researchers because it allows them to gather in-depth data on very specific topics.

Standards of Quality in Interviews

Interviewing seems deceptively simple – generate some questions, find a few interested and/or interesting participants, and then proceed. Experienced researchers know that this is a simplification of the process. For example, generating the interview questions can prove to be a real trial. "The key to getting good data from interviewing is to ask good questions; asking good questions takes practice" (Merriam, 1998, p. 75). Kvale (1996) provides these standards of quality for an interview:

- The extent of spontaneous, rich, specific, and relevant answers from the interviewee.
- The shorter the interviewer's questions and the longer the subjects' answers, the better.
- The degree to which the interviewer follows up and clarifies the meanings of the relevant aspects of the answers.
- The ideal interview is to a large extent interpreted throughout the interview.
- The interviewer attempts to verify his or her interpretations of the subject's answers in the course of the interview.
- The interview is "self-communicating" – it is a story contained in itself that hardly requires extra descriptions and explanations.

The issue of the researcher being the interviewer is frequently voiced in discussions about the limitations of self-study research. Typically, it is suggested that the interviewer be at arm's length from the interviewee. However, from experience, Clare has found that the students she taught and interviewed have been remarkably forthcoming. She attributes this to the good relationship that she has with them and their understanding that she really wants to learn from them. For numerous self-studies, she has interviewed her students because she felt that she was ideally suited to conduct the interviews because she knew the courses and program so well. In one study, Clare and another professor conducted interviews of the students she was teaching and they compared the data to see if there was a difference between those interviewed by Clare about her course and those interviewed by a third party. They could not detect any differences. In another study that examined the relationship between a student and the associate (cooperating) teacher, Yiola who was both the researcher and the associate teacher, interviewed her student teacher in order to deepen her own understandings of the nature of their professional relationship (Cleovoulou, 2008). By understanding the relationship and the perceptions of what made the relationship successful, Yiola was able to rethink and improve her own practice as an associate teacher. From that study, which generated rich information pertaining to the nuances of significant moments in the relationship, Yiola found that her student teacher was open, sincere, and ready to be involved in the research process.

Choosing the Type of Interview Questions

When selecting a type of interview, the researcher can choose from structured, semi-structured, and unstructured interviews, conducted either individually or in a focus group. Fontana and Frey (2000) distinguish between structured and unstructured interviewing as: "The former aims at capturing precise data of codable nature in order to explain behaviour within pre-established categories, whereas the latter attempts to understand the complex behaviour of members of society without imposing any *a priori* categorization that may limit the field of inquiry" (p. 653). When doing self-study research, all three types of interviews can be used effectively.

From our perspective and experience, semi-structured interview questions lend themselves well to self-study. For semi-structured interviews the researchers would identify the broad categories to be investigated and generate questions. A useful feature of semi-structured interviews is the use of probe questions. These are questions that are asked to extend comments, provide explanations, give the rationale for practice, and explore responses more deeply.

In the edited text, *Making a Difference in Teacher Education Through Self-Study: Personal, Professional, and Program Renewal* (Kosnik et al., 2006) many of the studies used semi-structured interviews. In each study, the researcher was central to what was being studied. Freidus (2006) "examined the Reading and Literacy Program at the Bank Street College of Education" (p. 167) where she had taught in this program for many years. She discovered through interviews with students and faculty that some of the goals for the program (e.g., reflection) were unclear to students and faculty tended to use educational terms in markedly different ways. McVarish and Rust (2006) analyzed "a new undergraduate teacher education program as an example of an educational innovation in higher education" (p. 185). They were the lead faculty in reconceptualizing and restructuring their teacher education program and wanted to find out how well it was working from the students' perspectives. They also charted their own levels of involvement, frustration, and successes in the initiative.

In unstructured interviews, the researcher "attempts to understand complex behaviour without imposing *a priori* categorization that may limit field of inquiry" (Fontana & Frey, 2000, p. 653). This completely open style may not lend itself well to self-study research because the researchers are likely studying a specific aspect regarding themselves (e.g., their courses). Merriam (1998) cautions that "[i]t takes a skilled researcher to handle the great flexibility demanded by the unstructured interview" (p. 74). In unstructured interviews, the goals for the research may not be addressed by the interviewees. Unstructured interviews used in ethnographic research are very open and although the researcher may be intimately involved with the interviewee, the work of the researcher is most likely not being studied. Self-study research rarely involves experimental or quasi-experimental studies with control groups and/or interventions. At times, self-study researchers may study a new approach to their courses or an aspect of the program but they most likely would not embark on a traditional quantitative study with comparison groups, using highly structured interviews.

Data Analysis

When analyzing interviews, a researcher can choose from a variety of approaches which reflect the theoretical perspectives that the researcher brings to the study (Gubrium & Holstein, 2002). Regardless of the approach used to organize, categorize and interpret interview data, we should take heed of thoughts offered by Gubrium and Holstein (2002) and Kvale (1996); that analysis of qualitative data applies from the very beginning of a research project, continues through the data collection process, and carries on after field and research texts have been compiled. It permeates all parts of the interview process. Indeed, Kvale (1996, p. 177) claims that the question of how to analyze transcripts should never be asked after the interview has been conducted; it is too late to start thinking about this important piece of the research puzzle.

Steps for analyzing interview data have been provided by, among others, Hycner (1985) and Kvale (1996). Explaining these in detail is beyond the scope of this chapter; however, interested readers could consult the aforementioned texts for further information. Data analysis that occurs recursively as the interviews unfold assists in the shape of the study (Glesne, 1999, p. 130). In the longitudinal study on beginning teachers described later in this chapter, the team conducted the interviews, analyzed the data, and built new and refined questions on that information. During the interviews notes were recorded on important points made and on non-verbal communication. Notes were also made at the conclusion of the interviews to record any reflections about the content of the interview. This process allowed them to add, monitor, and analyze the data as they went along (Merriam, 1998, p.88).

After transcription of the interviews, the researcher should bracket and reduce the data, ensuring that they are open to the emergence of unexpected meanings (Hycner, 1985). Kvale (1996) uses the term "meaning condensation" to describe this process. Initially, meanings will be categorized in a broad sense; however, those which are irrelevant to the research questions can be eliminated. Following this process, units of meaning can be categorized or clustered into themes. These themes are then interpreted and contextualized within broader frames of reference (Kvale, 1996). Some researchers may want to return to the participant with the interpretations from the initial interviews for a follow-up. Whether there is a second, third, or fourth interview depends upon the goals of the research. The analysis may continue and be returned to *ad infinitum,* and as with most research, the extent to which it is depends on the objectives and skills of the researcher.

If approaching the interview from a perspective based on previous studies or theories, the research questions are likely to be developed and subsequently analyzed according to specific principles. For example, Tim used a multi-component view of attitude (that is, that an attitude consists of affective, cognitive, and behavioural domains) to develop his questions and frame his analysis for a study on student attitudes toward physical education (Fletcher, 2008). When there is little prior research upon which to base a study, other strategies may need to be employed, such as those articulated in grounded theory (Glaser & Strauss, 1967).

Grounded theory, which Punch (2005) describes as "both a strategy for research and a way of analyzing the data" (p. 154) is a popular strategy for qualitative analysis (Gubrium & Holstein, 2002) and from our experience is compatible with self-study research. Since self-study research is focused on gaining an understanding, grounded theory is appropriate because it does not apply an *a priori* set of categories. "The rationale for doing a grounded theory study is that we have no satisfactory theory on the topic, and that we do not understand enough about it to begin theorizing" (Punch, 2005, p. 159). Grounded theory can be used with small sample sizes typical of much self-study work but it also can be utilized when there are a large number of participants.

The data analysis methods of grounded theory work well with interviews because the theory emerges from the data; the researcher keeps looking across the whole data set; the context of the research is considered; and subsequent data gathering (e.g., additional interviews) is informed by the emerging theory. The flexibility of grounded theory is highly compatible with interviewing because it allows the researcher to pursue areas of interest. One of the tenets of grounded theory is identifying relationships and in self-study research, identifying and understanding these relationships is pivotal.

Grounded theory allows the researcher to delay using the literature until analysis of the data begins and the literature can be seen as additional data for the study. This flexibility allows the researchers to move about the data in attempts to understand it fully. Throughout the analysis the researchers continually try to establish relationships; in self-study research this may be the connection between the interviewer's practice and the interviewees' knowledge and/or practice.

Grounded theory analysis tends to follow a three step process:
- Initially identify conceptual categories. This is done through open coding.
- Secondly, find relationships between these categories. This second set of codes which are called theoretical/axial are to interconnect the main substantive codes.
- And finally, account for and conceptualize these relationships at a higher level of abstraction (Punch, 2005, p. 204).

Although the whole notion of developing theory may be daunting, grounded theory does not necessarily require that the theory be applicable to others; it may be of use to the particular researcher but it does not have to extend across many settings. For example, in a self-study we conducted on a small learning community, our goal was to understand why this community worked so well (Kosnik, 2008). As we generated the theory, we had insight into us as members of the community. Although this theory is highly helpful for us, we did not assume that it would be directly applicable to other learning communities. We hope that our theory may help others studying their communities but we never conceptualized it as "the one and only theory" of community.

ANALYTIC STRENGTHS AND LIMITATIONS OF INTERVIEWS

Interviews take place in a setting between two individuals which can influence the interview process. Fontana and Frey (2000) refer to the work of Kahn and Cannel who recognize the social dimension of interviewing: "It is not enough to understand the mechanics of interviewing, it is also important to understand the respondent's world and forces that might stimulate or retard response" (p. 651). In the following section, we describe some of the strengths and limitations of interviews. Since many of the strengths of interviewing have been described in previous sections we go into greater detail regarding the limitations of interviewing.

Strengths

Interviews can be a very powerful tool in self-study research. "The great variety and flexibility of the interview as a research tool gives it wide applicability, with different types of interviews suited to different situations" (Punch, 2005, p. 176). Interviews allow the researcher and the interviewee to go into depth when appropriate and since the interviewer can choose the type of question (structured, semi-structured, and unstructured) there is opportunity to gather various levels of detail. Through the use of probe questions the interviewer can explore a particular aspect fully. Interviews allow the self-study researcher opportunities to pursue lines of inquiry that are relevant.

Both interviewer and interviewee can be changed by the process. "The qualitative research interview is a construction site of knowledge. An interview is literally an *inter view,* an interchange of views between two persons conversing about a theme of mutual interest" (Kvale, 1996, p. 2). Clare has found that student teachers and/or new teachers enjoyed the interview process and found it useful. Many have commented that rarely had anyone asked for their views or had someone actually listened to them so intently. Being an interviewee in a research study validated them as teachers. Further, the interview process requires the interviewee to put into words some of his/her thoughts, beliefs, and/or practices. Articulating these can be powerful because they can give shape to a budding philosophy or through articulation, the interviewees may come to understand their practice more fully. Our high retention rate in our studies (e.g., interviewing student teachers numerous times over the course of their program) suggests that they find the process very helpful.

For the interviewer, the process of setting the questions can be a real learning experience. The researcher needs to identify exactly what is to be studied. This process, although challenging at times, forces researchers to articulate and operationalize exactly what they want to learn. Obviously, the data analysis is a learning experience because the researchers gain insight into the views of others, especially in relation to their work.

Limitations

Interviewing, although it is a powerful research tool, has its limitations. One of the basic issues revolves around formulating the questions: are the "right" questions being asked; are the questions leading; are the questions clear. In self-study, as with many forms of qualitative research, the researcher may need to make the familiar strange and "detach" themselves from the topic being studied. There are also considerations of how appropriate the questions are for the individual being interviewed (e.g., Are they too personal? Does the individual have the knowledge to capably respond?). The intimacy of the interview is a strength, yet, it can also be a negative factor. Since the interview is done face-to-face (and often in self-study research the professor is the interviewer), there is the danger of interviewees providing the answer they think the interviewer wants to be heard. In both developing the questions and conducting the interviews our own biases come into play. For example, Clare is a strong believer that teachers need to develop the class into a learning community. When interviewing a teacher who emphatically stated that he ran his classroom based on competition, she immediately recognized that her bias could affect her analysis of his interview.

Post-modern research has helped us realize that the interview takes place in a social setting. Interviewers may think they understand the milieu but in fact may not appreciate subtle differences, messy dynamics, hidden mores, and so on. And language is the medium for the interview which in itself has limitations. "The more difficult problem concerns the correspondence between verbal responses and behaviour, the relationship between what people say, what they do and what they say they do, and the assumption that language is a good indicator of thought and action" (Punch, 2005, p. 176).

Although researchers may spend significant time developing their questions, they may not know which questions will elicit strong or insightful responses. Clare affectionately calls these "BINGO" questions. One year when she was interviewing her student teachers about the action research component that she had introduced to the program, she asked a rather innocuous question along the lines of, "Do you feel differently when you are teaching a lesson [in your practice teaching class] that is based on your action research project compared to when you are teaching a lesson prescribed by your Associate (cooperating) teacher?" The first respondent, Enza, shouted "Yes" which took Clare by surprise. Enza then went on to elaborate why she felt so much more in control when she was doing a lesson based on her action research because she knew why she was doing it and how it related to the students' needs. The next interviewee had the same emotional and positive response to the question. This question turned out to be a very powerful one but it took Clare by surprise. Over the years, she has had the same type of response to particular questions; some that she thought would be great prompts have turned out to be weak while others that she had not suspected to be so productive were highly valuable. Even with pilot testing, we cannot guarantee that the questions will be useful. Further, what interviewees say they do and what they actually do are not always fully congruent.

From our experience, classroom observations are required to triangulate data from interviews. In one study, we had a participant who from classroom observations we knew was an outstanding teacher, but who struggled in the interview to explain her practice. Consequently, the data from the interview did not reflect the interviewee's practice. Classroom observations add another layer to the process but we feel that they are essential

If the study is longitudinal the interviewer and interviewee develop a working relationship over time. In some cases this is positive but it can also descend into a combative stance. As feminist scholarship has pointed out, from the start, there is an imbalance of power between the interviewer and interviewee. This gap can be accentuated by the interviewer. In one of our research projects, one of the interviewers asked the interview questions as they were written but her body language and tone of voice were very negative. The interviewer had an extremely strong view of herself which she projected. From the transcripts, we could "see" how the interviewee was becoming anxious. We removed the interviewer because we felt the process was not beneficial for the interviewee.

When working within a research team, there are numerous concerns: although the interview questions are provided, all interviewers may not have the capacity to spontaneously develop probe questions or may not realize that a probe question should be asked. Fontana and Frey (2000) noted that in one study with multiple interviewers, the interviewers changed the wording to one third of the questions (p. 650). When research is done by a team, inter-rater reliability is an issue. For example, one of the researchers saw the interview in a similar manner to that described by Berg (2007), that is, as a conversation. She freely shared her views with the interviewee on all sorts of topics, which in other research projects may have been useful, but for the purposes of our research, disrupted the flow of the interview and resulted in her not actually asking the prescribed questions.

Fontana and Frey (2000) outline some additional cautions regarding interviews.

> Aside from the problem of framing real-life events in a two-dimensional space, we face the added problems of how the framing is being done and who is doing the framing. In sociological terms, this means that the type of interviewing selected, the techniques used, and the ways of recording information all come to bear on the results of the study. Additionally, data must be interpreted, and the researcher has a great deal of influence on what part of the data will be reported and how it will be reported (p. 650).

Regardless of the type of research, self-study or otherwise, some of the canons of research apply. Punch (2005) reminds us of issues of reliability and validity which he describes as follows:
- Reliability – in quantitative research, the consistency of measurement: [a] consistency over time – test-retest reliability; [b] consistency within indictors – internal consistency reliability. In qualitative research, the dependability of the data.
- Validity – the extent to which a measuring instrument measures what it is supposed to measure.

Ethical Considerations

Like all research methods, ethical issues must be addressed when conducting interviewing. In self-study research which often involves student teachers the concerns may be heightened. Fontana and Frey (2000) identify four ethical considerations when interviewing:
- Informed consent,
- Right to privacy,
- Protection from harm,
- Researcher's degree of involvement with the group/interviewee (p. 662).

The last point needs to be seriously considered by self-study researchers because they are often a member of the community they are studying. Kvale (1996) adds to Fontana and Frey's concerns. Although not writing specifically about self-study research, his concerns are relevant. For example, he flags the issue of "how deeply and critically the interviews can be analyzed, and whether the subjects should have a say in how their statements are interpreted" (Kvale, 1996, p. 111). Kvale further notes "the interviewer should also be aware that the openness and intimacy of the interview may be seductive and lead subjects to disclose information they may later regret. The personal closeness of the interview situation puts strong demands on the sensitivity of the interviewer regarding how far to go in their questioning" (1996, p. 116). This is of particular relevance for self-study research when we are studying our own students, many of whom we have developed strong, positive relationships with.

EXAMPLE: TEACHER EDUCATION FOR LITERACY TEACHING

In this section we describe the longitudinal study, *Teacher Education for Literacy Teaching,* which we conducted over a five year period. We were studying the impact of the preservice program, in particular the literacy courses, on the graduates of our teacher education program at OISE/UT. Clare teaches literacy courses in the program and was one of the Principal Investigators of the study along with Clive Beck. Yiola and Tim were research assistants on the project. Interviews were central to the research process.

Our research questions were:
– What impact does a teacher education program have on student teachers' theory and practice of literacy teaching?
– Is there a body of knowledge that student teachers need to be effective literacy teachers?
– How can universities and school systems provide more adequate support and mentoring for new literacy teachers?
– How can teacher preparation programs dovetail with the many large-scale school board initiatives in the literacy area?

Interviewing Student Teachers and Literacy Instructors

In the first year of the study, we interviewed 20 student teachers and surveyed all 600 students in the post-baccalaureate program. The interviews of the student teachers inquired into various areas, including: their experiences in the literacy courses and in their practice teaching placements; their vision for themselves as literacy teachers; the areas where they felt they needed to grow, their anxieties about teaching literacy; and so on. Clare conducted all of the interviews, which were congenial, but she had some anxieties about the students' responses from the first interview. As she continued to do the interviews, which were all later transcribed, she grew increasingly concerned because the student teachers seemed exceptionally naive. As we began sifting through the transcripts, we realized that the student teachers were very idealistic in their goals, were unrealistic about their own abilities, were exceptionally critical of the program, and many were unable to articulate their learning regarding literacy. We felt the data would have limited use because it was filled with jargon and platitudes. After many hours of work, reading and analyzing the data, we made the difficult decision to abandon this part of the research.

In this first year, we also interviewed 10 of the 11 literacy instructors. Clare again conducted all of these interviews and many of the questions were drawn from her previous self-study research as a literacy instructor. The questions addressed both the instructors' conceptual framework for their literacy courses and their day-to-day teaching. The broad areas for the questions were: their approach to their literacy courses, theoreticians who resonated with them, the readings they assigned, the influence of practice teaching supervision on their practice, the assignments they devised, and suggestions for improving the program. These interviews produced a strong data set, in part because Clare knew what to ask, and also because all of the instructors were thoughtful and articulate. With this background on the literacy courses we felt well prepared to study the beginning teachers, intending to make links between the literacy courses and the beginning teachers' practices.

Interviewing Beginning Teachers

We recruited 22 new teachers and planned to interview and observe them twice per year. Although we had clearly stated research goals, much to our surprise we struggled to develop interview questions to match them. Since we were not sure how to ask a question about the links between their preservice program and their practice without being too leading, the interview questions were often either too broad (e.g., how do you go about planning your literacy program?) or too specific (e.g., how would you define guided reading?). Furthermore, recognizing that beginning teachers are overworked and often disappointed with the gap between their ideals and their practices, we were extremely sensitive about the questions we asked. Since there were few longitudinal studies of this kind (Clift & Brady, 2005), we could not refer to the research instruments used by others. The interview questions addressed areas such as program planning, induction support, influence of the preservice program, overall reflections on their literacy program. We did include some questions that reflected our priorities (e.g., To what extent do you focus on building your class as a community?). We were not satisfied with the questions but were not sure what was wrong with them. Similarly, with the classroom observations, we devised a form to record basic information such as available reading material in the class and made notes as the teacher taught a literacy class but felt there was still "something" missing.

Much to our dismay, as we started analyzing the data, we discovered that the beginning teachers had limited recall of the specifics of their teacher education program, with many commenting "it is all a blur", "I don't remember the specifics," or dismissing it outright claiming, "it was a waste of time, I did not learn anything." Our plan to examine the influence of the preservice program on beginning teachers seemed to be disintegrating because our participants could not recall with any degree of accuracy much about the program.

In the second year of the study another key problem emerged. We tended to repeat many of the same questions attempting to determine change over time but the teachers found this repetitious and were becoming bored, feeling they had nothing else to add. We gathered our research team together and asked for their help. Since most were experienced teachers and many were working on their doctorates in education, they had some excellent suggestions. For example, they suggested abandoning the practice of repeating the same questions; moving to focus on the new teachers' practices rather than their reflections on preservice; looking more closely at the teachers' experience working in the division (e.g., grades 4 – 6); asking about changes in their motivation; and so on. These new questions led to interviews that were richer than those conducted previously.

Developing a Theory – Seven Priorities for Preservice Teacher Education

Since we were using a grounded theory approach, we began analyzing the transcribed interviews almost immediately. Working through the different systems of coding, we were able to see relationships and patterns. Consistent with grounded theory, we used the data to develop our theory. By the middle of the third year, we had identified seven priorities for teacher education which we see as a budding theory for teacher education:
- program planning,
- pupil assessment,
- classroom organization and community,
- vision for teaching,
- subject knowledge,
- professional identity,
- and inclusive education.

Identifying the priorities for teacher education was a turning point for the research process because we were no longer trying to figure out what we should be looking for; we now had a structure or framework, and knew the areas to pursue in our data gathering and analysis. True to the principles/tenets of grounded theory our "subsequent data collection should be guided by theoretical developments that emerge in the analysis" (Punch, 2005, p. 159). The interviews of the third-year teachers were dramatically different because there were questions about each of the priorities and the classroom observations were also based on the priorities. Below are the broad categories and examples of questions for each one. Some of the researchers had problems generating probe questions so we added these with the main question in bold type and the possible probe question in regular font.

Broad Categories and Sample Interview Questions:

- Brief Overview of Your Program and Experience
- **What has your experience been as a third year teacher?** How are you feeling about it?

- Approach to Teaching (Vision)
- **In what ways have you constructed or focused your literacy program this year?** Why did you make these changes? How is it different from what you have done in the past?

- Curriculum Resource Materials (Program Planning)
- **What are some of the main resources you use to plan your lessons?** Why do you use these?

- Specific Aspects of Program and Assessment (Assessment, Program Planning, Subject Knowledge)
- **Assessment is a challenge for teachers. In the past, you have used many forms of assessment. Which methods do you feel have given you the most reliable/useful information on the progress of your students? How have your assessment practices evolved these past three years?**

- Community and Connecting to the Broader Community (Inclusive Education, Classroom Organization and Community)
- **Can you tell me some of the ways that you establish your classroom environment?** In your three years of teaching, how have your views and practices of establishing a classroom environment changed? Why have you changed or stayed the same?

- Influences/Support/Professional Development (Professional Identity)
- **To what extent would you say that your literacy program matches the program of the teachers in your division/grade? Why is it different?** Over the past three years, would you say that your program has become more similar to or different from the programs offered by your colleagues?

- Confidence (Professional Identity)
- **Now that you are in your third year of teaching, how would you describe your motivation to teach compared to the last two years?**

- Your Development Over the 3 Years (Subject Knowledge)
- **What factors have helped you develop as a teacher?**

- Links with Preservice
- **In previous interviews you reflected on the strengths and limitations of your preservice and induction programs. Is there anything you would like to add about its strengths and weaknesses and how it might be enhanced?**

- Anything else you would like to add about teaching, preparation for teaching, or supports for new teachers?

In the teachers' fourth year of teaching, our questions evolved further. For example, we asked:

Think about the last four years and describe a "portrait" you might want to tell about this time. This portrait could be a description or picture of your journey the last four years or a description of your professional work. This does not need to be lengthy, involved, artistic, or groundbreaking; rather, we want to know how you might describe your story/experiences to someone thinking about going into teaching.

REFLECTIONS ON THE PROCESS

This complex research study produced a wealth of data. We gained tremendous insight into the link between the preservice program and the graduates' practices, we grew to more fully appreciate the challenges beginning teachers face in the current political climate, and we identified seven priorities for teacher education. We also increased our awareness of the challenge of working with such a large research team where doctoral students regularly came and left the team and interviewers interpreted their roles and the questions differently.

There was a need to provide on-going inservice for the interviewers (both new and experienced); we were challenged to develop appropriate research questions, and the sheer complexity of dealing with a staggering amount of data was at times overwhelming. The logistics of tracking 22 graduates required administrative support which we did not have. The time required to work on the data was significant and the knowledge required to analyze the data was extensive.

As an interviewer on this large scale project, Yiola found the ongoing inservice provided by Clive and Clare necessary and invaluable. She was reminded of the key goals of the project and of the ways to approach the interviews. Yiola found the team meetings highly informative as each researcher shared updates on issues such as: what questions in the interview yielded rich responses and which ones were less effective, new probe questions that worked, and interesting responses. The inservice kept a tight framework for conducting good interviews. Yiola recalls, "Because the study was related to my own practice, it was a constant challenge staying on task during the interviews because I wanted to share my insights and points of view with the participants. The inservice kept me focused and helped me stay on track".

Another challenge faced by Tim was finding a "good" balance in leading the interviewee in the questions he asked. In a previous study, he decided that he was not going to directly acknowledge the research problem in the interview items. Consequently, only two of the fifteen students he interviewed verbally recognized the problem he was investigating. While this led to information that he had not necessarily anticipated as arising from the interviews, he felt that the responses from his interviews had not given him the data to adequately answer his research questions. Tim learned that in order to have your research questions addressed, a certain amount of leading is almost certainly required; however, having the interview branch in different directions can also lead to new, unanticipated and interesting outcomes that may form the basis for new thoughts and investigations.

CHANGES TO OUR PRACTICES

As Laboskey (2004) has argued, self-study has to be improvement-aimed. Our initial plan was to conduct the research, write our report, and then revisit our work as teacher educators in light of the findings. This lock-step process evaporated instantly. Reading, analyzing, and writing about literacy education affected our work as teacher educators immediately. For example, many of the beginning teachers said they had been confused by all of the jargon and terminology in their literacy courses. So, Clare found an excellent glossary of literacy terms and distributed it to her current student teachers.

Beyond this simple tinkering with aspects of her courses, Clare took the dramatic step of reconceptualizing her literacy courses based on the priorities we identified, which led to a complete restructuring of every aspect of her courses. She felt that it would have been unethical to continue some of her practices (e.g., trying to cover the waterfront of all literacy topics) when she knew from the research that this approach overwhelms students and leaves them unprepared and confused. In the redesigned courses, she addresses five to seven main concepts rather than trying to do 12 topics; has selected readings that blend theory and practice; has a "Ticket Out the Door" system so that she can determine when students do not understand a concept; and has more small group-work. Each of these is directly related to our research on beginning teachers.

As the Teaching Assistant for Clare's course, Yiola witnessed and experienced firsthand the thoughtful processes of change. Clare systematically reconsidered every aspect of her teaching (planning, content, methods, structure, assignments, and assessment) in accordance with the findings from the longitudinal study. These changes not only occurred during the summer when the course was being prepared, but also Clare and Yiola reflected on their practice each week throughout the term; and, based on the research and students' needs, they adjusted their teaching accordingly. Consistent with self-study, Clare and Yiola, developed a research project to study these reconceptualized courses (Kosnik, Beck, & Cleovoulou, 2008).

True to self-study research, we intend to follow the student teachers from these reconceptualized courses to study their comfort level, their ability to organize a literacy course for their pupils, their comments on the preservice program, and so on. And we will use interviews as a data gathering tool!

REFERENCES

Berg, B. L. (2007). *Qualitative research methods for the social sciences* (6th ed.). Boston: Pearson.

Cleovoulou, Y. (2008). *A practicum experience in teacher education: Understanding a student teacher/host teacher professional relationship.* Saarbrucken, Germany: VDM Publishers.

Clift, R., & Brady, P. (2005). Research on methods courses and field experiences. In M. Cochran-Smith & K. Zeichner (Eds.), *Studying teacher education: The report of the AERA panel on research and teacher education* (pp. 309–424). Mahwah, NJ: Lawrence Erlbaum Associates.

Fletcher, T. (2008). *Attitudes, ability grouping and physical education.* Saarbrücken, Germany: VDM Publishers.

Fontana, A., & Frey, J. (2000). The interview: From structured questions to negotiated text. In N. K. Denzin & Y. S. Lincoln (Eds.), *Handbook of qualitative research* (2nd ed., pp. 645–672). Thousand Oaks, CA: Sage.

Freidus, H. (2006). Through a murky mirror: Self-study of a program in reading and literacy. In C. Kosnik, C. Beck, A. Freese, & A. Samaras (Eds.), *Making a difference in teacher education through self-study: Studies of personal, professional, and program renewal* (pp. 167–184). Dordrecht, The Netherlands: Springer.

Glaser, B. G., & Strauss, A. L. (1967). *The discovery of grounded theory: Strategies for qualitative research*. Chicago: Aldine de Gruyter.

Glesne, C. (1999). *Becoming qualitative researchers: An introduction* (2nd ed.). White Plains, NY: Longman.

Glesne, C., & Peshkin, A. (1992). *Becoming qualitative researchers: An introduction*. White Plains, NY: Longman.

Gubrium, J. F., & Holstein, J. A. (2002). Analytic strategies. In J. F. Gubrium & J. A. Holstein (Eds.), *Handbook of interview research: Context & method* (pp. 671–674). Thousand Oaks, CA: Sage.

Hycner, R. H. (1985). Some guidelines for the phenomenological analysis of interview data. *Human Studies, 8,* 279–303.

Jones, S. (1985). Depth interviewing. In R. Walker (Ed.), *Applied qualitative research* (pp. 45–55). Aldershot, UK: Gower.

Kosnik, C. (2008). Funny, this does not look like a community: Working collaboratively across borders and institutions. In A. Samaras, A. Freese, C. Kosnik, & C. Beck (Eds.), *Learning communities in practice*. Dordrecht: Springer Academic Publishers.

Kosnik, C., Beck, C., & Cleovoulou, Y. (2008). *We have the findings from our research on beginning teachers. How do we respond to them? Restructuring our teacher education courses in light of our findings. Proceedings of the seventh international conference of the self-study of teacher education. East Sussex, England.*

Kosnik, C., Beck, C., Freese, A., & Samaras, A. (Eds.). (2006). *Making a difference in teacher education through self-study: Studies of personal, professional, and program renewal*. Dordrecht, The Netherlands: Springer.

Kvale, S. (1996). *InterViews: An introduction to qualitative research interviewing*. Thousand Oaks, CA: Sage.

LaBoskey, V. (2004). The methodology of self-study and its theoretical underpinnings. In J. Loughran, M. L. Hamilton, V. LaBoskey, & T. Russell (Eds.), *International handbook of self-study of teaching and teacher education practices* (pp. 817–869). Dordrecht: Kleuwer.

McVarish, J., & Rust, F. (2006). Unsquaring teacher education: Reshaping teacher education in the context of a research I university. In C. Kosnik, C. Beck, A. Freese, & A. Samaras (Eds.), *Making a difference in teacher education through self-study: Studies of personal, professional, and program renewal* (pp. 185–202). Dordrecht, The Netherlands: Springer.

Merriam, S. (1998). *Qualitative research and case study applications in education*. San Francisco: Jossey-Bass.

Punch, K. (2005). *Introduction to social research: quantitative and qualitative approaches* (2nd ed.). London: Sage.

Samaras, A., & Freese, A. (2006). *Self-study of teaching practices*. New York: Peter Lang.

TOM RUSSELL

5. PERSONAL-EXPERIENCE METHODS

Re-Experiencing Classroom Teaching to Better Understand Teacher Education

Ritualized social routines are a necessary part of effective social interaction, but the problem is that they become embedded in beliefs that are self-fulfilling and designed to sustain the routines independently of any evidence that they are achieving their intended goals. . . . It is important to search out independent evidence that the widely accepted routines of teaching are in fact serving the purposes for which they are enacted. We need to find a critical vantage point from outside the routines and their supporting myths.

(Nuthall, 2005, p. 925)

A CONTEXT FOR SELF-STUDY OF PERSONAL EXPERIENCE

The decision seemed simple enough. In 1991, I was fast approaching the age of 50 and it had been 20 years since my days as a full-time high school physics teacher. With 13 years of experience teaching preservice science teachers, I was at the University of York for a year's sabbatical leave. In England at that time, the prevailing sentiment was that teacher educators should have "recent, relevant and successful" classroom experience. Provoked by this perspective, I wrote to a physics teacher back home in Kingston to ask if he would let me teach one of his physics classes in exchange for his teaching one of my two weekly physics method classes. My dean and his principal agreed to a simple exchange of services between the two educational institutions (school board and university) and my adventure was underway.

On every school day of the fall semester (September 1991 through January 1992), I left the university in time to be at the school to teach my afternoon class and then returned to my office soon after the class ended. Each class ran for 75 minutes. In exchange, the physics teacher traveled to the university once a week to teach one of my 2-hour physics method classes; I taught the other class each week in order to maintain contact with the students I would teach twice each week from February to the end of their preservice program in April.

I found the experience so stimulating and engaging that I arranged to continue the exchange agreement for a second year. Doing so proved to be central to learning from this self-study experience. Only in the second year did I come to understand what I had learned and re-learned in the first year, and I continue to

C. A. Lassonde, S. Galman and C. Kosnik (eds.), Self-Study Research Methodologies for Teacher Educators, 71–86.

wonder if this is not one of the reasons why new teachers find their first year of teaching so overwhelming.

Even though I had taught high school physics successfully many years earlier and even though I had been teaching preservice teachers for many years, the first year was a whirlwind experience, in part because I was teaching in an unfamiliar classroom with unfamiliar equipment and an unfamiliar textbook. Only by repeating the experience did I come to understand how centrally important it is to have first-hand knowledge of each and every textbook problem that students will be asked to solve.

It would be inaccurate to suggest that this self-study was driven by a profound set of research questions. I was confident that I would learn much that would be relevant to my teaching of preservice physics teachers and I was confident (most of the time) that I could be successful in the high school physics classroom. It seemed quite important at the time that I return to and re-experience the work that I was trying to help others learn to do.

Many years later I realize that the most crucial element in this account may be the fact that while I was re-experiencing a first year of teaching, I was doing so from the perspective of additional years of teaching experience as well as years of teacher education experience. I was hopeful that I could achieve some of the strengths and successes recalled from my last year in a high school. Inevitably, I was interpreting the experiences from the perspective of "Can I do what I ask my students of teaching to do when they become teachers?" As I taught, I always had to be asking myself how what I was doing compared to what I was advocating in the physics methods classroom.

METHODOLOGY FOR STUDYING PERSONAL EXPERIENCE

Methodologically, the term self-study had not yet appeared on the teacher education research scene. Qualitative research methods began to flourish after 1980, but the Self-Study of Teacher Education Practices special interest group within the American Educational Research Association was formed in 1993, after my 2 years of self-study of re-experiencing K-12 teaching. The academic year in England, 1991 through 1992, was my second 12-month sabbatical leave; as in my first leave, time spent in another teacher education program raised a variety of new and interesting issues. In 1992, when I was teaching Grade 12 physics for the second time, colleague Hugh Munby and I were beginning a research grant on the topic of case study research in teachers' professional knowledge.

This two-year self-study was two studies in one. One strand involved a study of my high-school teaching experiences. The first year that I returned to the physics classroom was as overwhelming as the first year of teaching, given that I was adding an additional 25 percent to my workload. Tracking that first year of experience in any systematic way quickly proved to be unrealistic, but in the second year I maintained a daily record of my experiences in enough detail that I can still recall many of the teaching moments that occurred more than 15 years ago. One fairly early discovery was that recording the events of the class soon after they occurred was an excellent way to formulate a plan for the next day, particularly in terms of how to begin the class to re-visit issues that required further attention.

The second strand involved a study of some of the preservice candidates in the physics method class, which I was sharing with the teacher during the 5 months that I was teaching at the school. In the fall of 1991, my return to high school teaching had no immediate or automatic effect on my preservice candidates, beyond providing them with the opportunity to observe my teaching whenever they wished to visit the school. My seeing them only once each week until February meant that relationships developed more slowly, and it was inevitable that they would enjoy the very practical tricks of the trade that the physics teacher provided each week. In the fall of 1992, I moved my weekly class to the high school and we met in my classroom just after the end of the school day. This would permit candidates to observe my class and then discuss it with me. While this was a potentially productive arrangement, it again did not appear to have a dramatic effect on those who were learning to teach.

LaBoskey (2004) has provided a definitive discussion of self-study methodology that is particularly helpful in considering research methods for studying personal experience. LaBoskey identifies five characteristics: self-initiated and focused, improvement-aimed, interactive, using multiple qualitative methods, and using trustworthiness to establish validity (p. 817). In the context of the self-study of my experiences returning to secondary school teaching, it is helpful to consider each of LaBoskey's characteristics in turn.

Self-Initiated and Focused

By returning to the secondary school, I hoped to learn first-hand the challenges associated with the teaching practices that I was recommending to new teachers. I initiated the experiences myself and I focused on my own learning from experience, yet it continued to be my professional obligation to provide the best possible learning experiences both for the Grade 12 physics students and for the prospective physics teachers. As LaBoskey notes (p. 843), while doing the research and studying oneself, the self is not the entire focus. Teaching is not an end in itself; the activities of teaching are meant to foster learning, and every teacher faces the daily challenge of fostering the most productive learning possible for her or his students. As I studied my own experiences returning to the school classroom, I necessarily had to study the quality of learning by the two different groups of students.

Improvement-Aimed

As I focused on developing a better understanding of how students learn physics and how preservice candidates learn to teach physics, my goal was to improve my own teaching practices so that future teachers would be helped to become the best possible teachers. For example, it has often been noted that prospective teachers have observed thousands of hours of teacher behaviour but they rarely have access to how teachers think about their actions and make decisions about those actions.

Loughran (2006) argues that teacher educators must take the lead in making explicit the reasons for their teaching actions. I believe that my opening myself to observation, by my preservice students and by others, while I was teaching in a secondary school has made it possible for me to be much more open with subsequent groups of teacher candidates about why I am teaching them as I do in the teacher education classroom.

Interactive

LaBoskey (2004, pp. 848–849) lists four ways in which self-study research is interactive, a term that she explicitly prefers over the term collaborative. Interaction with one's immediate colleagues frequently extends to interaction with teacher education colleagues in other universities. Interaction with one's students is a third form of self-study interaction, and a fourth form is interaction with relevant professional literature. In my self-study of my return to the classroom, I drew on all four categories of interaction. Interactions with my research colleague at Queen's and my school colleague who made it possible to return to the classroom were frequent sources of guidance. I was also in conversation with four new teacher educators (the Arizona Group: Karen Guilfoyle, Mary Lynn Hamilton, Stefinee Pinnegar and Peggy Placier) who were documenting their earliest teacher education experiences as assistant professors. Conversations with individuals in my two groups of students provided crucially important data, and it was natural that my activities in the classroom would be analyzed from a range of perspectives in the literature of teaching and teacher education.

Multiple, Primarily Qualitative, Methods

Typically relying primarily but not exclusively on qualitative research methods, self-study tends to draw frequently on action research, narrative research and dialogue with others about one's experiences in the world of personal practice. LaBoskey suggests that a "mix of mainly qualitative methods can enhance our understanding of our professional practice settings and help us to reframe our thinking and our teaching in appropriate and defensible ways" (p. 851). In my study I relied heavily on tape-recorded interviews of my preservice candidates, the daily personal record of my teaching experiences, and tape-recorded presentations to my colleagues about the nature of my experiences returning to the classroom.

Exemplar-Based Validation

LaBoskey draws on the work of others to construct an argument that self-study, like narrative knowing, seeks trustworthiness rather than truth as its primary criterion for validation of its research. She reports that one criterion of trustworthiness is the use of a study by others to guide their own research. Educational researchers have produced millions of research reports and published thousands of articles about teaching and teacher education, yet there is scant evidence that teaching and teacher education practices have changed significantly as a result (Cochran-Smith & Zeichner, 2005). The teachers I meet tend to reveal a distaste for research reports and a preference for practical activities that preservice candidates exhibit when they enter and leave a teacher education program. Personally, *coherence* has always seemed to be a crucial feature of a research report, and it is certainly the case that a research report must be read as trustworthy by others doing the same work (teaching or teacher education) in order to be judged as credible and potentially useful in one's own research inquiries and classroom practices. As with qualitative research, self-study research must provide exemplars that permit readers to form their own judgements of coherence, credibility and trustworthiness.

STRENGTHS AND LIMITATIONS OF THE METHODOLOGY

Standards for Quality in the Methodology

Self-study methodology is an important topic for many reasons, including the fact that self-study is a relatively new field within qualitative research. Perhaps the most deep-seated concern about self-study research is its reference to and study of the self, which has traditionally been associated with subjectivity. In contrast, quality in research has long been associated with objectivity. Issues such as objectivity may have led Bullough and Pinnegar (2001, p. 20) to offer the following perspective:

Self-study as an area of research in teacher education is in its infancy. Its endurability as a movement is grounded in the trustworthiness and meaningfulness of the findings both for informing practice to improve teacher education and also for moving the research conversation in teacher education forward. Like other forms of research, self-study invites the reader into the research process by asking that interpretations be checked, that themes be critically scrutinized, and that the "so what" question be vigorously pressed. In self-studies, conclusions are hard won, elusive, are generally more tentative than not. The aim of self-study research is to provoke, challenge, and illuminate rather than confirm and settle.

Self-study is about learning from experience and thus involves acknowledging and exploring the ways in which experience can have authority. Hugh Munby and I coined the phrase "the authority of experience" (Munby & Russell, 1994) when we analyzed and reported data provided by some of the preservice candidates who were in the class that I taught in 1992–1993, when I was teaching in the high school for the second time. Several years later we offered the following perspective as we explored the oft-cited tension between rigor and relevance:

In our view, Schön is correct in insisting that the knowledge of action resides within the action. We take this further by arguing that the idea of learning from experience offers too limited an account of how experience can teach. A better account would incorporate the idea that learning is *in* the experience. The authority of experience reminds us of the immediacy of this learning, just

75

as it also suggests that some of our students may not be ready to recognize and respond to that authority. Reports of data such as that presented here show that student teachers have met the conditions for significant professional learning. They have had experiences of sufficient depth and variety to begin to understand how they learn in and from experience—in short, to begin to recognize how experience has authority. Thus the data illustrate the instrumental value of the concept of authority of experience. We believe it is increasingly important for teacher educators to explore instrumental analysis of this type in order to better understand the basis for our claims to know in teaching and in teacher education. (Munby & Russell, 1995, p. 183)

Since that time, the published literature of self-study has increased rapidly and substantially. It continues to be important that those who undertake self-study include in their research reports their perspectives on their standards for quality.

Strengths and Limitations of Self-Study as Methodology

The strengths of self-study as methodology are also its limitations. Self-study is intensely personal, and those who reject research that is personal will always see this as a limitation. Yet the personal nature of self-study is also its strength. When research reported by others fails to speak to one's personal practice, self-study will never be disappointing. Including one or more critical friends adds considerable strength to self-study, protecting one from some of the personal intensity of self-study while also ensuring that data are interpreted from a range of relevant perspectives and that the interpretations are not self-sealing. Another strength of self-study in the context of teaching and teacher education emerges in richer and more open communication with one's students. Rationales for teachers' classroom behaviors almost always remain unavailable to students. As a teacher or teacher educator enters into self-study, it is essential to turn to one's students for data relevant to the research questions. While students might be regarded by some as unqualified to speak about their learning experiences, that is only the case because they have rarely been asked and have little experience of trying to judge the quality of their own learning. What some would judge to be a limitation can be a significant strength, both for the researcher and for the students being taught.

EXAMPLES OF PERSONAL-EXPERIENCE RESEARCH

Here I offer three examples. The first is my own, and the second is Jeff Northfield's self-study of a teacher educator returning to the classroom, similar in some ways to my own. The third is Graham Nuthall's critical interpretation of his personal experiences over 45 years as a classroom researcher; it has many self-study features but is not framed explicitly as a self-study.

Example 1: Studying Teacher Candidates' Responses to my Teaching in a Nearby School as I Studied those Teaching Experiences Myself

In the first of my two back-to-the-classroom experiences, I learned a great deal *in the experiences* but it was only through the second experience the following year that I came to understand what I had learned the first time. In that second experience I not only carried out a self-study of my learning but also studied the responses of my teacher candidates to my teaching in a school as I also taught them. Much as I might hope for enthusiastic responses to my school teaching and to my teaching of them, it was not to be.

Despite my teaching every day in a nearby secondary school, the candidates' initial expectations of preservice teacher education remained strong at least until the midpoint of their program. As in every such program, they were convinced that their most important learning would occur when they were placed in schools, but they believed that education classes could and should tell them how to teach. These continue to be strong expectations of teacher candidates in a preservice program and they continue to be resistant to teacher educators' efforts to change them. Watching me teach in the school seemed helpful before their first 2-week practicum placement but less so once they had teaching experiences of their own. At the midpoint of the program, I scheduled 30-minute interviews with each person in the class and data were analyzed from transcripts of conversations with those who agreed to the anonymous use of their comments. Qualitative analysis of the transcripts yielded four themes: expectations about learning to teach, observation skills, the credibility of a professor who teaches every day, and overall perspectives on teacher education. While discussing the data with Hugh Munby, who acted as critical friend for my teaching in the school, we suddenly noticed that we were speaking of the *authority of experience* and I continue to find value in the perspective captured by this term (Munby & Russell, 1994).

Other published accounts of my experiences focus on other elements of my self-study. In one account of the first year's experience (Russell, 1995a), I focus on rethinking the experience of the beginning teacher and my new insights into reflection-in-action (Schön, 1983). In a second account (Russell, 1995b), informed by the construct of the authority of experience, I frame my self-study from an action-research perspective focused on linking the teaching of secondary school physics to the teaching of those who are preparing to be physics teachers. Much more detail of my professional learning is presented below in the discussion of how this self-study research changed my practice.

Example 2: Inviting a Colleague to Interview Students and to Help Interpret Student Responses

In 1993, while holding an appointment as Director of Practice Teaching at Monash University, Jeff Northfield took himself back to the Year 7 classroom in a Melbourne suburb to teach science and mathematics. I had the good fortune to visit Monash University for 4 weeks that year, shortly after my own return to the physics classroom, and I was able to read portions of the daily teaching journal that

Jeff maintained. Jeff was assisted by a colleague who interviewed students and also helped him interpret classroom events from the students' perspectives. John Loughran then worked with Jeff to construct a book-length report and analysis of Jeff's experience (Loughran & Northfield, 1996). Northfield and Loughran (1997, p. 4) develop an important conclusion:

> The connection between school experience and improvement in teacher education is not clear. . . . We would argue that greater opportunities should exist for teacher educators to work in schools and classrooms, but the experience alone is not sufficient. Certain conditions for learning about teaching and teacher education need to be established to make the effort worthwhile.

They go on to offer 11 significant statements about the nature of self-study as methodology, as the following excerpts illustrate:

> 2. Effective self-study requires a commitment to checking data and interpretations with others. (p. 5)

> 6. A high level of self confidence is necessary as 'successful' experiences have unintended outcomes and closely held assumptions and ideas are queried. (p. 6)

> 7. Self-study outcomes demand immediate action so that the focus of study is constantly changing. (p. 6)

> 10. Dilemmas, tensions and disappointments dominate the data gathering and the attention in self-study. . . . Surprise and curiosity therefore spring from self-study, and shape it. (p. 6)

Jeff Northfield's self-study of his personal experiences as a teacher educator returning to the school classroom is among the earliest self-studies reported and his collaboration with John Loughran inspired many sound recommendations for how self-study should be conducted.

Example 3: Analyzing 45 Years of Personal Experience Conducting Research in Classrooms

Nuthall's (2005) extensive analysis and interpretation of his career studying classroom events is a significant account because it reveals his awareness of his evolving assumptions. A central feature is its focus on "cultural myths and realities":

> This article is about how culture shapes our understanding of both the teaching and learning process in ways that have proved extraordinarily difficult to identify and describe. What I want to recount in this article is the story of my own research journey and how, through nearly 45 years of research on teaching and learning in school classrooms, I have slowly become aware of how much of what we do in schools and what we believe about teaching and learning is a matter of cultural routines and myths. What is more, much of the research on teaching and learning in classrooms is itself

caught up in the same rituals and myths and sustains rather than challenges these prevailing beliefs. (p. 896)

When Nuthall and his research colleagues attempted to identify the differences that teaching experience made, they discovered none and attributed this finding to the basic patterns that characterize so much teaching:

To our surprise, however, there were no discernable differences between the experienced teachers, the beginning teachers we had trained in lesson analysis, and the untrained beginning teachers in either what they did or what their students learned. Being an experienced expert teacher apparently made no difference. Again, although we did not understand the significance of it at the time, we had stumbled across evidence that the basic patterns of teaching may be carried out in much the same way, with much the same effects, by novices and experts alike. (p. 898)

Nuthall's study of his own work and evolving assumptions also led to important insights about the nature of learning:

The most significant thing about learning is that it involves a progressive change in what we know or can do. What creates or shapes learning is a sequence of events or experiences, each one building on the effects of the previous one. This meant that the same experience might have quite different effects depending on where it occurred in the sequence of an individual student's experiences. The methods of data analysis that I and others were using in this research assumed that teacher and student behavior variables had stable effects regardless of when or where they occurred. Our methods were not sensitive to the possibility of constantly changing effects. (pp. 904–905)

It also dawned on me that the most important aspect of a student's experiences, from the point of view of conceptual learning, is the information (or meaning) that the student extracts from those experiences. Students cannot learn from information they are not exposed to, regardless of the kinds of questions the teacher is asking, the kinds of resources the student is exposed to, or the context in which the learning is taking place. . . . Since many of a student's experiences are hidden from the teacher, there is no way the teacher can know how often the student engages with relevant content.

With this kind of detailed analysis of the learning process it became clearer what role the teacher played and how the learning process was affected by interactions with peers and self-created learning experiences. (p. 911)

I quote extensively from Nuthall's lengthy (self-study) analysis of his long and productive career because I find the analysis so rich in new perspectives and so insightful about what happens in classrooms in the name of teaching and learning. I recommend it to all teacher educators for its important messages about how our teaching and teacher education practices are so deeply embedded in our culture that they are largely invisible to us as well as to our students. As we work to improve the quality of teaching and learning, both in schools and in preservice teacher education programs, we need to be guided by Nuthall's efforts to separate myths from realities. With these three examples as illustrations of self-study of personal experience, I turn now to an account of how self-study research using personal experience methods has changed by practice as a preservice teacher educator.

HOW RESEARCH USING PERSONAL EXPERIENCE METHODS CHANGED MY PRACTICE

What I Re-Learned about Teaching

I strongly believe that teaching is teaching, despite the obvious and important differences in the ages of individuals one may be teaching. A high-school physics teacher works with adolescents; a physics teacher educator works with adults who, in my case, have completed their undergraduate degree. These differences are important, yet building a productive teaching-learning relationship is not profoundly different between the two categories of students. I am drawn to Bain's (2004) analysis of the importance of how excellent teachers treat their students. Yes, a teacher is expected to know the subject being taught, but that is not the central point. If a teacher is completely new to a subject, teaching and learning are likely to be frustrating for everyone involved. If a teacher is familiar with a subject to a significant degree, knowing the answer to every possible question is quite unimportant. Subject-matter knowledge is important primarily for insights into how one might help others come to understand it.

Those who seek to become teachers seem to have great difficulty seeing teacher educators as real teachers, comparable to those obviously real teachers who teach children from Kindergarten through Grade 12 and must follow a prescribed curriculum set by the province or state. It seems unlikely that the absence of a prescribed curriculum for teacher education leads to the difficulty of seeing a teacher educator as a real teacher. I believed that this difficulty is closely linked to the fact that *the content of study is teaching itself*, and everyone in society is already very familiar with the behaviours of teaching. School teaches us about what teachers do as those teachers work to help us understand specific subjects. This is certainly not the point of school, but it is an inevitable consequence. Because teachers rarely explain why they are teaching as they do, prospective teachers experience an "apprenticeship of observation" (Lortie, 1975; Darling-Hammond, 2006) that conveys powerful messages about teaching without our realizing what we are learning. This unintended apprenticeship is also incomplete because the quality of what is learned is left entirely to chance. Only those who elect to prepare to become teachers feel the direct influence of those messages, and the influence is most apparent when they are placed in a school to be supervised as they begin to do the work of a teacher. Some take readily to a teacher's work, while others struggle at great length. Yet all prospective teachers can only come to understand the power of that unintended learning by observation if they are shown how to carry out self-study so that they may come to understand why they teach as they do.

What I Learned about Teaching New Teachers

The most immediate benefit of this self-study from the perspective of teaching future teachers came in the confidence that I did indeed possess "recent, relevant and successful" teaching experience that was comparable to the teaching they would soon be doing. Experience matters! All levels of schooling seem to minimize the significance of experience in learning, emphasizing instead the hoped-for potential of students extracting meaning from a teacher's spoken words and a textbook's written words. Important as they are, listening and reading are simply not enough. Watching someone else do something is better than listening or reading, but nothing can substitute for the meaning that can be developed through personal experience.

Some 15 years after the experience of returning to the physics classroom, the memories are still clear, though not as vivid as they once were. Teaching in a preservice teacher education program can, over time, reduce one's recollection of the range of pressures a teacher faces while trying to do the best possible teaching. It is only too easy to minimize the significance of experience in learning to teach, assuming instead that written and spoken words will adequately convey full meaning. Such practices implicitly assume that it is possible to talk over, around, and through the *experience gap* that separates those who know from those who do not and those who do have teaching experience from those who have little or none. Only at our peril do we ignore the reality that the preservice practicum is and always will be valued more highly than the education classes in a preservice program. Experience matters!

Thanks to this self-study and others I have conducted since, I now work to help my students see my education classes as experiences and I work to make those classes as experience-rich as possible. This means that I try to help them learn from the experiences we share in classes. Recently I was reminded of the significance of the experience gap when I showed a class of prospective physics teachers some of the simple equipment that can be used to demonstrate the phenomena that lead to our basic concepts of electricity and magnetism. Having worked with the equipment over several decades, I find it impossible to look at the equipment without immediately recognizing the concept each piece illustrates. In contrast, these university graduates seemed to be looking at the equipment for the very first time, and they could not begin to recognize or describe how the equipment might be used for teaching purposes. I now wonder if something similar happens when teacher candidates observe an experienced teacher: what they see is familiar, but do they know what to do with the teaching strategies they observe? Had I not studied my experiences returning to the school classroom, I doubt that I would now recognize and stress the central importance of learning from experience in the teaching of new teachers.

What I Learned about the Tensions between Schools and Preservice Programs

Over 30 years of teaching in a preservice program, I have supervised candidates in their school practicum placements in almost every year. This work does keep me familiar with the events that occur in schools and classrooms and it keeps me in contact with a number of teachers. Yet these supervisory experiences could never inspire the understandings generated by first-hand teaching experience from the start to the finish of a secondary-school course. It is easy for those who teach in preservice programs to be critical of those who teach in elementary and secondary schools. It is easy but unfortunate, even tragic, to view those learning to teach as those who will go forth and save the schools from themselves by finally introducing the new practices recommended by research. There are important reasons why schools do not change, just as there are important reasons why universities do not change (Sarason, 1996).

Just as preservice teacher education programs try to show new teachers how schools could be improved, so teachers in schools quite rightly try to show new teachers how to survive and thrive in schools as they are. It is not unusual to have teacher candidates report being greeted by a host teacher with the advice, "Forget everything they taught you at Queen's."

What I Learned about the Complexity and Rewards of Self-Study

Thanks to the experience of returning to the high school physics classroom at the midpoint of my career as a teacher educator, self-study has now become a natural and obvious activity. The rewards are almost exclusively intrinsic. Yes, self-study is intensive, time-consuming and often unflattering. We speak easily of the gap between theory and practice, as though theory somehow tells us what we should do but we fall short when it comes to enacting theoretical principles or research findings in our own classrooms. Self-study has shown me that the gap is not between theory and practice. The gap is between what we think we are doing and what our students perceive us to be doing. The gap is also between what teachers have always done and what teachers would like to do; overcoming the apprenticeship of observation is a huge challenge that can be overcome through self-study.

Self-study keeps me positive and optimistic because I see the improvements it has inspired in my students' learning and in my understanding of what I am doing deliberately to foster those improvements. Since discovering the writings of Seymour Sarason in the 1970s, his focus on the significance of the *culture of the school*, which certainly links to Nuthall's (2005) focus, has helped me to understand why calls for reform rarely produce change. I understand it now, but I was stunned when Sarason (1998) wrote after so many years that he no longer expected to see change in our schools:

> What finally convinced me was the recognition that no one—not teachers, not administrators, not researchers, not politicians or policymakers, and certainly not students—willed the present state of affairs. They were all caught up in a system that had no self-correcting features, a system utterly unable to create and sustain contexts of productive learning. . . . There are no villains. There is a system. You can see and touch villains, you cannot see a system. . . . The reform movement has been about parts, not about the system, not about how the purposes of parts are at cross-purposes to each other, not

about how the concept of purpose loses both meaning and force in a system that is amazingly uncoordinated and that has more adversarial than cooperative features. (Sarason, 1998, p. 141)

Like Nuthall (2005), Sarason (2002) has also produced an analysis of his 45 years in pursuit of educational reform; the subtitle of his book is "a self-scrutinizing memoir," a term that fits well with self-study. While self-study is no guarantee of change, it is an excellent methodology for recognizing personal and cultural assumptions and for focusing on the effects of our teaching practices by listening to our students. Self-study might well be said to be even more complex than the phenomena it studies; the rewards of self-study appear in improved understanding of one's practice and in improved learning by one's students.

What I Learned about a Daily Teaching Journal

Keeping a daily teaching journal was impossible in my first year, when everything about the experience was new, even though I was usually confident that experience would carry me through. Adapting to a new school means learning how attendance is taken, learning procedures for dealing with late students or late assignments, learning routines for photocopying, learning what to expect on parents' night and so on. The central focus of my first year was re-discovering what the students did and did not expect of me and discovering how a particular physics textbook could and could not be used to support student learning. The curriculum treadmill was laid out for me by my teaching colleague and I worked every evening to prepare to deal with student questions about a range of homework problems. Tests had to be marked for return to students the next day, and marks had to be entered into the same software program being used by my teaching colleague. I also had to learn where equipment was kept and what to expect in terms of students' laboratory reports.

In my second year, everything was different. I knew the routines of both classroom and school; I knew the ins and outs of the textbook. Keeping a daily teaching journal seemed natural and obvious, and I quickly discovered that writing to myself for 15 minutes every day after class generated a plan for the next day's class. The fact that writing each day helped me to plan the next lesson was an immediate bonus; over the long term, keeping the journal created a lasting record to which I could return at any time.

Interestingly, keeping such a teaching journal of my physics methods classes at the university has never happened in anything like the same way. Perhaps it is because there are only two classes per week. Perhaps it is because, quite unlike teaching high school physics, there is no set curriculum to follow. I have urged those who are preparing to teach to keep a journal as they teach, but success stories are rare. Russell & Hrycenko (2006) provides an example of a teacher candidate who maintained and shared a record of his practicum teaching. A graduate in 2008 who is now teaching at an international school in Latin America is writing about his teaching on a daily basis in a shared blog that we began during his practicum placements. Apparently, a daily teaching journal is for the few, not the many; a daily journal can be a unique exercise in studying and learning from one's teaching experiences.

What I Learned from Mistakes I Made

In the school, I was an outsider who had temporarily "moved in from the cold." Students, teachers, administrators and parents all expected me to act "just like a teacher." I recall no huge mistakes, but I am sure there were many little ones. Everyone was patient and helpful. In the classroom, I inevitably made mistakes with unfamiliar equipment. One of the most memorable and revealing moments of learning from a mistake came about 6 weeks into my return to the physics classroom. At the end of a class a student came to the front and in refreshingly candid fashion explained that my teaching was not preparing him to do the assigned homework problems. Later in the semester, on parents' night, his mother explained to me that all his teachers were familiar with his candid approach. The incident stands out, years later, because his comment was correct! In my preparation each night, I was solving the problems that they were solving, so that I would be ready to explain them the next day. I was not solving the next night's problems so that my lessons would include any details they might require that were not particularly obvious. One could argue that students can turn to their textbook for guidance, and I have never been one to believe in spoon-feeding. What this student perceived as a mistake on my part was a reminder of yet another challenge that a new teacher faces when confronted with one or more unfamiliar textbooks; all teachers face the same challenge when a textbook is changed. I soon found myself working problems a day earlier; in the second year, virtually all the problems were familiar and I had my solutions from the previous year as well.

What I Learned about Learning from Experience

Experience matters, and the learning is *in* the experience. Experience is particularly important if our focus is productive learning, yet learning from teaching experience can be inaccurate, incomplete, and hidden from view. Most of us readily learn from experience to avoid open flames, hot or sharp objects, loud noises, blinding lights, and other responses that involve our senses. Learning from experiences of teaching is quite different from learning how to live in our physical environment. We acquire patterns of behaviour by observing others around us and we are often unaware that our behaviours are changing. We come to teaching with a set of educational values, yet those values change in subtle and unnoticed ways as our behaviours change. While we may wish that our values will guide our behaviours, one of my most recent accounts of learning from self-study (Russell, 2007) is deliberately framed from the perspective of experience changing my values to emphasize the importance of attention to how and what we are learning from experience.

A new teacher's first goal might reasonably be described as survival with some measure of success. Most new teachers want to meet their students' expectations and most also want to fit in with the ways of their colleagues as well as those of their former teachers. As an experienced teacher and teacher educator returning to the school classroom, I too wanted to fit in. Yet the minute we start to fit in is also the minute that we begin to accept uncritically some of the myths of schooling that Nuthall (2005) described. As teachers and teacher educators, we are often criticized for our inability to create the powerful learning (Darling-Hammond et al., 2008) and the powerful teacher education (Darling-Hammond, 2006) to which we aspire. I am increasingly convinced that this inability is closely linked to our inability to make visible and act on the cultural myths and patterns in which we work. Self-study of personal experience can be a powerful and rigorous way forward.

REFERENCES

Bain, K. (2004). *What the best college teachers do.* Cambridge, MA: Harvard University Press.

Bullough, R. V., Jr., & Pinnegar, S. (2001, April). Guidelines for quality in autobiographical forms of self-study research. *Educational Researcher, 30*(3), 13–21.

Cochran-Smith, M., & Zeichner, K. M. (2005). *Studying teacher education: The report of the AERA panel on research and teacher education.* Washington, DC: American Educational Research Association.

Darling-Hammond, L. (2006). *Powerful teacher education: Lessons from exemplary programs.* San Francisco: Jossey-Bass.

Darling-Hammond, L., Barron, B., Pearson, P. D., Schoenfeld, A. H., Stage, E. K., Zimmerman, T. D., et al. (2008). *Powerful learning: What we know about teaching for understanding.* San Francisco: Jossey-Bass.

LaBoskey, V. K. (2004). The methodology of self-study and its theoretical underpinnings. In J. J. Loughran, M. L. Hamilton, V. K. LaBoskey, & T. Russell (Eds.), *International handbook of self-study of teaching and teacher education practices* (pp. 817–869). Dordrecht, The Netherlands: Kluwer Academic Press.

Lortie, D. (1975). *Schoolteacher: A sociological analysis.* Chicago: University of Chicago Press.

Loughran, J. (2006). *Developing a pedagogy of teacher education: Understanding teaching and learning about teaching.* London: Routledge.

Loughran, J. J., & Northfield, J. R. (1996). *Opening the classroom door: Teacher, researcher, learner.* London: Falmer Press.

Munby, H., & Russell, T. (1994). The authority of experience in learning to teach: Messages from a physics methods class. *Journal of Teacher Education, 45*, 86–95.

Munby, H., & Russell, T. (1995). Towards rigour with relevance: How can teachers and teacher educators claim to know? In T. Russell & F. Korthagen (Eds.), *Teachers who teach teachers: Reflections on teacher education* (pp. 172–184). London: Falmer Press.

Northfield, J., & Loughran, J. (1997, March). *The nature of knowledge development in the self-study practice.* Paper presented at the meeting of the American Educational Research Association, Chicago. ERIC Document Reproduction No. ED 408 353.

Nuthall, G. (2005). The cultural myths and realities of classroom teaching and learning: A personal journey. *Teachers College Record, 107*, 895–934.

Russell, T. (1995a). A teacher educator and his students reflect on teaching high school physics. *Teacher Education Quarterly, 22*(3), 85–98.

Russell, T. (1995b). Returning to the physics classroom to re-think how one learns to teach physics. In T. Russell & F. Korthagen (Eds.), *Teachers who teach teachers: Reflections on teacher education* (pp. 95–109). London: Falmer Press.

Russell, T. (2007). How experience changed my values as a teacher educator. In T. Russell & J. Loughran (Eds.), *Enacting a pedagogy of teacher education* (pp. 182–191). London: Routledge.

Russell, T., & Hrycenko, M. (2006). The role of metaphor in a new science teacher's learning from experience. In P. J. Aubusson, A. G. Harrison, & S. M. Ritchie (Eds.), *Analogy and metaphor in science education* (pp. 131–142). Dordrecht, The Netherlands: Springer.

Sarason, S. B. (1996). *Revisiting "The culture of the school and the problem of change."* New York: Teachers College Press.

Sarason, S. B. (1998). *Political leadership and educational failure*. San Francisco: Jossey-Bass.

Sarason, S. B. (2002). *Educational reform: A self-scrutinizing memoir*. New York: Teachers College Press.

Schön, D. A. (1983). *The reflective practitioner: How professionals think in action*. New York: Basic Books.

PATRICIA PAUGH AND ELIZABETH ROBINSON

6. PARTICIPATORY RESEARCH AS SELF-STUDY

An alternative would be to explore the possibilities of reimagining or redefining
the local as what Moshenberg (1996) called a "neighborhood" – a conceptual
space or vicinity in which the salient concern is not an essentialized identity but
rather one's location relative to others.

(Lytle, 2000)

"What counts as teacher education" in a postmodern era is often difficult to
capture. The rapidly shifting social and cultural spaces that define society greatly
affect what has been a traditional march through the institutional preparation,
recruitment, and retention of teachers. Such shifts mirror a world where students
move within and between schools, districts, and countries with increasing frequency.
They also reflect an ongoing struggle for control of education where economic
interests conflict with social and democratic practices. As teacher educators,
supporting teachers' work in such a world necessitates that we question relationships
and practices that have up until now been fairly clear. Our roles, responsibilities,
and goals are less certain as is the power connected to the designation of teacher
educator as "expert." The location of our work increasingly falls outside the
boundaries of the university. Yet our mission does not change: to educate teachers
to be intellectual workers who instruct with rigor and with a sense of social justice.

As teacher educators in a postmodern era we are increasingly called to reconsider
the locations of our practice (e.g. ranging from in-district degree programs to
global videoconferences) and our roles interacting with others in situated spaces
that create the context for those practices . In our exemplar study shared later in
this chapter, we illustrate how we drew on participatory research methods to
question our teacher education practices in relationship to: our goals, the goals of
the teachers in our courses, the outside standards and institutional constraints of
districts and states, and most importantly the diverse needs of the "students of our
students" (LaBoskey, 2004). In this chapter we illustrate how participatory
methods drawn from self-study, practitioner research, and action/participatory
action research together offer teacher educators a theoretical frame as well as tools
for studying the consequences of our participation in these contexts.

PARTICIPATORY ACTION RESEARCH, PRACTITIONER RESEARCH
AND SELF-STUDY WITHIN "CONTACT ZONES"

Studying our practices in teacher education necessarily involves the "purposes,
participants, and contexts" of our work (Loughran, 2004). As indicated above, the

*C. A. Lassonde, S. Galman and C. Kosnik (eds.), Self-Study Research Methodologies
for Teacher Educators, 87–106.*

choice of action/participatory action research as methodology for self-study research necessarily positions "self" *in relationship* to the context (LaBoskey, 2004). Teacher educators who hold an epistemological stance toward learning as socially constructed and an instructional stance prioritizing social justice and critical pedagogy find participatory action research a good fit for integrating research with teaching. This parallels practitioner research traditions that hold "emancipatory" positions (Feldman, Paugh, and Mills, 2004; Ziechner &Noffke, 2001). Briefly, these traditions include a critical questioning of the effects of power within social contexts, especially questioning the role of power and privilege in the education of teacher candidates, teachers, and students historically marginalized due to race, socioeconomic status, sexual orientation, language, or gender.

If we imagine social and dialogic spaces that include self-study, our unit of study not an essentialized "self" but the relational self (or selves). Lytle (2000) imagines these spaces as "contact zones" where:

> various discourses intersect and are systematically analyzed in ways where various constituencies recognize complementarity as well as difference and open up the productive possibilities of what Pratt (1991) referred to as oppositional discourse, resistance, and critique. The goal here is neither contentiousness nor consensus but rather acknowledging, understanding and drawing on the richness of roles and identities and searching for new language with which to talk and think about new social practices with which to structure and support the work. (Lytle, 2000, pp. 708 – 709)

For teacher educators studying their practices through critical and participatory methods, the units of analyses are evolving social spaces where participants continually interact with the goal of collective change (McTaggart, 1997). Below we describe participatory methods that include: action/participatory action research, practitioner research, and self-study, followed by suggestions for how they might together be useful to teacher educators seeking to study the multiple contexts of their practices. Although we discuss these as three separate traditions, it is important to consider their overlapping as well as distinct characteristics.

WHAT ARE ACTION RESEARCH AND PARTICIPATORY ACTION RESEARCH?

For our purposes we will merge these into a framework of action research/ participatory action research (AR/PAR). Any AR/PAR agenda is constructed through a cycle of data collection and analysis that leads to new cycles. In the literature, action research and participatory action research are confluent and divergent. Greenwood and Levin (1998) suggest that commonalities are linked to knowledge generation (research), participation, and action. That is, action research in education is the generation of knowledge that leads to democratic participation and the taking of responsibility by all participants in the research process. Facilitators work with members of school and community groups offering tools for full participation. "Because these people together establish the AR agenda, they generate the knowledge necessary to transform the situation, and put the results to work, AR is a participatory process in which everyone involved takes some responsibility" (Greenwood & Levin, 1998, pp. 7 & 8).

PAR diverges from AR in its link to an emancipatory agenda. It is often used in developing countries where researchers work as allies with populations living in extreme poverty or who are deprived of civil rights. The goals of the research are increased power for societal participation by group members. While AR usually involves some form of collaborative participation, PAR is specifically connected to collaboration with marginalized populations towards a critical praxis or raised consciousness of their positions in society and leading to the disruption of their marginalization (Freire, 1970; Kamberelis & Dimitriadis, 2005). With PAR there is always the focus on power and privilege within the collective and social consciousness, while this is not always the case with action research (Feldman, Paugh, & Mills, 2004). For teacher educators, including a PAR focus foregrounds questions of power within the AR cycle.

For teachers who are positioned in today's political contexts more as "implementers" of mandated curriculum rather than as professional decision-makers (Altwerger et al. 2004) AR/PAR methods invite a different relationship between teacher educators and teachers. AR/PAR questions the effects of power on teachers' and teacher educators' learning and questions this in the face of the social forces shaping today's educational environments. A critical PAR agenda adds ongoing questions of power and privilege to the change cycle.

WHAT DOES AN AR/PAR, PRACTITIONER RESEARCH METHODOLOGY OFFER TO SELF-STUDY?

Conducting research on teacher education practices with AR/PAR suggests cycles of studying dynamic roles and relationships. In the exemplar research to be discussed in this chapter the authors engaged in cycles of inquiry in relationship to critical friends, including co-instructors, teaching assistants, teachers, and teacher candidates in classrooms, schools and community sites. Here our "selves" were studied as relational, situated, and dialogic (LaBoskey, 2004). This view emerges from sociocultural theories that move away from "self" as an essentialized individual identity toward the more postmodern notion of "selves" as social and cultural constructions. This "social turn" (Gee, 1990) imagines "selves" in reciprocal relationship to context and "selves" constructed through power relations that determine what is said, who can speak, to whom, when, and in what situations (Bloome et al., 2005; Duesterberg, 1999).

Literature grounded in the field of practitioner research argues for a notion of self *in conversation* with others (Fecho et al., 2005) where multiple perspectives come into relationship, continually reshaping the context and participants. An excellent example of practitioner researchers collecting and analyzing data at the nexus of multiple perspectives is found in the critical teacher-research partnerships facilitated by Comber & Kamler (2005). When novice and experienced teachers together investigated their practices of teaching "at risk" students, their interactions reshaped classroom contexts away from deficit constructions toward instructional models based on student competence. Such dialogic investigation brought together "cross generational perspectives," foregrounding issues of power. Thus, current theories brought to classroom teaching by novice teachers came into relationship with the experience and knowledge of veteran teachers, with transformative consequences for struggling students. It is through this conception that we next offer guidance for developing self-study by teacher educators within the "contact zones" where we practice.

IS SELF-STUDY THE APPROPRIATE METHODOLOGY FOR MY STUDY?

> Social judgment is itself of a kind of democratic conversation in which the professional researcher has only one vote. (Greenwood & Levin, 2003)

Self-study research lends itself to the qualitative process (although methods both qualitative and quantitative fit this framework). LaBoskey (2004) reasons that self-study research is "iterative and responsive" (p. 858). That is, self-study necessarily engages in "an iterative process where questions and findings emerge within a *structured and ongoing examination of data* within the contexts of practice, with findings constantly being reexamined and retested as the contexts are transformed" (p. 850). Action research is an especially "appealing" framework for these goals. She explains,

> Inclusion of cycles of inquiry that incorporates the immediate practical application and testing of insights gained…this recursive and ongoing process allows for responsive adaptation with regard to the forms of data collected and the means of analysis. It is possible to subsume other strategies into this overall format. (p. 850)

These cycles of action research are "thought-action cycles" where the "testing of understandings collaboratively generated through actions that then become part of the next cycle of thought and planning" (Greenwood & Levin, 1998, p. 65). Cycles of critical inquiry enable all participants in the practice of teacher education to enter into *democratic conversations* that have local and as well as broader implications. This is the point of intersection between the methodological traditions of Action Research/Participatory Action Research (AR/PAR), Practitioner Inquiry (PI), and Self-study. For example, Cochran-Smith & Lytle (2004) offer the construct of teacher researchers as taking an "inquiry stance" toward their practice that recreates teaching as a "long term collective project with a democratic agenda." The notion of the "contact zone" helps us imagine spaces as well as the procedures by which to conduct *structured and ongoing examination* of data leading to democratic and emancipatory action resulting in intellectual growth for all participants. Participatory methods of self-study are well-suited for the complexity found in educational settings (Greenwood & Levin, 1998) and a critical focus embedded in these methods acknowledges the multiple perspectives and the power relationships that create knowledge in these contexts.

WHAT ARE THE PROCESSES THAT DRAW ON SELF-STUDY THROUGH PARTICIPATORY RESEARCH?

As critical self-study researchers, we draw on conceptual frames from the above traditions as *initial designers* of participatory research. This means that as we design initial cycles of research we "problematize" our practice in relationship to others. That is, we develop questions concerning its "purposes, participants, and contexts" and choose methods of data collection and analysis to structure our study (realizing that additional questions, methods, and participants may be needed as our research progresses through various cycles). We also realize that we are the designers and our methods justify our theories and intentions. That said, while participatory self-study research may have common methods, each researcher employs the methods in response to their theoretical framework and responsive to unique and local circumstances.

CYCLES OF DESIGN AND ANALYSIS

Designing initial cycles of "thought and action" may originate in two ways: A study may suggest itself due to "living contradictions" that emerge within a context or it may be initiated when designing new activities (such as a program or course or as the impetus for rethinking teacher/research networks, etc.). Procedures for initiating such study begin with identifying the "purposes, participants, and context" to be included. This is done realizing that the relationship between participation and the shaping of context is reciprocal. Imagining a "contact zone" helps define "participants" and "context" in participatory research. In the contact zone defined by Lytle above, multiple discourses intersect and new language develops.

Considering this intersection of discourses, a theory of discourse is required. For our study an understanding that language shapes and is shaped by the context was seminal (Rogers, 2004). Context as defined here is constructed through the effects of power. Social positions are constructed when discourses come into relationship. Thus the "participants" that come into contact can be present or distant, human or material. For example, in the on-site urban teacher education course in the exemplar study described below, the immediate context of the course was shaped through interactions between teachers and teacher educators physically present, but was also influenced distantly by test scores related to national No Child Left Behind legislation, by local press reports that consistently reported on the "underperforming" schools in the district, and in specific language found in the mission statement of the university program. These all represent discourses that came into contact and positioned the teacher educators, the teachers, and their students within the "zone" of the week-to-week activities of the course, sometimes creating conflicting positions.

In the initial planning of your own study, it may be helpful to consider the above in terms of categories of participation as primary (participants physically active in the research) and secondary (indirect discourses that may contribute to the context). These are not necessarily separate but such categories may be useful in prompting researchers to search for discourses not usually visible but important to shaping the social positions of those involved in the study.

Once initiated, new questions and actions emerge within the study. Additional cycles of the study are expected as it progresses. Researchers must attend to local circumstances as well as the progression of the research to determine how cycles will evolve. Figure 1 presents a framework for planning an initial cycle of an AR/PAR Study.

Purposes: What is the rationale for this study? What are the goals for research and action? What do you hope to accomplish?

Question: What are the initial questions that will focus the data collection and analysis? How and where do these questions arise?

Participants:

Primary: Who and what are the participants who contribute to the immediate contexts of the study?

Secondary: Who and what are the participants not directly involved in the data collection or analysis but contribute to the discourses that come into relationship in this study?

Context: What are the locations or spaces where participants come into relationship? What are the circumstances involved?

Methods:

Data: What are the sources of data that will be collected?

Analysis: How will that data be analyzed and by whom?

Figure 1. Planning an Initial Cycle of Data Collection and Analysis for your AR/PAR Self-Study

Those who engage in self-study research draw from a variety of qualitative research methods. Although unique to each project, there are specific focus questions that lend themselves to critical participatory studies as a whole. Extending the work of LaBoskey (2004) the following questions may provide helpful for designing methods of data collection and analysis. These include: questions of pedagogy, questions of collaboration, and questions of power. Linking these questions to standard qualitative methods to fit the purposes and goals of your participatory research is key to the initial and ongoing design.

QUESTIONS OF PEDAGOGY

Like practitioner researchers, teacher educators who engage in self-study include questions of pedagogy as "we do not engage simply for the purpose of theorizing but we have pedagogical imperatives, responsibilities to our current students as well as their students" (LaBoskey, 2004, p. 819). As models for our teacher education students, we strive to demonstrate an "inquiry stance" by collecting and analyzing data from our own teaching. Linking participatory research to participatory pedagogies fits a PAR model where researchers/facilitators collectively develop knowledge with students/participants through the power of collective dialogue (Dozier et al., 2006; Egan-Robertson & Bloome, 1989; Falk & Blumenreich, 2005; Kamberelis & Dimitriadis, 2005).

QUESTIONS OF COLLABORATION

Teacher educators who engage in participatory self-study naturally include methods that depend on collaborative communities of practice. That is they engage "critical friends" (Loughran, 2004) who serve to "confirm or oppose" the findings (Tidwell, 2002). Critical friends may includes students in their courses, members of the community, colleagues such as faculty or teaching assistants who practice within the same course, colleagues in the same university, or, "cross-institutional" colleagues such as teacher educators from other universities (Shuck & Segal, 2002). Participation structures may include: learning circles, participatory interviews, micro-teaching, "think-pair share", collaborative conversations, and opportunities for dialogue that involve ICT's (information and communication technologies such as email or ichat) (LaBoskey, 2004; Chryst, Lassonde, & McKay 2008).

QUESTIONS OF POWER

Teacher educators who engage in critical participatory research not only identify participation structures within their contexts but embed questions of power and privilege in their analyses. In the exemplar study below, language was key to the construction of our teacher education context. As we examined the power relationships between teaching faculty, doctoral assistants, teachers, and others in the national, state, and district, we wished to consider what Cochran-Smith and Lytle (2004) describe as "working the dialectic". That is, we focused on the effects of power generated in the spaces where university and school discourses came into relationship. To do this, it was necessary that we locate, learn about, and adopt specific methods of critical discourse analysis (Young & Fitzgerald, 2006) which we then refined during subsequent research cycles. The field of critical discourse analysis (CDA) offers multiple methodologies that may fit participatory self-study research. See Rogers (2004) for an excellent introduction to the field that provides multiple representations of critical discourse study.

ISSUES OF VALIDITY AND CREDIBILITY

As the goal is action, the primary test of effectiveness is to generate the "capacity to resolve problems in real-life situations." A key for all methodologies suggested in this chapter is for the research to *be internally and externally credible* (Greenwood & Levin, 1998, pp. 75–81). That is, to be internally credible, the knowledge generated must be suited to the local context. This addresses a critique heard from the teachers we meet in public schools who claim that theories and instructional methods suggested through outside research are not always suitable for their contexts. Yet, as LaBoskey notes for self-study research, Cochran-Smith & Lytle for practitioner research, and Greenwood & Levin for AR/PAR, there is a need for *external credibility*, that is, convincing those outside the context that the research enhances understandings of teacher education in general or contributes to larger research and policy conversations. AR/PAR and PI supports teachers' knowledge generation through systematic research. This extends and values teachers' perspectives and positions them authoritatively, in ways not always available when they are simply "recipients" and "implementers" of curriculum developed outside their school contexts (Cochran-Smith & Lytle, 2004). This view is often thought to be problematic by traditional researchers in the social sciences who value knowledge as generalizable across contexts (Cochran-Smith & Lytle, 2004; Greenwood & Levin, 2003). To be credible in addressing the purposes described above, participatory self-study must be transparent and clear about the value and limitations of its claims. In the section below we will discuss this further in terms of strengths as well as limitations for such research.

ANALYTIC STRENGTHS AND LIMITATIONS

Participatory methods such as those outlined in this chapter are well-suited for researching the complex social environments found in educational contexts. The theories behind these methods challenge embedded beliefs that sustain inequity in education. One embedded notion is that identity is individualistic and essentialized. Another is that theory is separate from practice. Instead, participatory methods consider intersecting perspectives that construct social roles within contexts, blurring the boundaries between researcher and researched. Such research is important in an era where educational settings include diverse social, cultural, political, and linguistic perspectives.

For teacher educators, the boundaries that define traditional university practices are rapidly shifting in response to changing social and political norms. In fact, Cochran-Smith & Lytle (2004) challenge university teacher educators to take an "inquiry stance" on their own work as they engage in preparing teachers to be critical professionals in Pre-K – 12 settings. PAR/AR methods support those who wish to research "with" rather than "on" school-based educators and students. As forms of self-study these methods encourage reflexivity that keeps us aware of ourselves as both subjects and objects in relation to others in our research and also keeps transparent the relationship between participants. Such reflexivity acknowledges what can be shifting and partial identities in the context of study and allows for mutual ground between researchers and research – realizing at the same time the instability and fragility of that ground (Kamberelis & Dimitriadis, 2005). These methodologies encourage teacher educators and university researchers to adopt a stance of vulnerability (Clifford, 1988 in Kamberelis & Dimitriadis, 2005) or what

Peter Murrell (2008) argues for as a need for "humility" by university researchers engaged in action and participatory work with urban communities.

This opportunity can be deceptive as it is difficult to assess our own positionality. Michele Fine (1994) warns that ignoring our own participation in our research – misusing our power as analysts to reproduce rather than rethink inequity – results in "othering" our collaborators. She also warns of an opposite extreme – looking inward and avoiding an ethical responsibility toward our world. Designing an AR/PAR self-study includes responsibility for the "discourses we inhabit and the histories we invoke" (Kamberelis & Dimitriadis, 2005, p. 904). Thus we must ensure that our design contains trustworthy checks to maintain such a balance, so as not to reproduce the social inequities we have set out to interrogate. McTaggart (1997) prompts us to maintain "appropriate communication" between participants to ensure that all identify with the work of collective change (p. 14).

Below we share an exemplary case where as authors involved in a school/ university partnership, we were compelled to remain responsible for the discourses we inhabited through our participation as course instructors and researchers working with urban elementary and middle school teachers in a high-stakes political context.

WHAT DOES AN EXEMPLARY CASE OF THIS METHODOLOGY LOOK LIKE?

This exemplary case in participatory self-study should not be considered a rigid model or template. Instead, we invite readers, as teacher educators, to observe and critically evaluate it as an emergent AR/PAR self-study. We outline several cycles of research and action where data were systematically and collectively analyzed with goals of social transformation. In this case, as university teacher educators we drew upon AR/PAR self-study methods to remain responsible to our stated mission of critical praxis as we participated as instructors for several courses in an off campus master's program.

BACKGROUND AND DESIGN OF OUR STUDY

The master's degree program in which we taught was a response to the NCLB legislation and our state's adoption of an English-Only law. This university program was developed through an alliance known as ACCELA (Access to Critical Content for English Language Acquisition). The alliance provided inquiry-based, on-site master's degree coursework to cohorts of district teachers seeking reading and ESL licensure in an urban setting. The mission included this language:

> The ACCELA Alliance professional development programs are unlike other programs in a number of ways. First, the theoretical perspective informing the work of ACCELA is grounded in a critical, praxis-oriented understanding of teaching, learning, assessment, and school change. This perspective highlights the necessity for educators to draw on students' linguistic and cultural resources in designing curriculum and instruction, reflecting on assessment practices, and developing students' abilities to use school-based

literacy practices to accomplish academic, social, and political work that matters to them and the communities to which they belong. (ACCELA Website, retrieved 3/3/08 from: http://www.umass.edu/accela/programs.htm)

Pat Paugh joined this alliance as a faculty member and Elizabeth Robinson as a doctoral student/research assistant. Over a three year period we worked collaboratively in several roles and relationships, as course instructor/TA and as co-researchers. We also held more separate identities, Pat as a member of the alliance faculty, primary investigator of a district/university professional development grant, and pre-tenure scholar. Elizabeth was a graduate project assistant to teachers in the program and to the ACCELA faculty, a doctoral student and pre-dissertation scholar. This PAR/AR study was designed when Pat (as faculty) and Elizabeth (as TA) taught the first course in the program, *EDUC 615X: Practitioner Inquiry*. The study eventually included three cycles of action-oriented research across two later courses *EDUC 697T: Content Literacy for L1 and L2* and *EDUC 687: Reading for L1 and L2*, and a grant sponsored district teacher-research conference (*ACCELA Teacher Quality Dialogues Half-Day Conference*). This spanned a three year period and included post-ACCELA activities such as conferences, presentations, and professional development in the district (Figure 2).

Spring 2005	Summer 2005	Fall 2005	Spring 2006	Summer 2006	Fall 2006	Spring 2007
EDUC 615X	EDUC 784	EDUC 684	Spanish	EDUC 670	EDUC 697T	EDUC 687

*(focus courses shaded in gray)

ACCELA TQ Dialogues
Half-Day Conference
(Spring 2007)

Post-ACCELA conferences, presentations, professional development activities
(Spring 2007 to Spring 2008)

Figure 2. ACCELA Cohort II & III Program of Study and Activities

STORY OF OUR QUESTIONS

Our overriding questions for this study emerged from dilemmas that we encountered while working with a previous ACCELA teacher cohort. As educators who aligned ourselves to the language of critical praxis and to a practitioner research orientation in our teaching, we felt compelled to remain responsible for interrogating our own "critical praxis." "Critical praxis" implied practicing critical literacy and developing an inquiry stance toward teaching. Our course assignments asked this of teachers in a highly charged political environment where they and their district colleagues were under public scrutiny due to press accounts that labeled them and their schools as "underperforming." These teachers were under pressure to adopt specific instructional mandates focused on high test scores. Within this environment we needed to question for ourselves and with the teachers, "What is the role of critical inquiry in a high-stakes political setting?" and "What are the consequences to teachers and their students of questioning dominant educational practices through critical literacy and practitioner research?" These questions demanded that we interrogate what counted as "critical praxis" for all participants in our "neighborhood" of the ACCELA district/university partnership (including ourselves) as we shared participation with teachers in the week-to-week course contexts.

PARTICIPANTS AND CIRCUMSTANCES

In addition to the co-authors, the primary participants over the course of our study included: other university colleagues such as faculty, doctoral course instructors, and doctoral project assistants, the cohort of approximately 25 ACCELA teachers, and at times their principals and district administrators. Indirectly, the Pre-K – 12 students in the ACCELA classrooms were also involved through the teachers' research. District and state policy makers, students' families, and authors of university and teacher research also contributed as secondary participants. Eventually "critical friends" from other university programs contributed directly to the self-study portions of our analysis. The AR/PAR process included three cycles of data collection and analysis during our teaching of three courses and organizing a district conference at which the ACCELA teachers presented. The "neighborhood" of ACCELA also connected with contact zones at the university and in teachers' classrooms. Eventually these contexts extended to conferences outside the district including the "critical friends" from other universities engaged in similar work.

DATA COLLECTION AND ANALYSIS

This study emerged as three cycles of data collection and analysis during ACCELA activities (including the teaching of the courses and the district conference) and eventually post-ACCELA conference presentations by instructors and teachers outside the district. Each cycle included reflection that connected research with action. Figure 3 illustrates how we drew upon three methodologies (AR/PAR, Self-Study, and CDA) for our analysis. AR/PAR provided structures for ongoing data collection and analysis of patterns of interaction as well as unexpected or "critical moments" that contradicted these patterns. As co-researchers the authors reviewed data individually as well as collaboratively, sharing and reviewing hunches, often then returning to check those hunches with ACCELA teachers through in-class dialogues and a focus group. We also used CDA for micro-analysis of language samples (writing or transcripts) suggested by the "critical moments" and hunches. The question, "What makes this a self-study?" required that we also question and check our own participation through these processes.

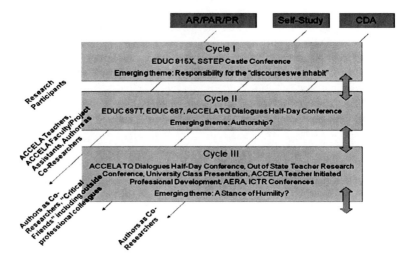

Figure 3. Methods of Analysis

Figure 4 provides an example from Cycle I of how our research design informed our ongoing pedagogy as well as our need to grow and learn as instructors and researchers. We will tell our research "story" below keeping in mind the questions of pedagogy, collaboration, power that were integral to the evolution of this study.

METHODOLOGIES	AR/PAR/Practitioner Research – Generating knowledge "of" practice (Cochran-Smith & Lytle,2004), creating 'critical praxis' (Freire, 1970))	Self-Study – "working the dialectic" (Cochran-Smith & Lytle, 2004)	CDA – Attention to Language and Power as realizing context (Young & Fitzgerald, 2006)
GUIDING QUESTIONS	*What knowledge "of" practice is systematically generated through ongoing data collection in our practices as teacher educators?*	*In what ways does this systematic analysis realize self-study?*	*What language realizes the critical mission of ACCELA within the context of our course?*
An example of emerging research and action:			
	"Critical moments" emerged from ongoing dilemmas during Cycle I classes (EDUC 615X). After noticing teachers' "side conversations" we analyzed video of "missing voices" in class discussions and teachers' writing. To respond we designed class "dialogues" to explore our own dilemmas as well as teachers' arguments that the teacher research articles we assigned were not valuable for them.	Reflexivity exposed potential conflicts between teachers' goals and ACCELA mission of "critical praxis". A reflexive stance forced us to pursue further knowledge to investigate conflicts. Included refining our methods to foreground teachers' perspectives in relationship to course goals, dominant perspectives in the district, and ACCELA teachers' own experiences and knowledge.	Examining the language of the public discussions and writing focused on a Latina teacher who did NOT participate in discussions. To do this we needed to stretch our own understandings of CDA as we worked with this data. In this teacher's writing – we identified language choices that: 1) preserved her professional authority supported by her experience as an immigrant and L2 English learner; 2) appropriated "No Child Left Behind" language used to validate her "talking back" to district policies; and 3) appropriated new language of "practitioner research" that she encountered in her initial efforts to take up an "inquiry stance" in her own teaching.

Figure 4. An Example of the Interrelated Methods of Analysis and One Example of How the Analysis Shaped Both Action and Research

CYCLE I: TAKING "RESPONSIBILITY FOR THE DISCOURSES WE INHABIT"

This cycle centered on our teaching of the practitioner inquiry course (EDUC 615X). Using methods of AR/PAR we followed a hunch reflected in our weekly teaching memos, noting that teachers resisted what we imagined would be an "empowering" experience – encountering course readings written by teacher researchers. We were surprised when several vocal members of the class complained about one of the assigned articles. The author of the article (a teacher researcher) argued for the need to read research, but from a teacher's perspective. The ACCELA teachers were not convinced, responding that the language used in the piece was "too academic" and disconnected from their experiences as real teachers in real schools. One teacher responded to the key argument (that teachers continually needed to challenge themselves with new theories) by stating "and I'd rather not!" Drawing on our AR/PAR design we used this data to design an in-class dialogue on "What counts as research and theory of practice?" to address the perspectives shared in the article, the teachers' critiques, and our own reasons for choosing the reading. Next, while reviewing a video-tape of this discussion, we noticed that public participation was limited. That is, there were ongoing side conversations among groups of teachers especially a group of four Latina teachers who did not speak publicly. This prompted us to investigate "missing voices" by extending our analysis to other modes of language – teachers' written responses to the assignments.

Using CDA we conducted microanalyses of the language of vocal and non-vocal teachers. One of the "missing voices" in the large group, Carmen, wrote strongly and passionately. Our analysis identified multiple discourses in her texts that reflected Carmen's adult immigrant experience, seeking a degree while also learning English as a new language. She also included language of accountability (the discourse of NCLB policies). That is, she appropriated terms that were valued by the district and gave her credibility (such as *language proficiency, student achievement, intervention*) when publicly addressing the needs of her students. Finally, we recognized language of teacher research (such as *triangulation*) that constituted the discourses recently introduced in our class.

What was powerful was Carmen's control of what we had been considering "oppositional discourses" – combining them in ways that retained her "authority of experience" while adding new language to extend that authority. She appropriated what she needed across multiple discourses. This was a powerful insight for our own teaching – it pushed us to consider the complexity of critical authority and exposed our assumptions that "critical" meant rejecting one ideology to adopt another. It forced us also, through the questions provided by self-study, to refine our understanding of CDA methods. Such analysis led us to recognize and respect teachers' authority in relation to the needs of the students in the district, the goals of our teaching and our program, and our own power as course instructors. It also alerted us to be vigilant that our discourses about teacher research did not serve to drive vital perspectives underground. Carmen's personal experience of developing

L2 academic literacy in a culturally unfamiliar setting was an example to us. Such personal discourses provided essential knowledge that supported the goals of the program, which were to create access to equitable education for struggling readers and English Language Learners. This cycle was bounded by action, derived from systematic and collaborative data collection and analysis, and led to new ways of teaching and learning. We shaped our later classes to include similar dialogues. For many teachers (like Carmen) appropriating new language from the courses encouraged further questioning of their own classrooms and district policies.

CYCLE II: INVESTIGATING AUTHORSHIP

The next cycle focused on two teaching events – a two course sequence (EDUC 697T and 687) that culminated in a district conference where ACCELA teachers presented their classroom research. Our roles in teaching these courses shifted slightly. A colleague (doctoral candidate) was the lead instructor in the first course[1]. Pat was co-instructor in the first course, lead instructor in the second and PI for the grant-sponsored district conference. Elizabeth contributed as one of ten doctoral project assistants, attending all classes and supporting the teachers' classroom research. As in the first cycle, we collected and reviewed data as part of the teaching process. Email interactions between the instructors served a primary role for both communication and planning among instructors as well as between instructors and students. Systematic storing of dated email became an important source of data for both teaching and research.

During this cycle, we again drew upon AR/PAR methods by creating and sharing memos and adjusting class sessions in response. We designed the syllabi and the individual course sessions based on our analysis of Cycle I as well as ongoing review of course data. Teachers' stated need for research to fit the realities of their teaching remained a focus. For example, we used a critical literacy model to structure the practitioner research requirements for EDUC 697T where teachers developed and taught a content unit. We required teachers to include a "reflection" tool as part of their course portfolio but invited them to design this reflection to meet their own needs. Despite some continued public resistance to this assignment, the reflection tool became an important text for many of the teachers as they taught the unit and worked with instructors on upcoming research presentations. The reflections served as the key texts around which instructors and ACCELA teachers negotiated the district-wide conference presentations.

We used CDA to examine the language teachers used in their reflection tools. For some, instructors were the audience. These "neat and clean" reflections were limited lists of activities hinting that the purpose was simply "completing the assignment". Others were less linear, and served multiple purposes such as noting technical aspects of teaching (e.g. specific ideas or materials needed for lessons), self-reflection (e.g. comments ranging from venting about scripted curriculum to more theoretical self-questions), memos about planning and conducting classroom research (e.g. ideas about data collection), and critical analysis (e.g. fieldnotes or quotes from children accompanied by questions related to race, family background, language difference). When we analyzed the reflection texts, using qualitative and CDA methods, we developed a deeper understanding of the teachers as authors of their own teaching. Subsequently, analysis of our feedback (including feedback/ grading comments and email exchanges with students) provided additional images of how each teacher was making meaning about this project in relation to us as instructors. Thus, drawing on AR/PAR and CDA methods, the theme of "co-authorship" of the teachers' conference presentations came into focus. This prompted us to question our power as instructors with a "critical" agenda and explore teachers' power as they authored public presentations of classroom research for a district audience – an event that for teachers could be both professionally empowering and risky. Self-study demanded that we attend to the contradictions in our own roles as we guided teachers' authoring of these presentations (Kamberelis & Dimitriadis, 2005).

CYCLE III: ASSUMING HUMILITY

This cycle continued to focus on the presentations at the district conference that took place in mid-semester of the second course. The design of the second course included four classes of "workshops" where teachers revised course one research into presentations for their principals, invited district administrators, university faculty, and colleagues on a Saturday morning in January. The cycle also continued to follow participants as they continued to present their research beyond this event. For example, five of the teachers revised and presented at an out-of- state teacher research conference, another presented in an on-campus university literacy class, another organized extensive in-school professional development around her research almost a year later, and the authors organized several professional conference symposia with colleagues at other universities.

In all of these cases, the question of authorship that emerged during Cycle II was significant to teachers' and to our learning. For example, Carmen was eager to use evidence from her teaching of a science unit to deliver a strong message to the district science department. She was one of several ACCELA teachers who often sought feedback from instructors as she planned her presentation. As instructors we invited her to present a draft to the class during a revision workshop. She framed her presentation with two key points intended to "question the system" – exactly the "critical praxis" encouraged by the ACCELA program. As an ESL instructor she found it frustrating and unproductive for her students when language and science were taught in isolation. Therefore, her research presentation questioned a policy that separated science and language instruction (Figure 5).

Contexts and Challenges

- Hands-on vs. Reading and Writing?

District frowns on development of reading and writing skills in science. Wants
focus to be on hands-on content learning. (Observations, experiments and discussions).

This kind of instruction ends up highlighting curricular activities (hands-on)
rather than developing depth in core concepts. Besides, it forgets the need that
ALL students (especially ELLs) have to receive explicit instruction in written
genres that naturally associate with science education.

Figure 5. Slide from Carmen's Presentation

She supported this with classroom data demonstrating that including reading and writing in science promoted academic growth for her ESL students. A classmate challenged her and us – indicating that it was "unfair" to publicly critique the science program. Yet as instructors we supported Carmen's argument and she kept it in her presentation. While space limits a full discussion of this example, it is indicative of the conflicting and multiple discourses that came into relationship as teachers authored their ongoing work. Here primary (classmates, instructors) as well as secondary (district norms) participants contributed to the teachers' presentation texts. In this case, discourses connected to the critical focus of the course (questioning the system), as well as embedded norms for teachers' participation in the district (not publicly critiquing or participating in authorship of the science and ESL curriculum) shaped the eventual choices teachers such as Carmen made in creating a presentation text.

AR/PAR research, enhanced by attention to language using CDA helped us understand the multiple influences on teachers' authorship of their classroom research, and also prompted us to question our involvement and privilege as instructors, especially when, unlike Carmen, some ACCELA teachers made choices that did not fit our advice or expectations. Transparency in understanding how we and the teachers controlled the context in relationship to each other forced us across all the cycles to increasingly realize the paradoxical relationships (Kamberelis & Dimitriadis, 2005) that sometimes existed as we worked with the ACCELA teachers toward our goals and towards the goals they desired from participating in the program. Participatory self-study encouraged us to take up a stance of "humility" (Murrell, 2008) and an ethical responsibility to understand the choices made by teachers as they enacted their research. This knowledge assisted us as instructors in deciding when and how to be supportive and when to step aside and learn from our students as they took their research "public" beyond our program.

WHY IS THIS CASE EXEMPLARY?

> By studying the communities we are part of, we have the opportunity to explore the ways we and our students and colleagues co-construct knowledge; we can investigate issues of language, culture, and literacy; and, we have a chance to analyze the contexts that support the work of inquiry communities and the professional development of teachers across the life span. (Cochran-Smith & Lytle, 2004)

This case is exemplary in that it combined action and research. It is credible in that it achieved intended goals through action (Greenwood & Levin, 1998). For example, the research informed and recreated the local context through university instructors' adjustments and ongoing course design. Drawing on traditions of AR, PAR, and practitioner research, courses were designed to keep multiple perspectives visible and in relationship. PAR and CDA methods necessitated that power within those relationships was continually questioned. The actions involved were substantive and recordable through the research process. Ongoing questions and themes suggested further cycles of the research process.

Self-study was intentional in this research design as theoretically all participants engaged in what Cochran-Smith & Lytle (2005) define as "working the dialectic" – that is, "where there are no distinct moments when we are only researchers and practitioners…rather these activities and roles are intentionally blurred" (p. 635). Thus methods of self-study provided necessary research tools. Inviting the involvement of "critical friends" was integral within and beyond our local relationships. For example, at several points in the process, we presented at international and national conferences. At the S-STEP Castle Conference in 2006, feedback from our university peers prompted us to further question "what makes this self-study?" Self-study posed new questions for our own learning and resulted in our increased efforts to extend and deepen our methodological and theoretical frameworks (Cochran-Smith & Lytle, 2005). We audited courses and read widely as we challenged our own knowledge of Critical Discourse Analysis and related theories through subsequent cycles. Feedback from other university colleagues at the 2007 Annual Meeting of the American Educational Research Association (AERA) and the 2008 International Conference on Teacher Research (ICTR) provided perspectives on our developing themes in relation to research being done by teacher educators with similar interests. For example, comparing "resistance" from our course data with colleagues provided a helpful perspective in linking our analyses to the larger conversations in the field.

As teacher educators interested in creating research relationships *with* and *across* school/university contexts, the methodologies provided by AR/PAR self-study were invaluable assets for understanding, extending, and negotiating our roles as critical teachers and creating socially just literacy education. While enacting and representing such research is non-linear and challenging, it is also powerful in addressing the complexity involved in social contexts where practices and power are continually shaping the social practices of the participants.

NOTES

[1] We acknowledge the work of our colleague, Dr. Andres Ramirez, who instructed and participated in analysis of the data during this cycle.

REFERENCES

Altwerger, B., Arya, P., Jin, L., Jordan, N. L., Martens, P., Wilson, G. P., et al. (2004). When research and mandates collide: The challenges and dilemmas of teacher education in the era of NCLB. *English Education, 36*(2), 119–133.

Bloome, D., Carter, S. P., Christian, B. M., & Shuart-Faris, N. (2005). *Discourse analysis and the study of classroom language and literacy events.* Mahwah, NJ: Lawrence Erlbaum.

Cochran-Smith, M., & Lytle, S. (2004). Practitioner inquiry, knowledge, and university culture. In J. J. Loughran, M. L. Hamilton, V. K. LaBoskey, & T. Russell (Eds.), *International handbook of self-study of teaching and teacher education practices* (pp. 601–650). Dordrecht: Kluwer Academic Publishers.

Comber, B., & Kamler, B. (Eds.). (2005). *Turn-around pedagogies: Literacy interventions for at-risk students.* Newtown: Primary English Teaching Association.

Chryst, C., Lassonde, C., & McKay, Z. (2008). The invisible researcher: New insights into the role of collaboration in self-study. In L. Heston, M. Tidwell, D. K. East, & L. Fitzgerald (Eds.), *Proceedings of the seventh international conference on self-study in teacher education practices: Pathways to change in teacher education: Dialogue, diversity and self-study, England* (pp. 50–53).

Dozier, C., Johnston, P., & Rogers, R. (2006). *Critical literacy critical teaching: Tools for preparing responsive teachers.* New York: Teachers College Press.

Duesterberg, L. (1999). Theorizing race in the context of learning to teach. *Teachers College Record, 100*(4), 751–775.

Egan-Robertson, A., & Bloome, D. (1998). *Students as researchers of culture and language in their own communities.* Cresskill, NJ: Hampton Press.

Falk, B., & Blumenreich, M. (2005). *The power of questions: A guide to teacher and student research.* Portsmouth: Heinemann.

Fecho, B., Graham, P., & Ross, H. (2005). Appreciating the wobble: Teacher research, professional development and figured worlds. *English Education, 37*(3), 174–199.

Feldman, A., Paugh, P., & Mills, G. (2004). Self-study through action research. In J. J. Loughran, M. L. Hamilton, V. K. LaBoskey, & T. Russell (Eds.), *International handbook of self-study of teaching and teacher education practices* (pp. 943–978). Dordrecht: Kluwer Academic Publishers.

Fine, M. (1994). Working the hyphen: Reinventing self and other in qualitative research. In N. K. Denzin & Y. S. Lincoln (Eds.), *Handbook of qualitative research* (pp. 70–82). Thousand Oaks, CA: Sage.

Freire, P. (1993/1970). *Pedagogy of the oppressed.* New York: Continuum.

Gee, J. (1990). *Social linguistics and literacies: Ideology in discourses.* New York: Falmer Press.

Greenwood, D., & Levin, M. (1998). *Introduction to action research.* Thousand Oaks, CA: Sage.

Greenwood, D., & Levin, M. (2003). Reconstructing the relationships between universities and society through action research. In N. Denzin & Y. Lincoln (Eds.), *The landscape of qualitative research* (pp. 131–166). Thousand Oaks, CA: Sage.

Kamberelis, G., & Dimitriadis, G. (2005). Focus groups: Strategic articulations of pedagogy, politics, and inquiry. In N. Denzin & Y. Lincoln (Eds.), *Handbook of qualitative research* (3rd ed., pp. 887–908). Thousand Oaks, CA: Sage.

LaBoskey, V. K. (2004). The methodology of self-study and its theoretical underpinnings. In J. J. Loughran, M. L. Hamilton, V. K. LaBoskey & T. Russell (Eds.), *International handbook of self-study of teaching and teacher education practices* (pp. 817–870). Dordrecht: Kluwer Academic Publishers.

Loughran, J. J. (2004). A history and context of self-study of teaching and teacher education practices. In J. J. Loughran, M. L. Hamilton, V. K. LaBoskey, & T. Russell (Eds.), *International handbook of self-study of teaching and teacher education practices* (pp. 7–40). Dordrecht: Kluwer Academic Publishers.

Lytle, S. (2000). Teacher research in the contact zone. In M. Kamil, P. Mosenthal, P. D. Pearson, & R. Barr (Eds.), *Handbook of reading research: Volume III* (pp. 691–718). Mahwah: Erlbaum.

McTaggart, R. (1997). *Participatory action research: International contexts and consequences.* Albany, NY: State University of New York Press.

Murrell, P. (2008). Keynote address given at the 40th annual meeting of the New England Educational Research Organization (April 2008), Hyannis, MA.

Rogers, R. (Ed.). (2004). *Critical discourse analysis in education.* Mahwah: Erlbaum.

Shuck, S., & Segal, G. (2002). Learning about our teaching from our graduates, learning about our learning with critical friends. In J. J. Loughran & T. L. Russell (Eds.), *Improving teacher education practices through self-study* (pp. 88–101). London: Routledge Falmer.

Tidwell, D. (2002). On stage: The efficacy and theatrics of large group instruction. In C. Kosnick, A. Freese, & A. P. Samaras (Eds.), *Making a difference in teacher education through self-study. Proceedings of the fourth international conference on self-study in teacher education practices. Herstmonceux. East Sussex, England* (Vol. 2, pp. 117–120). Toronto, ON: OISE, University of Toronto.

Young, L., & Fitzgerald, B., (2006). *The power of language: How discourse influences society.* London: Equinox.

Zeichner, K., & Noffke, S. (2001). Practioner research. In V. Richardson (Ed.), *Handbook of research on teaching* (pp. 298–332).Washington, DC: American Educational Research Association.

JULIAN KITCHEN AND DARLENE CIUFFETELLI PARKER

7. SELF-STUDY COMMUNITIES OF PRACTICE

Developing Community, Critically Inquiring as Community

Good conversations feed the spirit; it feels good; it reminds us of our ideals and hopes for education; it confirms that we are not alone in our frustrations and doubts or in our small victories...Conversation gives us as teachers a room of our own.

(Clark, 2001, p. 179)

The first year has left us with an appreciation for the authority of each member, a strong sense of community, and a desire to continue to work together both as a self-study group and as members of an education faculty. Also, the dynamics are beginning to change as members become familiar with self-study as a method for studying their teaching practices.

(Kitchen, Ciuffetelli Parker, & Gallagher, 2008 p. 167)

INTRODUCTION

Conversation, collaboration, and community can have a powerful impact on teachers' confidence, capacity for professional growth, and willingness to share their practices with others. Clark (2001) discovered this through his work with teacher conversation groups. Similarly, when we formed a self-study community of practice for new teacher education professors at Brock University, we found our individual and collective voices grew stronger. Practical conversations about teacher education in this "room of our own" improved our teaching, contributed to institutional change, and advanced our scholarly work.

Collaboration among teacher educators has been part of self-study from its inception and is viewed as one of the defining characteristics of self-study (Lighthall, 2004). Insights from a collaborator can help individual practitioners notice patterns in their practices and directions for professional growth. As collaborative self-study becomes increasingly accepted, an emerging area of practice and inquiry is self-study communities of practice.

In this chapter, we begin with a description of self-study communities of practice. This is followed by a review of procedures, with a particular emphasis on standards of quality for self-study communities. Strengths and limitations of this methodology are considered. Finally, our work within a self-study community of

C. A. Lassonde, S. Galman and C. Kosnik (eds.), Self-Study Research Methodologies for Teacher Educators, 107–128.

practice is critically examined as an exemplary study. We conclude with the effects on our practices and implications for teacher education.

DESCRIPTION OF METHODOLOGY: WHAT IS A SELF-STUDY COMMUNITY OF PRACTICE?

Self-study emerged from dialogue among teacher educators who were uncomfortable with the *status quo* in teacher education. "Questioning the nature of teacher education" led some teacher educators to "look more carefully at their own practices" (Loughran, 2002, p. 240). Teacher educators in S-STEP were able to converse about their practices and develop an international community committed to understanding, improving, and disseminating critical inquiry into teacher education practices. As self-study grew, collaborative self-studies increasingly shared space with individual self-studies and collaboration became a defining characteristic of self-study. Now that self-study has established itself as a viable methodology for teacher education practice and scholarship, there is a need to widen its influence within education colleges and across the field of teacher education.

While there are many notable collaborations within institutions, these practitioners represent small groups of collaborators within large education colleges. Similarly, self-study collaborations across institutions tend to be small in scale. Self-study groups of four or more teacher educators are largely absent from the self-study literature. We have coined the term *self-study communities of practice* to refer to groups of at least four members committed to working together to study their teacher education practices.

We interpret *methodology* in two ways: first, as a how-to guide and, second, as an inquiry process. As self-study communities of practice are not very common, the chapter can be read as a how-to guide to developing self-study communities. The chapter, however, focuses primarily on self-study as an inquiry process that can lead to the further development and enactment of a pedagogy of teacher education (Russell & Loughran, 2007) on both a small-scale and more broadly. The exemplary study, by critically inquiring into the characteristics of a new self-study community of practice, serves both purposes.

The term *professional learning communities* (PLCs) has received considerable attention in recent years, as innovative educational leaders have established them in schools as a means to engaging teachers in education reform (DuFour & Eaker, 1998). Principles that characterize PLC schools include improving teaching practice through shared expertise, collaboration, life-long learning, care, respect, and commitment to and reflection upon continuous renewal (Elmore, 1997). Unlike teachers in schools, however, teacher educators must balance improving practice with contributing to the scholarship of teaching. The term *self-study communities of practice* is intended to convey both the teaching and inquiry dimensions of such communities. Each community must also be adapted to the particular institutional culture in which it operates to sustain its members and overcome barriers to teacher education practice as a form of scholarship.

Self-study communities take many forms. We have identified three general locations in which these communities are situated. First, there are communities of teacher educators working together in a specific instructional team. The efforts of a team at George Mason University are examined to see how such a self-study community works to collaboratively improve a particular teacher education cohort or program. Second, there are teams working within the same institution but not as an instructional team. These include our community at Brock University and a well-established community at the University of Northern Iowa. Third, teacher educators can support each other across institutions through critical reflection. The correspondence of the Arizona Group, four professors who had studied together at University of Arizona, is used to illustrate the richness possible in dialogue among teacher educators in different locations.

Four standards of quality are used to critically examine self-study communities of practice: (1) establishing conditions for research, (2) creating educational knowledge, (3) recreating teacher education, and (4) the public discourse of communities of practice. In the Procedures section, self-studies from George Mason, Northern Iowa and the Arizona Group illustrate these standards. These standards of quality are then used to frame the exemplary study of the first year of our nine-member self- study community at Brock University.

What Is the Relationship between Self-Study Communities of Practice and Teacher Conversations?

There are many similarities between self-study communities of practice and teacher conversations as documented by Clark and his colleagues. The core idea underlying teacher conversations is that "sustainable professional development for teachers must be led by teachers themselves and be intrinsically satisfying, voluntary, and inexpensive" (Clark & Florio-Ruane, 2001, p. 4). Bodone, Guojonsdottir, and Dalmau (2004) cite similar reasons for collaboration among teacher educators aiming to transform themselves and their practices. In our exemplary study, we draw upon the teacher conversations literature to identify characteristics that were critical to the development of our self-study community at Brock University.

The main difference is that collaborative self-study involves teacher educators as practitioners and researchers committed to disseminating our findings beyond our immediate contexts. As scholars engaging in self-study, we explicitly engage in a public discourse of collaborative self-study, whether it is through individual or collaborative self-studies by group members (Bodone et al., 2004). The co-authors, for example, have prepared wide-range of conference papers and journal articles: individual inquiries, collaborations with colleagues, and studies of our community of practice. Another crucial difference is that the study of the self of the practitioners is an explicit part of self-study methodology, and there is a conscious intent to challenge the dominant positivistic discourse within teacher education (Loughran, 2002).

What Is the Relationship between Self-Study Communities of Practice and Collaborative Self-Study?

Collaborative self-studies by pairs and triads are common. There has been much research on and by such collaborative teams. There is little research published on the work of collaborative self-study teams comprised of four or more practitioners. It is our belief that communities of four or more members possess different characteristics and need to be distinguished from smaller, more close-knit groups. Each additional member increases the complexity of the web of relationships and increases the likelihood that not all members will have their personal and professional needs addressed. Also, as membership widens to include individuals from different research traditions, there is a greater need to negotiate group dynamics and shared understandings.

The establishment of trust and the structuring of a self-study process were critical to the formation of a self-study community involving a diverse instructional team at George Mason University (Samaras, Kayler, Rigsby, Weller, & Wilcox (2006). Similarly, at the University of Northern Iowa, where there are many overlapping and intersecting self-study teams, core members were very concerned with ensuring that the necessary conditions for effective self-study communities of practice were maintained (East & Fitzgerald, 2006).

In our exemplary study, most of the eight characteristics that we identify as important to self-study communities involve negotiating the relationships among members of a group consisting of nine members, many of whom were unfamiliar with self-study. If self-study is to move from small-scale initiatives to a movement involving large numbers of teacher educators within institutions, nationally and internationally, there needs to be more attention given to developing communities of practice and critically inquiring into the work of these communities.

When Is It Useful to Create a Self-Study Community of Practice?

Teacher education "has low status and is rewarded poorly in terms of tenure, promotion, and merit pay" (Beck & Kosnik, 2001, p. 946) in most universities. The mystique of the esoteric life of professors committed to scholarship often causes education professors to focus on scholarship rather than preservice teacher education (Ducharme, 1993). This tendency is reinforced by the recognition and rewards systems within universities, which may validate scholarly achievement more than contributions to preservice courses and programs. These forces are "a constant source of tension, frustration, and challenge" (Cole, 1999, p. 284) for teacher educators who are primarily committed to practice and to those who wish to make strong contributions to both scholarship and practice. Self-study of teacher education practices has enabled some of us to simultaneously improve practice and make scholarly contributions. The self-study of teacher education practices (S-STEP) has played an important role in linking isolated individuals through its international network.

There is a need, however, for stronger communities of self-study practitioners within education colleges and across institutions. Such communities, in addition to supporting existing self-study practitioners, can draw more teacher educators into self-study. Inquiry into practice on a larger scale can, in turn, lead to the further development and enactment of a pedagogy of teacher education (Russell & Loughran, 2007).

It is important, however, that at least some of the members of the self-study community have engaged previously in self-study work. In the case of Samaras and colleagues (2006), the experienced and widely published Anastasia Samaras helped structure the inquiry activities in a manner that contributed to future success. At the University of Northern Iowa, the principal members developed a number of strategies that have proven successful in their context (East & Fitzgerald, 2006). In our exemplary study, two of the co-chairs were familiar with self-study and spent considerable time and energy developing understandings of self-study and community. Of the four self-study communities of practices discussed in this chapter, only the Arizona Group was established without outside assistance; the efforts of these four teacher educators to seek assistance later led to the formation of the S-STEP.

PROCEDURES

Self-study communities of practice composed of members who are highly diverse in their interests. Self-studies by individuals, sub-groups, and the community as a whole are subject to the same criteria as any other self-study inquiries. Teacher educators establishing or working within self-study communities of practice are advised to look at the procedures for the inquiry methods they are employing within the self-study community. For example, the four members of our self-study community who shared their personal narratives (Figg, Lu, Vietgen, & Griffin, 2007) examined life history methods as they developed their paper.

In this section, we focus our attention on procedures for developing self-study community and critically inquiring as community. We begin by identifying standards for quality in self-study communities of practice and then illustrate these with examples from three self-study communities of practice. Meaningful critical inquiry into self-study communities should address one or more of these standards for the work to be of significance to other teacher educators. In preparing critical inquiries as self-study communities, it is important that data be collected and analyzed thoughtfully and that the research findings are meaningfully represented.

Standards for Quality: Establishing Conditions for Research

Many teacher educators are interested in improving and studying their practices, yet most are neither introduced to self-study nor provided with opportunities to develop a program of research in this area. As a result, there is a need for self-study scholarship that identifies the conditions for research and, perhaps more importantly, illustrate ways in which these conditions have been established.

The Arizona Group formed due to an absence of conditions that supported their interest in teacher education practices and research. As they struggled to understand their experiences as beginning academics in four universities, members turned to former colleagues from graduate school for support (Guilfoyle, Hamilton, Pinnegar, & Placier, 2004). An interest in studying teacher education practices and a willingness to dialogue provided the necessary conditions for this voluntary community of former classmates teaching at different universities to be successful. Despite a "divergence of interpretations, analysis, methodology, and level of commitment" (Guilfoyle et al., 2004, p. 1110), they were able to help each other "negotiate multiple layers of institutional politics and policies" (Guilfoyle, Hamilton, Pinnegar, & Placier, 1995, p. 37) as they sought to be educators and scholars of teacher education. In their numerous publications, they illustrate how to establish the conditions for collaborative self-study through their work generally and, in particular, through their writings on dialogue in self-study groups.

The University of Northern Iowa self-study community established firm foundations for community despite an amorphous membership. The necessary conditions established and maintained by the core members of the community ensured there was a common identity that transcended the individual members. A fundamental condition for them was wanderfarh, a term invented to describe the loose, non-linear nature of their group work (East & Fitzgerald, 2006). In describing how wanderfarh manifested itself in their discussions, they wrote:

> While we were often intensely engaged in grappling with issues of practice we also strayed off topic or *wanderfarhed*. We were very productive, but ironically not vigilantly task-oriented. We allowed ourselves to enjoy working together rather than being single-mindedly focused on completing a product. We found our digressions to be generative and refreshing. (East & Fitzgerald, 2006, p. 73)

The wanderfarhed was balanced with a professional intimacy that made their communities of practice very rich environments for personal, professional, and community growth (Fitzgerald, East, Heston, & Miller, 2002). This intimacy helped them move beyond the practical to considering at times the personal and spiritual components of their professional lives. It also provided members with support as they dealt with forces of accountability in the university, forces that were often not receptive to the kind of evidence that demonstrated the value of the work they did with teacher candidates (Fitzgerald, Farstad, & Deemer, 2002). By reporting on their ways in which they established conditions for self-study, members of this community made a significant contribution to self-study internationally.

Standards for Quality: Creating Educational Knowledge

At the heart of self-study as a research methodology is the creation of knowledge that can improve teacher education practices. Research on self-study communities of practice should illustrate how collaborative efforts to understandings about teacher education are practiced in our classroom contexts.

The George Mason University study, for example, contributed to educational knowledge by examining how the collaborative self-study process improved the practices of a team of instructors. It also described their research method of being interviewed, reading and rereading interview transcripts, meeting to discuss impressions, and thematically analyzing the results with the assistance of Wilcox and Samaras. They also contributed to inquiry into self-study communities by identifying and examining dominant themes that emerged from their experience.

One contribution to educational knowledge by the self-study groups at Northern Iowa involved the use of learning circles for students in many of their courses. They have not only developed learning circles, but discussed them at length in their groups and collected data together to assess the merits of the pedagogical innovation (Fitzgerald, Farstad, & Deemer, 2002). They have also developed a wide range of techniques for assessing the effectiveness of their teaching. The data collected from these sources acted as an alternative form of accountability to the more formulaic surveys conducted by the administration (Fitzgerald, East, Heston, & Miller, 2002). This educational knowledge has been shared by a large number of faculty at Northern Iowa and, through articles in scholarly publications, with educators in many other institutions.

Standards for Quality: Recreating Teacher Education

Self-study begins with teacher educators improving their own practices but, as Hamilton (2002) suggests, its impact must extend beyond our classrooms to the wider communities of teaching and teacher education. The George Mason self-study had an impact first and foremost on the practices of the faculty team itself. They also hoped that this self-study would "entice other faculty teaching teams in [the Master's program] to use a self-study methodology to examine their practices" (Samaras et al., 2006, p. 55) and have implications at the education college level:

> At a program level, this research on faculty professional development and program development has rekindled consideration of the authenticity of our *Beliefs and Principles*...regarding work on teams...Thus, we continue to study our teaming and teacher education practices and how well they align with our beliefs and principles. (p. 55)

By helping faculty team members enact their pedagogy of teacher education more effectively, the self-study activities reported in this paper illustrate the power of self-study as a vehicle for teacher education reform.

The beginning professors in the Arizona Group initially focussed on ensuring their teacher education practices would be congruent with their conceptions of teacher knowledge and student learning. The questions that emerged prompted broader questions about the nature of the programs in which they taught. On an intellectual level, this led to a symposium at AERA in 2002 on teacher education reform (Guilfoyle et al., 2004, p. 1110). At the institutional level, it led members to advocate for significant changes in their programs to focus on teacher experiences and contribute to social justice. Hamilton, as director of teacher education in her college, acted as a change agent promoting equity, diversity, and social justice. In a self-study paper on the resistance she experienced, Hamilton (2002) reflected on the challenges of bringing about instructional reform. Interestingly, her reflections led to greater sensitivity towards those who resisted her efforts. She remained a change agent but became acutely aware of "insights to be gleaned from the process" (p. 187) of institutional reform.

Standards for Quality: Public Discourse of Communities of Practice

Improving one's teaching and contributing to teacher education reform in our institutions are reasons enough for teacher educators to engage in self-study communities of practice. The need to improve teacher education on a larger scale, however, means that self-study communities can contribute to the public discourse of self study.

Samaras had already contributed through her individual self-studies (e.g., Samaras, 2002), other collaborative self-studies at George Mason University (e.g., Samaras, DeMulder, Kayler, Newton, Rigsby, Weller, & Wilcox, 2006) and cross-institutional self-studies (e.g., Samaras, Beck, Freese, & Kosnik, 2005). The publication of their self-study made an important contribution to dialogue within the knowledge community of self-study.

Belonging to an international self-study community allows teacher educators to extend their discourse beyond their university and country. This is evident from the "liberating shift of perspective" experienced by Fitzgerald, Farstad, and Deemer (2002) when they shared their concerns at the International Conference on Self-Study of Teacher Education Practices. The validation received from the self-study community renewed their "commitment to collaborative engagement with colleagues" (p. 214). Their problem reframed, they continued with a renewed sense of purpose. The self-study practitioners at the University of Northern Iowa have made major contributions to self-study internationally through their writing about teacher education practices and communities of practice. Their greatest contribution, however, may be the service they provide the international self-study community by editing three volumes of the proceedings of the International Self-Study Conference of Teacher Education Practices in 2004, 2006, and 2008. These double-blind reviewed, carefully edited, and attractively designed volumes are treasure-troves of self-studies, and the first self-study publication for many teacher educators. Members of this community have also edited books that help define the field of self-study (Tidwell & Fitzgerald, 2006; Tidwell, Heston, & Fitzgerald, 2009).

Arizona Group members have made an enormous contribution to the scholarship of self-study internationally through their work as a self-study community and their individual contributions. Stefinee Pinnegar, for example, has written on her own experiences (1995), collaborated with her education students (Pinnegar, Lay, Bigham, & Duldue, 2005), and contributed to the meta-literature of narrative inquiry (Pinnegar & Daynes, 2007) and self-study (Bullough & Pinnegar, 2001). Similarly, Mary Lynn Hamilton has used self-study to explore social justice issues

(Hamilton, 2002), was a co-editor of the *International Handbook of Self-study of Teaching and Teacher Education Practices*, and has edited a number of self-study volumes.

Data Collection and Analysis

Drawing on shared expertise to improve practice is central to all forms of PLC's. As self-study communities combine the improvement of teacher education practices with critical inquiry into practice, it is important that members consider methodological questions from the outset. In particular, the collection and analysis of data should be discussed as the community forms, as specific projects are developed, and upon beginning a new academic year. The data collected can take many forms, depending on the specific inquiry questions asked and the self-study methods employed by community members. Particular attention, however, should be given to the collection and analysis of data concerning the work of the community itself. Even if a specific research question does not emerge in advance, data should still be collected for possible use in the future.

The Arizona Group maintained a record of its written communications over more than a decade; this data set formed the basis for much of their writing about teacher education reform and self-study dialogue. At times, particular inquiry questions drove their letter writing; at other times, lines of inquiry emerged from an analysis of themes that organically emerged from the letters. By writing and saving their letters, however, they accumulated a rich data set on which to draw for ongoing research and for retrospective studies of their interactions as a community.

Similarly, the Northern Iowa community kept careful records of their meetings, and many members engaged in inquiry regarding their meetings and group dynamics. Research was embedded in their ongoing activities and members were regularly standing back from their experiences to reflect and analyze. For example, when institutional demands for greater accountability prompted Fitzgerald, Farstad, and Deemer (2002) to critique checklist rating of performance, they each wrote reflections on student evaluations which provided data on the issues and their self-perceptions. Analysis of this data set led them to identify key themes and critically examine implications in scholarly articles. Members of this self-study community also maintained records of their meetings, which they were then able to examine retrospectively in order to identify characteristics of their collective interactions (Fitzgerald, East, Heston, & Miller, 2002). Data emerging from meetings can take a variety of forms, including personal reflections, letters between members, recordings and transcriptions, and minutes of meetings.

As with other self-study methods, there may also be value in collecting other forms of data such as feedback from students and classroom artifacts, then analyzing for common themes and relationships using methods outlined in other chapters. Interviews of three team members at George Mason, for example, formed the basis for data analysis by the larger research team (Samaras et al., 2006).

Representation of Research Findings

While scholarly papers may be written by one or two people, it is important that representation of self-study research findings on communities of practice offer a multiplicity of voices. The members of the Arizona Group, for example, all provided insights into the questions under consideration, and much of the interest generated by their work concerned the interplay between members. Similarly, the George Mason team, by offering reflections by all members, conveys the complexities of collaboration in larger communities.

It is also important that the representations of research findings engage with important questions in self-study and/or the self-study communities of practice. East and Fitzgerald (2006), for example, explore how "collaboration has taught us to trust the authority of our experiences" (p. 74) by illustrating ways in which the group mind extended their thinking as a community at the University of Northern Iowa. Similarly, the Arizona Group drew on its correspondence to examine questions about the relationship between improving practice and reforming teacher education at the institutional level. Effective representations of self-study communities of practice in action have the potential to contribute to broad discourses in self-study and teacher education while presenting intriguing examples of self-study communities engaged in inquiry.

STRENGTHS AND LIMITATIONS

Developing and critically inquiring into self-study communities of practice can be very powerful. Collaboration with colleagues can both support individual teacher educators grappling with ways of improving their practices and help them to critically examine these issues within the larger contexts of their institutions. A community of four or more both widens the perspectives of its members and provides a place in which to introduce neophytes to the possibilities offered by self-study methodologies and the benefits of working within a professional learning community.

These strengths, however, are off-set by some limitations. In particular, it is not easy to establish a self-study community of practice that is safe and promotes critical inquiry. It requires an investment of time and energy in establishing conditions for success, sustaining the group over time, critically inquiring into one's own teaching, and supporting the critical inquiry of others. Also, by disseminating their critical inquiries, community members risk having their doubts and shortcomings exposed . The exemplary study that follows addresses many of the strengths and limitations of self-study communities of practice, and offers ways in which to maximize strengths while minimizing limitations.

EXEMPLARY STUDY

Self-study communities of practice have been described, along with its methodology and procedures, in the preceding sections. To illustrate how one might develop and critically inquire into a self-study community of practice, we present as an exemplar a self-study we conducted at the end of our first year at Brock University. This self-study is developed more fully in "Authentic Conversation as Faculty Development: Establishing a Self-Study Group in an Education College" (Kitchen, Ciuffetelli Parker, & Gallagher, 2008).

Overview

Through the exemplary study, we illustrate practical methodologies for establishing and sustaining self-study communities of practice. In this section, we examine the Brock University self-study group as a case to demonstrate how self-study communities of practice can be formed and sustained, and how engaging in a critical inquiry moves forward self-study communities of practice.

At Brock University, a small group of new faculty formed a self-study community in September 2006 as a way of nurturing alternative ways of conceptualizing the pedagogy of teacher education (Loughran, 2006) and our identities as new tenure-track professors of education within a changing teacher education department and the wider education college. We recognized that professional development, focused on the improvement of student learning, is particularly difficult in the university context due to internal obstacles such as lack of time, limited institutional commitment to reforming programs, limited rewards, and isolationist university cultures. While we welcomed the freedom associated with academia, we valued the "norms of collaboration and community" (Cole, 1999, p. 294) we had experienced in schools and remained dedicated to meeting student needs while we pursued our scholarly interests. We sought to learn together through conversations about our teacher education practices and scholarship. In this respect, we were akin to faculty learning communities (Cox & Richlin, 2004) consisting of faculty, graduate students, and professional staff engaged in active, collaborative programs to improve teaching and learning.

New professors in our self-study group experienced tension as we sought to balance our commitment to teacher education with our scholarship. One of the attractions of the group was the prospect of resolving this tension. Darlene, in her second year teaching elementary instructional methods, had been a teacher, literacy consultant, and school administrator. Julian, in his first year teaching professionalism and law, had been an adjunct professor at the University of Toronto after leaving the classroom. Tiffany Gallagher, in her second year teaching educational psychology, had been an administrator and diagnostician in private practice supplemental education. Peter Vietgen, a former art education consultant, was in his third year teaching visual arts education. Candace Figg, in her first year teaching instructional technology, had been an assistant professor in two American universities. Louis Volante, prior to his two years teaching assessment and evaluation at Brock, held faculty appointments at Concordia University and the University of Hawaii. Lorenzo Cherubini, in his second year teaching secondary instructional methods, had been a teacher and administrator. Chunlei Lu, in his first year teaching health and physical education, had taught in Chinese, American, and Canadian universities.

Newly hired music educator Shelly Griffin was a former teacher who had lectured at two Canadian universities.

In examining the make-up of our self-study community, we identified eight characteristics that we considered critical to the development of self-study communities. Our identification of these characteristics was informed by our reading of the work of the Arizona Group (Guilfoyle et al., 2004) and Clark's (2001) work on the discourse of dialogue. We drew on their understanding of critical inquiry in the discourse of dialogue and authentic conversation. *In this chapter, we use the four standards for quality presented earlier as a frame for organizing the eight characteristics the group identified as critical to the development of self study communities.*

In *establishing conditions for research:*
- Self-Study Community Involvement is Voluntary
- Self-Study Community Happens on Common Ground
- Self-Study Community Requires Safety, Trust, and Care
- Self-Study Community Members Share Struggles through Conversation

In *creating educational knowledge:*
- Self-Study Community Members Explore Their Teaching through Dialogue
- Self-Study Communities Critically Examine Their Group Processes and Dynamics

In *recreating teacher education* and *contributing to the public discourse of communities of practice:*
- Self-Study Communities Explore Teacher Education Reform
- Self-Study Communities Move Toward the Future

Establishing Conditions for Research

The self-study community at Brock University was formed at the beginning of the 2007-2008 academic year. Darlene and Tiffany, two of the co-chairs, identified the need for a support group for new faculty who were grappling with the tensions inherent in being new faculty members at a time of rapid institutional change. In particular, they and the three other professors hired in 2006 struggled to balance the high teaching and service expectations of a department. They asked Julian, a newly hired faculty member with experience in self-study (Kitchen, 2005a; 2005b), to join them in developing a letter inviting colleagues to join a self-study group for faculty in their first two years. Although we did not have experience in collaborative self-study, we three drew on our experiences working in other collaborative groups to establish conditions for community and critical inquiry.

Community involvement is voluntary. A self-study community should be founded on a common sense of purpose among teacher educators who find the conversations professionally meaningful (Clark, 2001). We invited nine other professors to join a self-study of teacher education practices group. The letter of invitation highlighted the community's purposes, which included: (1) encouraging self-study practices and scholarship; (2) studying the collaborative self-study process; (3) critically reflecting and inquiring into each others' work; (4) being critically reflective; (5) moving our self-study work towards scholarship and changes in practice; and

(6) making a contribution to teacher education scholarship nationally and internationally.

The six who accepted the invitation to attend monthly meetings for the academic year were attracted to the opportunity to simultaneously improve practices, develop a support network, and generate scholarly publications. This reasoning was reinforced by the bonds many members had already established in their short time at Brock.

Members demonstrated commitment by forming smaller clusters to work on collaborative self-studies of particular interest to them. Darlene and Tiffany, for example, formed a cluster as they began to advise graduate students through their exit research projects. Similarly, three of the new faculty members and a third-year professor initiated a collective self-study of their experiences as new faculty (Figg et al., 2007). Several pairs also worked on self-study projects on topics of common interest.

Self-study community happens on common ground. Common ground is crucial to the establishment of a shared discourse community. While diverse perspectives and strong voices should be accepted, good conversation requires a space in which the authority of each member's voice is valued. The authority of each other's voices is more likely to be respected when there is common ground in terms of values, ideas, fears, and shared experiences (Clark, 2001). While common ground is not sufficient for good conversation, it increases the chances that community members will be committed to each other and to attending group meetings.

Although members of our community were not well acquainted with each other's work, we shared the experience of being new professors in an education college undergoing considerable change. Each of us needed a space in which to confide our impressions, ideas, and questions. Shared concerns regarding tenure and promotion were particularly helpful in establishing common ground. In designing the first sessions of the group, efforts were made to ensure that the discussion topics addressed areas of common concern. Julian's opening presentation opened possibilities for combining the improvement of teaching education practices with scholarship on practice. This common gathering place beyond formal education college meetings helped us to know each other and support each other's work. Norms of respect and a safe space, which are examined later, helped people discover their commonalities while respecting their differences in perspective. On common ground there was greater opportunity to honor each other's voices and discuss common issues in a manner that was respectful of all members.

In subsequent sessions, an individual or group presented perspectives on issues related to teacher education practice or the experience of being a new professor. Regardless of the topic, there was sufficient common ground for each group member to resonate with the discussions at hand. Darlene's reflections on her duty as co-ordinator of the teaching methods courses, for example, resonated with Tiffany's duty as coordinator of the educational psychology courses. Illumination of the tensions of new faculty assuming these roles was made evident through sharing stories regarding the responsibilities that were associated with being a course coordinator.

A basis for relating to others' experiences contributed to the cohesion of the group and was critical to establishing the conditions for authentic conversations about teacher education research and practices. Participation afforded members the opportunity to reflect critically on their respective roles in the department and to move forward from this new perspective. Once this common ground was established, members used this space to probe more deeply into their individual and collective self-studies of teacher education practices.

Self-study community requires safety, trust, and care. The authentic quality of our conversations as a self-study group would not have been possible without safety, trust, and care (Clark, 2001). As we wrote after our first year:

> The opening presentations by Julian and Darlene, in which they made explicit their tensions as teacher educators, encouraged openness. The thoughtfulness of the oral and written responses, modeled in part by the facilitators, also created a safe place for sharing and further research. (Kitchen et al., 2008, p. 163)

Finding time to meet in a safe place was particularly challenging given the competing and ever-pressing demands of teaching, scholarship, and service. Darlene reflected

> I think everyone appreciated the natural extension and flow of conversation that linked our last session with this one. It was a nice feeling of communal effort/safety in sharing our work. I am noticing that the more we gather in our group, the safer, more collegial, friendly and exciting it is becoming. (Darlene, Reflection, January 17, 2007)

Although a safe atmosphere must be cultivated not commanded (Clark, 2001), one of the factors that contributed to a trusting and caring atmosphere was a predictable structure for meetings during the first year. Everyone knew that there would be a short presentation, time for questions, and opportunities for discussion. We were surprised at the degree of trust that emerged from resonating experiences. The care with which members attended to each other's stories and research also ensured that the self-study group was a welcoming place for everyone.

In order to create a safe environment for presenters, we sought to establish an attentive, listening environment in which they could present their work without interruption. Afterward, the other members of the group asked questions and reflected on the implications for our shared practice as teacher educators and scholars. Darlene noticed in the presentations "a sense of 'formality' yet also a sense of safety... [and] an awareness of trust... about sharing our thoughts on practice" (Darlene, Reflection, January 17, 2007). Similarly, as members were sensitive to each other in the discussion phase, members were increasingly willing to share their perceptions.

Self-study community members share struggles through conversation. As a self-study community becomes established, it needs to engage in meaningful dialogue related to more sensitive topics and experiences. As Guilfoyle and colleagues (2004) emphasize, "Conversation moves from beyond mere talk to become dialogue when it contains critique and reflection—when ideas are not simply stated but endure intense questioning, analysis, alternative interpretations, and synthesis" (pp. 1155–1156).

For the sharing of struggles to be an equitable process, it is crucial that all members participate actively in group conversations by sharing perspectives and stories of practice. During the first sessions of the Brock group, we monitored discussions closely to ensure attentive listening, appropriate feedback and full participation. Well-meaning interjections into conversation were monitored to ensure that presenters were comfortable and other members of the group were encouraged to speak. As experienced facilitators, we were also attentive to the verbal and nonverbal cues from others. Initially we were concerned that Chunlei was more a reflective listener than a vocal participant in dialogue. Once Darlene urged Chunlei to contribute, he was a very active participant in the next discussion. Julian reflected, "I was glad that Darlene drew Chunlei out at the very end. It is important that everyone contribute, and that some of us monitor our contributions so others may contribute more" (Julian, Reflection, December 13, 2006). Later, Chunlei reflected that sharing concerns in the self-study group "significantly helps us survive in the difficult initial years, and provides strength ready for the years to come" (Chunlei, Reflection, February 28, 2007). A shared sense of community also led members to discuss their concerns about the university's tenure and promotion process.

"Dialogue is not owned by any participant....The one 'requirement' is that it be sustained through active participation, keeping the ball in the air," according to Guilfoyle and colleagues (2004, p. 1333). While the safe environment helped individuals present ideas with which they were struggling, it was through the subsequent dialogue that inquiry became a collective struggle in which everyone contributed through critique and reflections.

Creating Educational Knowledge

Collective dialogue within a self-study community should centre on educational knowledge and improving our teacher education practices. As Clark (2001) stresses, "the heart of conversational learning for teachers is about ourselves" (p. 177) in relation to the learning needs of our students.

Self-study community members explore their teaching through dialogue. As academics in the Brock group, we sought to be both practical and scholarly in our inquiries. This balance was established in the first session, in which Julian presented a self-study into providing reflective feedback (Kitchen, 2008). His presentation sought to illustrate how inquiring into typical teaching situations could both improve practice and contribute to scholarship.

The self-study presentations, which focussed on specific issues emerging from a member's teaching practice, resonated with members of the community. A particularly lively collective dialogue was prompted by Louis's collaborative self-study inquiry with Darlene on preparing feedback to teacher candidates during practica. After Louis expressed concerns about the assessment tool he was required to use, Darlene encouraged him to inquire into the issue using self-study methodology. Together, they documented their experiences and reflected on the frustrations they experienced using the same detailed checklist used by supervising teachers. Dialogue in response to this presentation was very lively, as everyone had just returned from evaluating the first practicum. All had experienced frustration with this assessment tool, and members with experience in other universities offered alternative approaches to providing feedback. Tiffany wrote, "All members are intently listening to this conversation. This discussion had the potential to alter the very purpose of our role as faculty counsellors and require a complete examination of the whole organization of the department" (Tiffany, Reflection, December 13, 2006).

Although Louis was new to self-study, he was able to combine his expert knowledge of assessment with reflection to present a forceful, scholarly, and personal inquiry into practice. This reinforced a sense that everyone in the group was capable of presenting self-studies with resonance for other members of our self-study community and to contribute to the wider field of teacher education. After further data collection, reflection, and critical analysis, their article was accepted for publication (Ciuffetelli Parker & Volante, 2009). The journal editors identified the pairing of self-study and assessment as a valuable new contribution to the field. This served as a further indication that our self-study dialogue fostered meaningful scholarship.

Studying our teacher education practices in a self-study community both deepened our understandings of practice and developed a mutually respectful community of practice among new faculty. We modelled collegiality within a scholarly learning community and, through our publications in peer-reviewed journals, received external validation for our explorations of teaching through collective dialogue.

Self-study communities critically examine their group processes and dynamics. As conversation groups develop, according to Clark (2001), "participants find their voices, the conversational floor opens to greater complexity, depth, and tolerance of uncertainty" (p. 179). In the first year, members increasingly found their voices as they became comfortable in the group and with self-study. This was most evident when the four members least familiar with self-study formed their own self-study group to explore their professional identities as teacher educators. As Candace, Chunlei, Peter, and Shelley conversed among themselves, while engaging in the larger group discussions, their confidence as scholars of practice deepened (Figg et al., 2007).

Pleased with our first year as a self-study community, we presented a three-paper symposium presented at the International Study Association for Teachers and Teaching conference (Figg, Lu, Vietgen, & Griffin, 2007; Gallagher, Ciuffetelli Parker,

Kitchen, & Cherubini, 2007; Kitchen, Ciuffetelli Parker, Gallagher, & Volante, 2007). The opportunity to reflect and critically examine our processes and dynamics as a group, along with the feedback from those who attended, helped us to both celebrate our successes and consider ways in which we could move forward as a group. We were reminded of the work of the Arizona Group who, through the process of writing together, "unintentionally pushed [themselves] into a breakthrough from one level of discourse on research to another" (Guilfoyle et al., 2004, p. 1135).

Just as the Arizona Group "walked through a variety of discourses" in their "progression" in "discourse as a way of knowing" (Guilfoyle et al., 2004, p. 1135), we examined our group processes and dynamics to make adaptations in our second year as a self-study community:

> The first year has left us with an appreciation for the authority of each member, a strong sense of community, and a desire to continue to work together both as a self-study group and as members of an education faculty...All members have contributed conference papers based on their self-study work during the year, with several journal submissions in progress. The group is also open to further development in our second year. (Kitchen et al., 2008, p. 167)

Recreating Teacher Education and the Public Discourse of Communities of Practice

The Arizona Group, after dialoguing about their professional identities and classroom practices, "moved back to using self-study and dialogue to help us understand change in teacher education" (Guilfoyle et al., 2004, p. 1154). Explorations of their own teacher education practices reinforced their perception that faculty members need to "rethink learning and teaching from alternative perspectives, including a social justice and equity view" (p. 1154). They began to be seen as change agents as they advocated for teacher education reform in their institutions. Teacher education reform was also a recurring theme in our self-study group at Brock.

Self-study communities explore teacher education reform. As new faculty in a department undergoing a significant program review, we were aware of areas for improvement. As most of us were curriculum coordinators for the course we taught, we recognized that we are well positioned to reform teacher education at the classroom level.

The discussion of Darlene and Louis's work on practicum supervision was a significant moment in developing a sense of ourselves as teacher education reformers. The feedback from the group validated their reflections and analysis. The group's encouragement also prompted Darlene and Louis to present and discuss their findings to the department chair and the program committee chair. The result was that Louis and Darlene were asked to form an *ad hoc* committee to formally review and revise the existing faculty practicum evaluations. A final report to program committee was presented in February 2008, and a revised evaluation form has been accepted.

The self-study community as an incubator of teacher education reform was articulated at a self-study meeting on December 12, 2007. Shelley suggested that it "fosters and enhances our understanding" while "in the midst of tension.... This is a chance for us to highlight some of the backgrounds and strengths that we bring as pre-tenured faculty members." Julian agreed, suggesting that "the self-study group is a home or a safe harbor. The group meetings are the only place to talk about certain issues. This was also a time of great opportunity as now there is recognition that change is needed." Darlene extended this notion when she said, "The self-study group offers us a common and critical voice." Candace echoed that "there was power in the new voices to impact change."

We believe that studying our teacher education practices through self-study enhances our understanding of the intricacies of teacher education and promotes a community of practice within our faculty. Our work as teacher education reformers, however, has only just begun. Ongoing discussions have prompted members to become active in modifying course curriculum to incorporate more equity work, scholarly readings, and authentic assessment practices.

Self-study communities move towards the future. Authentic dialogues, in addition to contributing to the immediate personal and professional needs of the participants, "become a means for organizing ourselves for future action in our classrooms and schools" (Clark, 2001, p. 180).

The power of the self-study group as a place for authentic dialogue among teacher educators has motivated Darlene and Louis to make this dimension of practice a priority in their scholarship and to advocate for reforms to existing practices in the program. This echoes the experience of Candace, Peter, Chunlei, and Shelley, who reaffirmed their commitment to teaching. They highlighted conversations in the self-study group as a powerful force for constructive program reform efforts. They wrote, "Understanding how to successfully work in this new context became easier simply because we used each other as a sounding board to work out ideas for best ways to work within the existing structure" (Figg et al., 2007, p. 47).

The power of self-study as a vehicle that propels teacher educators forward is illustrated by Darlene and Louis's self-study of practicum assessment approaches. In the previous year, self-study proved to be a means for addressing their shared concerns about the "program and how assessment features fit into the program at large" (Ciuffetelli Parker & Volante, 2009). The larger self-study group, however, helped them advance their work: "We learned that the key to studying our teacher education practices – in this case of assessment strategies – was to ask the question that affected our practice most, and then begin collecting and reflecting on experiential data (Ciuffetelli Parker & Volante, 2009).

Julian, Darlene and Tiffany have brought the group's experience to a public discourse and have published on how to establish a self-study community in an education college (Kitchen et al., 2008). There have been several conference present- ations and proceedings to date at both national and international levels.

CONCLUSION: HOW SELF-STUDY COMMUNITY INFORMS OUR (AUTHORS')
PRACTICE

Being part of a self-study community provided us with a sense of belonging and community. Darlene reflected, "There was always awareness of trust and at the same time excitement about sharing our thoughts on practice" (Darlene's Journal, January 17, 2007).

The self-study community sustained our commitment to teacher education practices by providing us with a supportive community that values teacher education and is committed to improving practice. Julian reflected:

> While tenure and promotion procedures state that teaching, scholarship and service are all considerations in earning tenure, the reality is often quite different. Of the three, scholarship has the most rigorous measures of success, as they are dependent on the rigorous judgements of professional journals and funding agencies... It is not surprising then, that professors tend to favour scholarship when the incentives offered by the university are clearly skewed in that direction. Self-study and the support of members of the self-study group have helped me to resist these forces, while maintaining my deep commitment to teacher education and the scholarship of practice. (Julian's Journal, September 17, 2007)

Our commitment to teacher education reform was also strengthened by the self-study community's support and collaboration. Together we have identified many strengths in our teacher education and areas for improvement. More importantly, our dialogues have helped us become agents of change. Darlene reflected:

> I never would have imagined that my collaborative self-study with Louis Volante in assessment practices would have sparked a view to change assessment procedures for teacher candidate evaluations. I am encouraged by the faith and trust of first our self-study community and, later, all faculty have placed on our work and the work that we continue to contribute as a result of our collaborative self-study. It offers an example and a concrete legitimacy of self-study of teaching and scholarship and the inter-section between the two. (Darlene's Journal, April 3, 2008).

While many teacher educators engage in self-study on their own or with a few trusted colleagues, we believe that self-study can have a greater impact if more practitioners develop self-study communities of practice. Practitioners of collaborative self-study, by engaging with colleagues in developing self-study communities of practice, are better able to question the conventions of the academy and their institutions, and enact alternative approaches to teacher education. Unless we challenge the shared symbols and rules that underlie conventional approaches to teacher education practices and educational research, the normal process of community formation will continue to perpetuate them.

Self-study communities of practice have an important role to play in developing and enacting effective teacher education pedagogy. We hope that this review of methodologies for community development and critical self-study will encourage teacher educators to establish and sustain self-study communities.

REFERENCES

Beck, C. & Kosnik, C. (2001). From cohort to community in a preservice teacher education program. *Teaching and Teacher Education, 17*, 925–948.

Bodone, F., Guojonsdottir, H., & Dalmau, M. C. (2004). Revisioning and recreating practice: Collaboration in self-study. In J. J. Loughran, M. L. Hamilton, V. K. LaBoskey, & T. Russell (Eds.), *International handbook of self-study of teaching and teacher education practise* (pp. 193–246). Dordrecht, The Netherlands: Kluwer Academic Publishers.

Bullough, R. V., & Pinnegar, S. (2001). Guidelines for quality in autobiographical forms of self-study research. *Educational Researcher, 30*(3), 13–21.

Ciuffetelli Parker, D., & Volante, L. (2009). Reconciling summative teacher candidate evaluation within a formative assessment framework: A collaborative self-study of practicum supervision by faculty. *Studying Teacher Education.* In Press March 2009.

Clark, C. M. & Florio-Ruane, S. (2001). Conversation as support for teaching in new ways. In C. M. Clark (Ed.), *Talking shop: Authentic conversation and teacher learning* (pp. 1–15). New York: Teachers College Press.

Clark, C. M. & Florio-Ruane, S. (2001). In C. M. Clark (Ed.), *Talking shop: Authentic conversation and teacher learning* (pp. 1–15). New York: Teachers College Press.

Cole, A. L. (1999). Teacher educators and teacher education reform: Individual commitments, institutional realities. *Canadian Journal of Education, 24*(3), 281–295.

Cox, M. D., & Richlin, L. (2004). *Building faculty learning communities.* San Francisco: Jossey-Bass.

Ducharme, E. R. (1993). *The lives of teacher educators.* New York: Teachers College Press.

DuFour, R., & Eaker, R. (1998). *Professional learning communities: Best practices for enhancing student achievement.* Bloomington, IN: National Educational Service.

East, E., & Fitzgerald, L. M. (2006). Collaboration over the long term. In L. M. Fitzgerald, M. L. Heston, & D. L. Tidwell (Eds.), *Collaboration and community: Pushing the boundaries through self-study. Proceedings of the sixth international conference on self-study of teacher education practices* (pp. 72–75). Herstmonceux, Sussex, UK.

Elmore, R. F. (1997). *Investing in teacher learning. Staff development and instructional improvement in community school district #2, New York City.* National Commission on Teaching and America's Future.

Figg, C., Lu, C., Vietgen, P., & Griffin, S. (2007). Navigating the way: Balancing the challenges of new faculty. In *Proceedings of the international study association for teachers and teaching* (pp. 36–52). St. Catharines, Ontario, Canada, July 2007. Retrieved June 26, 2008, from http://www.isatt.org/ISATT-papers/ISATT-papers/Gallagher_EstablishingaSelf-StudyGroupinaFacultyofEducation.pdf

Fitzgerald, L. M., East, E., Heston, M., & Miller, C. (2002). Professional intimacy: Transforming communities of practice. In C. Kosnik, A. Freese, & A. Samaras (Eds.), *Making a difference in teacher education through self-study. Proceedings of the fourth international conference on self-study of teacher education practices* (pp. 77–80). Herstmonceux, Sussex, UK.

Fitzgerald, L. M., Farstad, J. E., & Demer, D. (2002). What gets "mythed' in the students evaluations of their teacher education professors? In J. J. Loughran & T. Russell (Eds.), *Improving teacher education practices through self-study* (pp. 208–221). London: RoutledgeFalmer.

Gallagher, T., Ciuffetelli Parker, D., Kitchen, J., & Cherubini, L. (2007). Establishing a self-study group in a faculty of education. In *Proceedings of the international study association for teachers and teaching* (pp. 2–20). St. Catharines, Ontario, Canada, July 2007. Retrieved June 26, 2008, from http://www.isatt.org/ISATT-papers/ISATT-papers/Gallagher_EstablishingaSelf-StudyGroupinaFacultyofEducation.pdf

Guilfoyle, K., Hamilton, M. L., Pinnegar, S., & Placier, P. (1995). Becoming teachers of teachers: The paths of four beginners. In T. Russell & F. Korthagen (Ed.), *Teachers who teach teachers: Reflections on teacher education* (pp. 35–55). London: Falmer Press.

Guilfoyle, K., Hamilton, M. L., Pinnegar, S., & Placier, P. (2004). The epistemological dimensions and dynamics of professional dialogue in self-study. In J. J. Loughran, M. L. Hamilton, V. K. LaBoskey, & T. Russell (Eds.), *International handbook of self-study of teaching and teacher education practise* (pp. 1109–1168). Dordrecht, The Netherlands: Kluwer Academic Publishers.

Hamilton, M. L. (2002). Change, social justice, and re-liability: Reflections of a secret (change) agent. In J. J. Loughran & T. Russell (Eds.), *Improving teacher education practices through self-study* (pp. 176–189). London: RoutledgeFalmer.

Kitchen, J. (2005a). Conveying respect and empathy: Becoming a relational teacher educator. *Studying Teacher Education, 1*(2), 194–207.

Kitchen, J. (2005b). Looking backwards, moving forward: Understanding my narrative as a teacher educator. *Studying Teacher Education, 1*(1), 17–30.

Kitchen, J. (2008). Using written feedback to promote critical reflection: A teacher educator responds to reflective writing by preservice teachers. *Excelsior, 2*(2), 37–46.

Kitchen, J., Ciuffetelli Parker, D., & Gallagher, T. (2008). Authentic conversation as faculty development: Establishing a self-study group in an education college. *Studying Teacher Education, 4*(2), 157–177.

Kitchen, J., Ciuffetelli Parker, D., Gallagher, T., & Volante, L. (2007). The Brock self-study group in action: Examining teacher candidate evaluations. In *Proceedings of the international study association for teachers and teaching* (pp. 21–35). St. Catharines, Ontario, Canada, July 2007. Retrieved June 26, 2008, from http://www.isatt.org/ISATT-papers/ISATT-papers/Gallagher_ EstablishingaSelf-Study GroupinaFacultyofEducation.pdf

Lighthall, F. F. (2004). Fundamental features and approaches of the s-step enterprise. In J. J. Loughran, M. L. Hamilton, V. K. LaBoskey, & T. Russell (Eds.), *International handbook of self-study of teaching and teacher education practise* (pp. 193–246). Dordrecht, The Netherlands: Kluwer Academic Publishers.

Loughran, J. (2002). Understanding self-study of teacher education practices. In J. Loughran & T. Russell (Eds.), *Improving teacher education practices through self-study* (pp. 239–248). London: RoutledgeFalmer.

Loughran, J. (2006). *Developing pedagogy of teacher education: Understanding teaching and learning about teaching*. London: Routledge.

Pinnegar, S. (1995). (Re) Experiencing student teaching. In T. Russell & F. Korthagen (Eds.), *Teachers who teach teachers: Reflections on teacher education* (pp. 55–67). London: Falmer Press.

Pinnegar, S., & Daynes, J. G. (2007). Locating narrative inquiry historically: Thematics in the turn to narrative. In D. J. Clandinin (Ed.), *Handbook of narrative inquiry: Mapping a methodology* (pp. 3–34). Thousand Oaks, CA: Sage.

Pinnegar, S., Lay, C. D., Bigham, S., & Dulude, C. (2005). Teaching as highlighted by mothering: A narrative inquiry. *Studying Teacher Education, 1*(1), 55–68.

Russell, T., & Loughran, J. (Eds.). (2007). *Enacting a pedagogy of teacher education: Values, relationships and practices* (pp. 182–191). Abingdon, UK: Routledge.

Samaras, A. P. (2002). *Self-study for teacher educators: Crafting a pedagogy for educational change*. New York: Peter Lang.

Samaras, A. P., Beck, C., Freese, A. R., & Kosnik, C. (2005). *Focus on Teacher Educations Quarterly, 6*(1), 3–5 & 7.

Samaras, A. P., DeMulder, E. K., Kayler, M. A., Newton, L., Rigsby, L. C., Weller, K. L. et al. (2006). Spheres of learning in teacher collaboration. In C. Kosnik, C. Beck, A. R. Freese, & A. P. Samaras (Eds.), *Making a difference in teacher education through self-study: Studies of personal, professional, and program renewal* (pp. 147–163). Dordrecht, The Netherlands: Springer.

Samaras, A. P., Kayler, M. A., Rigsby, L. C., Weller, K. L., & Wilcox, D. R. (2006). Self-study of the craft of faculty team teaching in a non-traditional teacher education program. *Studying Teacher Education, 2*(1), 43–57.

Tidwell, D., & Fitzgerald, L. (Eds.). (2006). *Self-study and diversity*. Rotterdam, The Netherlands: Sense.

Tidwell, D., Heston, M., & Fitzgerald, L. (Eds.). (2009). *Research methods for the self-study of practice*. Dordrecht, The Netherlands: Springer.

SALLY GALMAN

8. TRADING IN FABLES

Literary and Artistic Methods in Self-Study Research

...even these readers persisted in wondering. They wondered about human nature, human passions, human hopes and fears, the struggles, triumphs and defeats, the cares and joys and sorrows, the lives and deaths of common men and women! They sometimes, after fifteen hours' work, sat down to read mere fables about men and women, more or less like themselves, and about children, more or less like their own.

(Dickens, 1854, p. 37)

Listen carefully. Can you hear them? The scratching of their pens and pencils, the clatter of their keyboards? At this moment, all over the world, people are preparing...more stories and defining a movement. Are you sitting comfortably?

(Gravett, 2005, p. 9)

INTRODUCTION

Nussbaum (1995) asserts that the literary imagination, or "fancy," is the ability to construct self and other generously. Fancy allows us to "testify to the value of humanity as an end in itself" via cultivating the "ability to imagine what it is like to live the life of another person who might, given changes in circumstance, be oneself or one's loved ones" (pp. 3–5). She uses Dickens' *Hard Times: A Novel (1854)*, quoted above, to illustrate the humanizing power of the literary imagination. While she is speaking to a judicial audience, Nussbaum's assertion is also applicable in the terrain of social science inquiry. In short, it is the work of reflection, of seeing oneself and the other in terms of positive possibility that emphasizes connection and resists oversimplification of experience. Nussbaum's analysis demarcates the difference between a life driven by quantitatively derived "efficiency" and economy and one seen "through the tender light of fancy" (p. 10) or human imagination. While she does not dismiss the former, her thesis is that "science should be built upon human data" such as found in the "mere fables" (p. 11) of literature and art.

In arts-based self-study research, a term I use to encompass the literary, visual, and performing arts in research, we trade or barter in fables—we utilize the arts to help us focus on human meanings and experience and arrive at "reason ...through the tender light of fancy" or moral and intellectual imagination (Nussbaum, 1995,

C. A. Lassonde, S. Galman and C. Kosnik (eds.), Self-Study Research Methodologies for Teacher Educators, 129–149.

p. 10). With regard to the science of self-study research, examining one's own practice through the arts can be a route to both a) deepened understanding of our own teacher education practices and b) improved student learning. It can also be joyful, deeply satisfying, and powerful work.

This chapter will begin with a description of arts-based research methodology in the self-study context, followed by a detailed procedural overview and a discussion of the unique strengths and limitations afforded by this approach. Finally, an analysis of an exemplary study and its effects on my practice as a teacher educator precede concluding remarks.

DESCRIPTION OF METHODOLOGY: WHAT IS ARTS-BASED SELF-STUDY RESEARCH IN THE TEACHER EDUCATION CONTEXT?

Arts-based self-study research is about using the power, economy, and reflective/ transformative potential of the arts to conduct and deepen inquiry and to represent and disseminate its findings. As Weber and Mitchell (2004) write,

> one of our main contentions is that certain theoretical stances and practical methods derived from cultural studies, visual studies, and the visual arts are particularly important to self-study in teacher education because they hold up another mirror to facilitate self-reflection, and force critical consideration of the social and cultural dimensions of personal experience. And further, using the visual and the artistic can make self-study highly meaningful and pleasurable. (pp. 979–980)

Using images in educational research has a long history, but it is important to note, as Weber and Mitchell go on to suggest, the casual addition of illustration to a research article does not arts-based research make. In arts-based research, including arts-based self-study research, the arts occupy a central space in the work of inquiry and in analyses and representation of findings. Particularly useful in teacher education, the arts are adept not only at providing a site for reflexivity but also for "awakening us from our stock responses" (Eisner, 1993, p. 2), with unique power to disrupt "personal and cultural responses that have come to be taken for granted...recasting the contents of experience into forms with the potential for challenging (sometimes deeply held) beliefs and values (Barone, 2001, p. 26).

Some key features of arts-based research that emphasize its good fit with the goals of self-study in teacher education include 1) **its inherent, complex reflexivity** that "connects to the self yet distances us from ourselves" (Weber & Mitchell, 2004, p. 984); 2) **its capacity to communicate** in ways beyond and including historically dominant research prose with dynamic accessibility; 3) its natural emphasis on the always complex, often intricately "nested" (Lubeck, 1989), **personal, social, political, and other contexts** in self-study work; 4) its generous construction of and emphasis on **the importance and depth of the ordinary;** and 5) its capacity to **transform the goings-on of the private domain into a public conversation** (Weber & Mitchell, 2004).

What Is the Difference between Arts-Based Research in General and Arts-Based Self-Study Research?

> While the methods and methodologies of self-study are not much different from the other research methods, self-study is methodologically unique . . . although participant observation, ethnographic, grounded theory or statistical methods might be used in any single study, self-study involves a different philosophical and political stance . . . researchers who embrace self-study through the simple act of choosing to study their own practice, present an alternative relationship to the researcher and the researcher. (Pinnegar, 1998, p. 31)

Self-study methodologies are highly context-specific, they can be idiosyncratic and related more to the inquiry project than to any "one true way" (Loughran, 2004, p. 17). For those of us most comfortable with being handed a recipe card or toolbox for how to "do" a particular kind of research, this can be frustrating. Similarly, if I were to suggest that doing arts-based self-study is rather like doing arts-based research in general, and that one need only "add" and account for the self like an extra cup of flour, that would probably be equally inadequate. Yet the truth is this: the differentiating factor with self-study research methodology is the shift in "philosophical and political stance" of a researcher who chooses to study her own practice and problematize/contextualize the researcher's gaze upon the "researched" to settle, instead, upon her self and practice (Pinnegar, 1998, p. 31). Implicit in this shifted stance is the requirement that the researcher must be comfortable, at least initially, with the messy work of *not* knowing, with the idiosyncratic nature of inquiry in the hyper-contextualized space and the possibly disorienting sensation of taking the intellectual risks inherent in being both researcher and researched, and laying out one's laundry for general inspection, unaware of what you or others might find. This is work that, at least for some, falls in the margins (or off the page entirely) of what feels like safe, predictable, canonical Research. However, even though it requires the researcher to take an intellectual and emotional risk, to step into those margins, the possibilities for that work may also extend beyond the canonically expected into a different kind of nuanced, highly-responsive kind of inquiry. The same risk and reward synchrony can be true of literary and artistic research approaches—both in the practice of conducting inquiry and in presenting and disseminating findings.

What Are the General Guidelines for Doing Arts-Based Self-Study Research?

Part of my agenda in my self-study work, especially in the graphic novel work I will discuss later in this chapter, is the attempted resolution of a fragmented self, in which teaching selves are often held separate from other selves or facets of an integrated self. This is reflected in my recurring tendency to create dueling guidelines for my work in arts-based self-study; I find myself tempted to think about the aesthetic and artistic goals of a project on one hand and the self-study

Table 1. Guidelines for Arts-Based Self-Study Research
Developed from Eisner (1997), LaBoskey (2004) and Weber & Mitchell (2004)

Goals	Illustration/Operationalization
Emphasizes the complex work of reflexivity with an eye toward improvement	• Arts-based methods "act as a mirror" "connects to the self yet distances us from ourselves" (Weber & Mitchell, 2004, p. 984), emphasizing the relationship between autobiography, history and practice (Eisner, 1997) • Is improvement-aimed with a focus on transforming ourselves as teacher educators "first so that we might be better situated to help transform our students, their students, and the institutional and social contexts that surround and constrain us" (LaBoskey, 2004, p. 820-821) and to that end focused on the central work of improved teacher education practices • Creates opportunities for the researcher and the audience to think more deeply about themselves and their learning (Weber & Mitchell, 2004)
Maximizes the arts' potential descriptive and transformative power to communicate, contextualize the work of inquiry	• Facilitates alternative representations and descriptions of complex contexts and of difficult-to-operationalize concepts and phenomenon • Enables appreciation and realization of the highly contextualized nature of self-study • Underscores a commitment to aesthetic quality in the name of communication and understanding • Creates opportunities, "in the doing or the viewing [of the art] leading to new ways of being" (Weber & Mitchell, 2004, p. 1027)
Promotes readability and accessibility through effective use of arts across data collection and/or interpretation and dissemination of findings	• High-quality work in alternative aesthetic formats may command special attention, enable greater accessibility with more diverse, wider audience (Eisner 1997) • Communicates and emphasizes the humanity of the work (Eisner 1997)

Table 1. Continued

	• Focus on dissemination of findings; particularly concerned with widening debate and discourse, sharing and developing methodology and re-examining tentative findings and emerging theories
Is holistic in focus and practice	• Communicates simultaneously the whole and its parts • Speaks not only to static realities but also dynamic possibilities
Highlights complexity while maintaining clarity of purpose and broadening the scholarly conversation	• May be able to relate nuanced complexity with economy and clarity • Brackets the "ordinary", providing generous construction of the seeming "ordinary" with depth and complexity and most importantly, possibility. • Themes and evidence are clear • Representation of findings should advance understanding even further, carry on the conversation and contestation across and between discourses, highlighting the complexity of phenomena and making the scope of inquiry bigger rather than reduced (Eisner, 1997); providing opportunities for "useful re-framings" for other teachers and scholars in the field (Weber & Mitchell, 2004; p 1027)
Promotes interaction and collaboration across and beyond the lifespan of an inquiry project	• Creates spaces for multiple forms of interaction and collaboration • Lays the groundwork and provides structures for collaboration and interaction in the future.
Stresses the importance multiplicity of methods, perspectives and possibilities in project design, implementation, interpretation and dissemination	• Employs multiple methods and multiple means of representation through the arts relating not only to project design and data collection but also to the "quality of the story told" (LaBoskey, 2004l, p. 853). • Allows for multiple voices, outcomes, truths and perspectives to exist simultaneously and privileges that multiplicity as part of the richness of the context and the work.

research goals and objectives on another—and never the twain shall meet. This is, however, unnecessary. Just as our selves and lives outside of the classroom are inextricably connected to our teaching selves, lives, and practice, guidelines for arts-based self-study research should consider the aesthetic and research objectives as intertwined and mutually focused on the larger goals of the project.

Weber and Mitchell (2004) frame their work in arts-based self-study research in terms of the autobiographical tradition within the visual and performance arts as well as the rich history of visual work in social sciences (p 979). To resist the temptation of dueling guidelines and two-handed purposes, I typically use a chart to keep my planning and practice unified (see Table 1). This table is derived from Weber and Mitchell's (2004) guidelines for practice, combined with Eisner's (1997) recommendations for the artistic representation in research, and LaBoskey's (2004) foundations of self-study.

When Is Arts-Based S-Step Effective to Use?

High-quality self-study work in teacher education uses the arts in both inquiry and representation to realize our desire to 1) teach in ways that model good teaching practices for our teacher education students, or the ways in which we hope they will teach (Loughran, year, p. 10) as well as 2) the ways in which we want to explore our practice as a facet of ourselves, our histories, and our identities.

The former (1) entails experimenting with new discourses and new ways to demonstrate knowing. The arts-based approach to self-study is connected, therefore, with the modeling of diverse teaching and learning modalities for students, and showing them both the depth and the rigor of such ways of thinking and being in the classroom. However, modeling is often tricky (LaBoskey, 1997). As Loughran (2004) describes,

> Her self-study was driven by a purpose to do herself that which she asked her students to do. In participating in the process in the same way as her students, by placing herself in the same vulnerable position as her students and, in doing so in a public forum that was real and risky for her, she was modeling actions that she hoped would explicitly illustrate (to her students) the value of being seriously involved in the process of learning through developing a teaching portfolio. At the same time she was also conscious that her modeling could be misinterpreted as offering a 'model' or 'prototype' for the 'right way' to construct a portfolio and how to respond to questions about it, despite the fact that she explicitly intended her modeling to be a way of helping to show the value in the process (of portfolio construction) through real and personal involvement. (p. 11)

Modeling that particular teaching practice helped this researcher understand the nature of students' experience with that teaching strategy and her effectiveness as a teacher.

The latter (2) is a function of the desire to engage in meaningful reflection toward transformation of self and practice with the goal of improved teaching. Working with the arts the terrain of self often requires a different kind of thinking that may create deepened, more nuanced understanding. "The point of working within artistic frameworks," write Weber and Mitchell, "is that they are more symbolic and representational than traditional formats…self-expression using these methods leads to deeper understanding of teaching and learning processes even when the ostensible focus is not on teaching practices" (2004, p. 1026). In my own work, discussed briefly in the exemplary study section that follows, the question is not what my history has to do with being a teacher and teacher educator but rather what can I learn about my practice and my self by radically altering my perspective through the use of the arts—in my case, taking that connection for granted and taking the time to treat self and practice as a symbolic whole.

Procedures

Arts-based self-study is hardly uniform. Like much of self-study research, there are as many incarnations of design as there are researchers and research questions. However, as many practitioners have noted, it is not simply a case of "add art and stir" (Fischman, 2001; Galman, 2008; Weber & Mitchell, 2004). Its appropriate use is governed by the extent to which the systematic and rigorous application of the aesthetic standards of the arts to the terrain of self-study inquiry provides uniquely deepened understanding, accessibility, and deep connection. However, that said, the notion that representation of research findings must be connected to research design is central: There should be a connection between the questions that drive inquiry and how the research findings are presented. Additionally, the researcher should keep in mind that the kinds of understandings that anyone might construct are closely related to the methodological and artistic decisions made in the course of the work (Eisner, 1993; LaBoskey, 2004).

Data Collection and Analysis

Data collection should emphasize multiplicity: This means a space for multiple voices, multiple interpretations and multiple perspectives that can be divergent but occur simultaneously. Arts-based methods are particularly well-suited at framing multiple perspectives and acknowledging the inherent complexity of realities as they coexist in the life of an inquiry project and in the lives of participants. So also data analysis procedures emphasize both complexity and collaboration: As Loughran (2004) emphasizes, the work of checking data interpretation is best a shared task to address the issues inherent in the researcher's close personal involvement. A central part of my interpretation of the strengths of arts-based research is its capacity to create a space for that shared discourse around data, impressions, and interpretation. In my collaborative work I have used a dialogic journal, peer debriefing and collaborative data analysis with colleagues who occupy divergent roles and positionalities (Lincoln & Guba, 1985; Rosenberger, Galman & Pica, 2008). Similarly, in one of the arts-based projects discussed in the exemplary study section of the chapter, I collaborated with teacher education students to comment on the truthfulness and authenticity of my work and our collective insights.

Standards for Quality: Authenticity and Truthfulness

Out of collaboration, conversation, and the privileging of multiplicity comes a concern for standards of quality, or the state of the evidence for the "findings" at hand. Our procedures must be systematic and our evidence must support what we say we have learned. The standards for research quality, validity and reliability, are often discussed in terms of "truthfulness and authenticity" in arts-based self-study research. Authenticity can be addressed as whether or not the person or persons assuming authorship are present in the "story" being told. Were they present in any reasonable way to actually bear witness by fully participating? Validity is understood as "truthfulness", or the extent to which the data support purported findings. Reliability, meanwhile, can be best understood not as replicability (as duplication of findings is generally not relevant as a standard of rigor) but rather as an attempt to "satisfy the underlying principle of voice and its relation to a desired [study effect]" (LaBoskey, 2004, p. 847).

Standards of authenticity and truthfulness can be maintained by 1) explicitly including the author(s) in the "story" being told and providing details of the precise contours of that involvement across the project lifespan and being clear about the evidence, 2) being explicit about evidence and its connection with the evidence and the themes or findings that emerge from analysis and 3) using systematic procedures to examine and analyze data. However, in addition to these kinds of safeguards, one other measure of quality, "cathartic validity" (Lather, 1986), might be especially appropriate for arts-based self-study research. This entails comparing the "story" of the project and findings to its impact on actual practices, its realization of transformative potential for both the researcher and the audience and the extent to which it has created a space for more and wider dialogue. To these measures of authenticity we would also add Feldman's (2003) admonition that for self-study work to be trustworthy it must also acknowledge the moral and political weight of the work of teacher educators doing self-study work, and therefore be transparent with regard to method.

It is also important to note that while many scholars who do arts-based inquiry assume the contemporary wide-acceptance and legitimacy of this work there has been some debate about the overall quality of arts-based inquiry in educational research in general. Issues related to its acceptance in the tenure structure, the unique dilemmas related to its publication, and dissemination and development of unique interpretations of rigor have required some defense. As music/performance-based researcher Peter Gouzouasis (2008) suggests,

> Our stories about lived experiences—experiences in all aspects of music—are the most powerful 'data' we can use in our research . . . just because they are written in one style or another, a scientific or literary style, shouldn't define or establish their validity as serious research...even though some qualitative

researchers have tried to work with traditional notions of validity…[ultimately] validity is 'not valid; in the assessment of [arts-based] research. (p. 110)

Representation of Research Findings

As reflected in Table 1, using an arts-based approach in self-study research underscores the importance and potential impact of representation on two fronts: 1) representation of the multiplicity and complexity inherent in the diverse perspectives that may influence the findings and the voice(s) in which the author may speak and 2) the power of the representation of research findings with regard to their effective dissemination, impact, and accessibility. While it is useful to think about standards of research quality in terms of truthfulness and authenticity, these are not useful terms to describe representational issues in arts-based self-study research. Instead, I prefer to think about how we go about representing our voices, our experiences and the experiences of involved others as a function of faithfulness:

> Being faithful, unlike being true or authentic, implies a commitment to an idea or thing in which that entity is the center and yardstick against which claims of value are measured. A researcher can strive to be faithful to participant stories and experiences, presenting a faithful rendering of their original form and being faithful to participant meanings and understandings. Also implicit in the goal of faithfulness is the idea of the limitations of striving—which is to say that though the researcher will strive to be faithful, the limitations presented by their individual subjectivity, however closely audited, must still be taken into account. (Galman, in press)

While ultimately the central participant in arts-based self-study is one's self, or selves, the admonitions for representing the self in the context of practice are similar to those we might make in the context of representing participant voices in qualitative research. For self-study, rendering a faithful representation of the self, with honesty and with transparency, is an essential measure of quality and integrity as is being faithful to the multifaceted research context. Both speak to the quality of the evidence and to the power of the project to have an effect, but even more importantly, faithfulness in this regard underscores the individuality of experience, the centrality of that individual yardstick and attention to limitations of our striving as human beings. As Weber and Mitchell (2002) say of their critical memory work, it is ultimately not the accuracy of the memories that is the focal point, but rather the ways in which memories of the past are rendered usable: "remembering in the service of future action . . .what and how we remember things provides clues to how we think now, windows of sorts into our emotional and cognitive restructuring of experience and testimony to how the past shapes us" (p. 122) by asking questions that cause us to pay attention to the faithfulness with which we interpret experience.

Analytic Strengths, Limitations, and Other Issues

The strengths of high-quality arts-based self-study research are many. Its almost automatic reflexive potential, its emphasis on the complexity and centrality of contexts, its emphasis on connection between individuals and with one's own self and practice, and the opportunities its dissemination provide for high individualized meaning-making are all important procedural, analytic, and interpretive strengths. Additionally, many scholars in self-study work have suggested that the issues of trust, vulnerability, and positive risk it brings to the fore may also be a strength (Cahnmann, 2003; Galman, 2006; Weber & Mitchell, 2004). These issues, as well as the foregrounding self-study research in general gives to the intellectual and even personal risks that may be perceived parts of this kind of inquiry, suggest that the act of publicizing the private and scrutinizing self are positive, pro-reflexivity strengths.

However, seeing the "sense of vulnerability necessary to genuinely study personal conflicts and the sense of dissonance that is so often the driver for self-study as a professionally rewarding experience" (Loughran, 2004, p. 23) may also be a limitation if not properly bracketed. Just as my collaborative work drawing with teacher education students brought their issues of vulnerability to the fore in positive and negative ways, it also required a thoughtful response on my part unique to the risks inherent in doing art as inquiry. As Cahnmann (2003) writes, "poetry is risky business" (p. 30)—and not necessarily because of its marginal status in the universe of scientific inquiry. Rather, poetry in research, like all arts in research, take participants to a place where they may not be comfortable, where the results can be unpredictable and the feelings of vulnerability even counter-productive at times. To avoid having the gift of risk become more of a curse than a blessing, careful planning is necessary. For my students, I provided scaffolded options for participation, and modeled those options with them in a classroom environment carefully structured for community, support and safety. For myself, the same must be true of the people with whom I engage in the work of inquiry.

One other issue that comes up is the fact that reports of arts-based self-study research are constrained by publication and presentation structures and may be unable to offer as explicit a methodological discussion as is necessary for new and senior scholars alike to adequately engage in dialogue and learn about best practices. Though this is certainly changing thanks to the arts-based research community's efforts, continued transparency and specificity are needed.

STUDY EXEMPLAR

To more concretely demonstrate what arts-based self-study research might look like, the following paragraphs present my own work using the graphic novel as one exemplar of literary/visual arts-based self-study based. In my discussion, I will first provide a short description of the genre and some background information for its application in self-study research context. A detailed description of data collection and analytic procedures follows.

Background: What Is the Graphic Novel in the Self-Study Research Context?

The graphic novel is what we might call a hybrid text genre; it features contiguous text and images and is considered by some artists to be a sub-genre of the comic book. It is distinguished from the "comic" by its typically much less hero-oriented, fantastical, mythic and exaggerated style and content, and features instead an often more detailed, nuanced and flexible approach to telling stories about everyday life and experience. Most graphic novels feature a diverse array of narrative and visual composition, which in many cases leads to greater flexibility and a wider application than the standard, linear comic—including popular culture, research and other diverse possible applications. While it still remains somewhat undefined as a genre, it continues to gain legitimacy as a versatile text in academic and other circles, due in part to the crossover success of many works that previously would have been relegated to comic status; Art Spiegelman's *MAUS* series is particularly notable for its early popular success, and in more contemporary arenas of popular appeal Marjane Satrapi's *Persepolis* stands out as an important and influential text (Galman, 2008; McCloud, 1992; LeFevre, 2000; Satrapi, 2003, 2004; Spiegelman, 1986; 1987).

Part of this legitimacy may be related to the accessibility and potentially democratizing effect of the text genre. For example, the sound of "scratching pencils" to which Gravett (2005) beckons us in the introductory quote emphasizes that, unlike participation in the comparatively closed culture of long-legitimated writing and knowing, the history of comics and graphic novels as a sub-culture of literary practice existing in the margins of acceptable discourse creates a space for wider participation, this movement trades in the currency of Dickens' fables of ordinary men and women. Fundamentally, the assertion that one's story is worth telling and that one's words and images and memories have a right to the space they take up (and in the case of publication, the right to the large PDF files that accompany, enrich, and complicate tidy prose manuscripts) and that words may not, in fact, be adequate, is a powerful assertion of the primacy of self and experience, and the right of the knower to be heard. This may be especially true for pre-service teachers, who are often not afforded with the time, space, and opportunity to engage in the affirmation of self that is arts-based reflection, expression and inquiry.

In this discussion, I am treating the graphic novel as an exemplar of two types of arts-based self-study work: both literary and visual-arts methods. I will be discussing it methodologically as 1) a literary method according to tenets of narrative inquiry and autobiography and with an emphasis upon the central power of metaphors in literary inquiry; and 2) a visual-arts method emphasizing the use of images alone and in connection with tandem text with an emphasis upon the economy and versatility of the image in both process and "product" of self-study research. Both facets of the project I will describe present different possibilities for an approach to examining self and practice as teacher educator and the process of modeling arts-based and reflective processes for one's teacher education students. The former is an adaptation of "critical memory work" (Weber & Mitchell, 2002) in which found objects, including photographs, become prompts for autobiographical reflection and inclusion in the hybrid text narrative in tandem with an analysis of my own "story" of teaching based on eclectic data collection and documentation processes. The latter is rather like the work of LaBoskey (1997), who sought to model particular practices for teacher education students by doing what she asked of them herself, and subsequently by (publicly) experiencing that uncertainty, vulnerability and potential reward.

How to Do It: Methodology Step-By-Step

I will be talking about a project that has been ongoing over several years and incorporates my work with different groups of preservice teachers, critical friends, and colleagues in teacher education. My research question was relatively straightforward: *What is the difference between what I know are best practices in teacher education and what I do as a teacher educator, and what is the relationship between my own autobiography and identity as a critical teacher educator, my memories of becoming a teacher, and how I engage in my work?* It later grew to include inquiry into the effects of working collaboratively to reflect on story, autobiography, and critical memory with teacher education students, and that expansion would entail a great deal of modeling and trust. In the step-by-step presentation of procedures that follows, I will first discuss my own self-study work using the graphic novel. This will be followed by a discussion of how I modeled the work for teacher education students.

Part One: Working with My Own Story and Practices

In working with my own story I spent a great deal of time engaging in critical conversation with colleagues and friends—rather like what Lincoln and Guba (1985) describe as "peer debriefing" (p. 308)—as I sought to see the relationship between autobiography, intention, and practice, rather like a lengthy game of connect-the-dots. While Lincoln and Guba suggest that the appointed peer should be "disinterested" and that debriefing should occur "in a manner paralleling an analytic session" (p. 308), the many peers, colleagues, and ultimately, students, with whom I shared my critical memory and autobiographical work were not required to be disinterested or strictly analytic in focus, but rather collaborators with whom I interacted repeatedly to help refine the contours of my research practice, the clarity of themes, and the quality of reflection.

Step one: Sketching out formative theories. Before I began thinking about collecting any data I sketch out (literally using contiguous text and images, or sometimes only figuratively using word-processing on the computer) the parameters of my research question as formative theory. This includes, what my "picture" of my own practice is—i.e., what I believe best practices are, what my theoretical foundations are and "whether or not [my] practice is consistent with [my] evolving ideals and theoretical perspectives" (LaBoskey, 2004, p. 820). I remember this "formative theory" began to look a little bit like a map, and blew up a copy to post on the office wall, keeping another smaller copy in my data files for reference during analysis.

Step two: Initial data collection. Data collection would include two stages and multiple forms of evidence. The graphic novel panel[1] is both a product and representation of the inquiry process and the process of my own reflection. The kinds of data I collect on my own practice includes but is typically not limited to transcripts of email communications, relevant interactions and conversations and other text-based discourses, including an online, collaborative journal I keep with one or two colleagues and, when possible, video or audio recordings of my teaching; my ongoing reflective autobiographical and critical memory work, which includes creating a narrative and looking at significant found images; and more structured researcher journal-keeping methods related to my own practice and reflection (Seidman, 1998; Schensul, LeCompte & Schensul, 1999). The precise procedures for collecting such data are summarized in Table 2, Initial Data Collection Plan.

Table 2. Initial Data Collection Plan[1]

Data Type	Collection Procedure
1. Email, audio/video and conversational/interactional transcripts and other field texts	I examine my own cache of professional correspondence, notes, course syllabi and other field texts, organizing these into folios for reflection and analysis
2. Researcher reflective journal	In addition to maintaining an individual record of reflective practice, I create a collaborative online journal in which I and, frequently, some critical teacher educator colleagues and friends write in dialogue.
3. Reflective autobiography and image collection	I am continually in the process of authoring a reflective autobiography as a teacher educator, which is added to the field text folio for analysis along with relevant found images. This is recorded in my ongoing artists' notebook where I record images that might contribute to my construction of the central metaphor with which I work as a theme or themes for analysis, representation and dissemination of findings.
4. Peer debriefings (usually recorded in notes and transcripts as field texts similar to Item 1)	Conversation and sharing about my research and the fruits of the analysis in conversation with colleagues and critical friends. This became especially important as themes emerged in the data through recursive analyses as well as in the "final" product.

---

[1] This is adapted from methodological discussion in Rosenberger, Galman & Pica (2008).

In previous studies in which I was working with the graphic novel around participant-student data and my own experience I have conducted one verbal interview (focusing on narratives of experience and self) prior to creating images/texts with participants. During the drawing session the participant and I would typically go over the interview tape or a transcription if that was available, presenting, as we listened, each participant with the task of representing the story they knew and they told in the interview, and the memories and beliefs of that story into a narrative of contiguous texts and images. I would often encourage participants to focus on illuminating a central metaphor or theme that they felt was important in their data and then using images and words to show how that theme worked through memory, story and interpretation to create a multi-layered, multi-vocal text that they would then analyze as a graphic novel panel.

In the case of doing self-study work with the graphic novel I analyze the data collected in Table 1 to create the equivalent of the verbal interview text, and in conjunction with further peer debriefing I begin creating the graphic novel panel from that analysis.

Step Three: Working with the graphic novel to create/represent/analyze/isolate themes. In beginning to put the pen to paper, I focus on 1) themes that emerge/are emerging from data analysis and 2) how I might create a composition that accomplishes my goal of juxtaposing a narrative of self with what I saw as its historical and personal antecedents. One finished panel appears in Figure 1, below.

Figure 1.

This figure represents one section of one page of what was a much longer piece that focused on my exploration of the gendered self(ves) and roles at play in my becoming a teacher, and ultimately leaving the K-12 classroom to become a teacher educator. I have chosen to highlight this section of what is ultimately a very large (4' x 5') piece because it is a place where I incorporate found images, personal history, and contemporary selves as antecedents of practice in a narrative that features many different perspectives simultaneously. I have shared this work with teacher education students, and many have been taken aback at the deeply personal nature of the stories, their non-linear narrative format and the surprising relevance of the themes of growing up as a "good girl" in a white, Southern family and the behaviors associated in that culture with "women's work" to my practice as a teacher and later as a teacher educator. This is ultimately a story of finding myself in my students, and examining a lot of my uninterrogated assumptions about their aspirations and the "semi-professional" (Etzioni, 1969) and gendered nature of elementary-level teacher's work. Seeing my own history and how it connects with my current practice was a way to more generously construct both myself and my students.

Part Two: Modeling Arts-Based Self-Study for Teacher Education Students

Creating opportunities for pre-service teachers to engage in arts-based self-study means gently encouraging their buy-in and participation, and the core of this coaxing is the act of modeling. Somewhat more aggressive than the act of merely presenting my own work, step-by-step as I did in Part One, above, and encouraging them to explore their own stories and do their own narrative inquiry, it often begins with "selling" them on the power and rigor of arts as method by showing them in concrete terms the effects of this inquiry on my practice in teaching *them*. Often, providing opportunities for creating hybrid texts using drawing or collage[2] in a workshop environment in class rather than as an assignment creates a space more conducive to participation—simply because there are others there who are also engaged in the act of suspending disbelief.

I've also used a couple of different layers of modeling depending on student needs, trust levels, atmosphere and so on. One I called the collaborative graphic novel approach where we would draw together—something I also call dialogic writing or drawing, or drawing in two voices. This can work out beautifully or it can be disastrous. One reason for the former is that it provides some degree of reciprocity and mutual risk-taking, in addition to the idea of safety in numbers; participants are able to see the antecedents of my own practice as a teacher and teacher educator, and how that is similar and different, and includes similar resonant themes as their own. They also feel comforted in the risk of drawing by seeing my willingness to make my personal history both public as well as relevant to the work that they are currently doing as pre-service teachers. This latter is also part of the disastrous possibility: it becomes very clear very quickly that I am someone with a degree of artistic training, practice and facility and this can be daunting. In the case of the latter, trading off, or finding "found" images might be a useful alternative. Still other students are sensitive to being "watched" while they are at different stages of data collection and text creation, and despite my desire to insist on the in-class workshop, really need private time. Finally, I have also encountered times when I have felt uncomfortable using the graphic novel method in the context of a graded course environment, and I have experimented with the idea of offering it outside of the course, as an elective opportunity.

Figures 2 is an example of one product of modeling the inquiry process for students. This is an example of a collaborative piece done with an undergraduate teacher education student. She was uncomfortable drawing, and so instead elected to "trade off" with me, ultimately incorporating a range of images we devised together. The central metaphor with which she worked was the cardboard box classroom, which is to say the play-school she constructed as a little girl in which cardboard boxes "stood" for students as she imagined herself as a teacher. The image of the cardboard box, juxtaposed with her own journal writings from high school and college and the narrative of the "scary school" and "real students" come together to tell her story of being unsure that the role she had "always wanted" would really "fit" in the cardboard boxes she clung to, even at the time of the project. She would return to this metaphor, and other themes that came out of creating the piece, time and time again.

Figure 2.

DATA ANALYSIS

There are two levels of analysis: as mentioned, one level takes place before creating the graphic novel panel—it is itself, then, both a data elicitation and analytic tool—and then the analysis of the panels themselves. Analyzing the products of initial data collection is reminiscent of the Strauss & Corbin's (1990) grounded theory procedure, moving rather rapidly from the "open coding" phase to the isolation of central categories or themes in an adaptation of "selective coding". Regardless of the extent to which these initial analytic procedures progress by the proverbial "book", they serve to create an opportunity to delve into the data and focus on what lies there. This is also a space for initial attention to the faithfulness of how I represent the process, and myself.

The process of creating the graphic novel panel is about presenting the "findings" of the first tier of analysis, but it is also a "text" for reflection and analysis, albeit this time treated as a narrative for literary text analyses of important, recurring themes and central metaphors (Lakoff & Johnson, 1980; Scholes, 1985) and image content analyses including frequency counts (Chalfen, 1998). Concurrent with these analyses are my own ongoing reflections and interpretations, and the practice of returning periodically to peer-debriefing procedures. Lastly, I return to my initial "sketch" or formative model and examine any relationships. Findings from these analytic procedures typically include the elucidation of important themes and key metaphors that may drive my practice and illuminate discrepancies between belief and practice, and suggest ways in which I might become more effective.

Why Is This Case Exemplary?

As I stated before, there are as many incarnations of high-quality arts-based self-study as there are researchers and research questions to occupy them. So, I highlight some of my work as an example of *one* way in which some of the guidelines for arts-based self-study might be effectively realized and the benefits of arts-based work might be maximized. It is important to note that my exemplar case is not intended to be representative of method or interpretation for all arts-based self-study work, but is instead only one possible exemplar of how it might be operationalized in a visual-arts context. To more explicitly illustrate the ways in which the case I provide could be considered exemplary I have refitted the guidelines laid out in Table 1 as Table 3: Exemplary Case Analysis.

Other arts-based projects incorporate the literary or performing arts to realize the transformative potential of self-study. Literary projects might include a prose novel or novella or poetry, and could draw on the traditions of narrative inquiry and the roots of autobiography as a pillar of self-study work. Both of these foreground the centrality of human narratives of experience, emphasize reflection and treat research as a potentially collaborative activity in which texts are created around the understandings gleaned from reflecting on and engaging with one's own narrative of personal history (Connelly & Clandinin, 1990; Kitchen, 2002). Similarly, the performing arts, including theatre, performance art and music incorporate the work of critical reflection and autobiography, mostly through the use of metaphor.

Theatre, treated as both a performance and a text, creates theoretical positions through the use of metaphor "all the while contextualizing them within the mundane everydayness in which they are grounded" (Weber & Mitchell, 2002, p. 122).

Table 3. Criteria Developed from Eisner (1997), LaBoskey (2004) and Weber & Mitchell (2004)

Goals (from Table 1)	In the exemplar case
Emphasizes the complex work of reflexivity with an eye toward improvement	The visually complex text resists an oversimplified "skimmer's" read but speaks with clarity to the connections and themes that emerged from the multiple stages of data analysis. Similarly, the systematic and rigorous process by which the pieces are created were embedded with multiple opportunities for formal and informal reflection
Maximizes the arts' potential descriptive and transformative power to communicate, contextualize the work of inquiry	Uses the graphic novel's unique non-linear narrative format, complex symbols and versatile contiguous text to isolate, illustrate and communicate important themes related to the personal, political and instructional context.
Promotes readability and accessibility through effective use of arts across data collection and/or interpretation and dissemination of findings	The graphic novel format is immanently readable, drawing the audience to engage with both the text and the image in a system not unlike "co-duction" (Booth, 1988), a process by which the reader inserts his or her interpretation between and across his or her experience of the text; in this instance, the reader connects prose and images to make meaning.
Is holistic in focus and practice	Addresses history, autobiography, experience and identity as interconnected antecedents and contemporary factors of practice, creating a text that is simultaneously one and many concurrent and interconnected narratives
Highlights complexity while maintaining clarity of purpose and broadening the scholarly conversation	The non-linear narrative structure and text/image configuration allow for the flexibility to address multiple factors, voices and interpretations while at the same time clearly communicating the important themes and questions emerging from inquiry.
Promotes interaction and collaboration across and beyond the lifespan of an inquiry project	The structures of peer-debriefing and collaboration put in place to do the work, as well as the practice of modeling both the graphic novel process and the sense of vulnerability inherent in the work created a new level of trust, new collegiality and new instructional energy in the teacher education classroom and beyond
Stresses the importance multiplicity of methods, perspectives and possibilities in project design, implementation, interpretation and dissemination	The non-linear narrative structure and text/image configuration allow for the flexibility to address multiple factors, voices and interpretations; The graphic novel format allows for a different level of dissemination and interaction with the audience.

CONCLUSION: TRADING IN FABLES, OR HOW MY PRACTICE CHANGED

My practice as a teacher educator is constantly evolving in response to both formal self-study efforts and my work as an artist in the graphic novel genre and my daily interactions with students and colleagues. However, as I revisited study exemplar project and the artifacts connected with it, I have had the opportunity to reflect upon what synthesizing, and ultimately creating my own "mere fables" has meant in terms of my practice. As per the reflections of Hamilton, LaBoskey, Loughran, and Russell (2002), I will structure my learning as "artifacts of personal development" (p. x) similar to how Mary Lynn Hamilton frames her own learning in that piece. In keeping with the thrust of this chapter, I have chosen to see not artifacts or exemplars but rather multiple retellings of a single story, or "mere fable": my own evolving narrative of self-as-teacher-educator as revealed through my process of reflective arts-based self-study using the graphic novel. Taking inspiration from Nussbaum, I use the word *fable* despite its connotations (indeed, I am anything but a "fabulist" here) to underscore the connection of this work to its impact on the audience as well as its connection with critical memory.

1. The Fable of Fragmentation: As a new teacher, and later as a novice teacher educator, I separated the teacher self from the other parts of myself—the artist self, the mother self, and so on. Part of this was the result of being overwhelmed and therefore not having an opportunity to revisit my own ideals and evaluate my practice. Instead, I was lost in the daily crash and fray of "getting the job done."

2. The Fable of Resistance: Thus fragmented, I was unconsciously ventriloquated by facile, though popular, characterizations of pre-service teachers; I resisted reflective practice and the understanding that teaching was emotional, intellectual, and potentially transformative work. I didn't engage in critiquing these discourses or reflecting upon the young people—mostly women—with whom I worked as knowers making pragmatic, powerful choices. I also didn't see myself and my trajectory as connected with their work and possibility, except in a buried past as a teacher that I kept divorced from my contemporary life and work.

3. The Fable of Connection: Through encouragement from critical colleagues and friends, I began to connect my work as an artist and my other selves with my teacher-educator self, and I began to see how the fragmented self that began in K-12 teaching created the conditions for my ventriloquation and also for resisting reflective practice. The central metaphor of fragments or fragmentation emerged as important. In creating the graphic novel panels of the project, and modeling the telling of my story for my students, the emotional and intellectual terrain, my connections to my students and to the K-12 classroom, and ultimately my connections across selves became a clear and holistic portrait of my practice emerged. This was also a way to begin connecting others to the powerful work of teachers, which so few people remember from their own apprenticeships of observation with critical accuracy or the generous construction that Nussbaum (year) describes.

GALMAN

4. The Fable of Relevance: I began to see my autobiography, and that of my students, as relevant and essential antecedents to practice, analyzable as data for improved teaching. Continued critical memory work leaves me with continued questions around the structure of memory and how that structure continues to shape my identity and my practice—even of things that are not overtly relevant to my classroom work (Weber & Mitchell, 2002; 2004). I was able to return to my ideals and theoretical perspectives, to move beyond a fragmented, reactive stance.

The power of heeding my own "mere fables" has given me an enriched, generously constructed fable of my work, the work of others, and the possibilities for inquiry, transformation, and change.

NOTES

1 I refer to the single page or pages I typically work with in the beginning as panels because they are usually not at full book or novella-length, and may be works-in-progress on multiple levels.
2 Though this is problematic on several levels due to the limited "source" material, and they should be encouraged to be critical in terms of where their images come from and what ideologies may be implicit in source material, etc.

REFERENCES

Barone, T. (2001). Science, art, and the predispositions of educational researchers. *Educational Researcher, 30*(7), 24–28.
Cahnmann, M. (2006). Reading, living, and writing bilingual poetry as scholARTistry in the language arts classroom. *Language Arts, 83*(4), 342–352.
Chalfen, R. (1998). Interpreting family photography as pictorial communication. In J. Prosser (Ed.), *Image-based research*. London: Falmer Press.
Dickens, C. (1854). *Hard times: A novel*. London: Harper & Brothers.
Eisner, E. (1993). Forms of understanding and the future of educational research. *Educational Researcher, 22*(7), 5–11.
Eisner, E. (1997). The promise and perils of alternative forms of data representation. *Educational Researcher, 26*(6), 4–11.
Etzioni, A. (1969). *The semi-professions and their organization: Teachers, nurses and social workers*. New York: Free Press.
Feldman, A. (2003). Validity and quality in self-study. *Educational Researcher, 32*(3).
Fischman, G. E. (2001). Reflections about images, visual culture and educational research. *Educational Researcher, 30*(8), 28–33.
Galman, S. (2006). Rich white girls: Developing critical identities in teacher education and novice teaching settings. *International Journal of Learning, 13*, 3–13.
Galman, S. A. C. (2008). The truthful messenger: Visual methods and representation in qualitative research in education. *Qualitative Research*.
Gouzouasis, P. (2008). *Toccata on assessment, validity and interpretation: Validity in a new tonality*. Paper presented at the 2nd Annual Arts-Based Educational Research Conference. Bristol, UK: July 5–7, 2007. Partially reprinted in Perryman, L., Conference report: Way too much fun? *Arts and Humanities in Higher Education, 7*(105).
Gravett, P. (2005). *Graphic novels: Everything you need to know*. New York: Harper-Collins.
Hamilton, M. L., LaBoskey, V. K., Loughran, J. J., & Russell, T. (2002). *Have five years of self-study changed teacher education? Artifacts of our personal development as teacher educators*. Paper presented at The Fourth International Conference on Self-study of Teacher Education Practices. Herstmonceux Castle, East Sussex, England.

Hoffman, D. (2007). Personal communication.

Kitchen, J. D. (2002). *Becoming a relational teacher educator: A narrative inquirer's self-study.* Paper presented at The Fourth International Conference on Self-study of Teacher Education Practices. Herstmonceux Castle, East Sussex, England.

LaBoskey, V. K. (1997). Teaching to teach with purpose and passion: Pedagogy for reflective practice. In J. Loughran & T. Russell (Eds.), *Teaching about teaching: Purpose, passion and pedagogy in teacher education.* London: Falmer Press.

LaBoskey, V. K. (2004). The methodology of self-study and its theoretical underpinnings. In J. J. Loughran, M. L. Hamilton, V. K. LaBoskey, & T. Russell (Eds.), *International handbook of self-study of teaching and teacher education practices.* Dordrecht: Kluwer Academic Publishers.

Lakoff, G., & Johnson, M. (1980). *Metaphors we live by.* Chicago: University of Chicago Press.

Lather, P. (1986). Issues of validity in openly ideological research: Between a rock and a soft place. *Interchange, 17*(4), 63–84.

LeFevre, P. (2000). The importance of being published: A comparative study of comic formats. In C. Magnussen & H. Christiansen (Eds.), *Comics & culture: Analytical and theoretical approaches to comics* (pp. 91–106). Copenhagen: Museum Tusculanum Press.

Lincoln, Y., & Guba, E. (1985). *Naturalistic inquiry.* Thousand Oaks, CA: Sage Publications.

Loughran, J. J. (2004). A history and context of self-study of teaching and teacher education practices. In J. J. Loughran, M. L. Hamilton, V. K. LaBoskey, & T. Russell (Eds.), *International handbook of self-study of teaching and teacher education practices.* Dordrecht: Kluwer Academic Publishers.

Lubeck, S. (1989). Nested contexts. In L. Weis (Ed.), *Class, race and gender in American education.* Albany, NY: SUNY Press.

McCloud, S. (1992). *Understanding comics.* New York: Kitchen Sink Press.

Nussbaum, M. C. (1995). *Poetic justice: The literary imagination and public life.* Boston: Beacon Press.

Pinnegar, S. (1998). Introduction to methodology. In M. Hamilton (Ed.), *Reconceptualizing teacher education* (pp. 31–33). London: Falmer.

Rosenberger, C., Galman, S. A. C., & Pica, C. (2008.) Equity, complacency, compliance and conformity: Teacher educators, pre-service teachers, and social justice practices. Proposal presented at the American Educational Research Association Annual Meeting, New York City, March 24–28, 2008.

Satrapi, M. (2003). *Persepolis: The story of a childhood.* New York: Pantheon Books.

Satrapi, M. (2004). *Persepolis 2: The story of a return.* New York: Pantheon Books.

Scholes, R. (1985). *Textual powers: Literary theory and the teaching of English.* New Haven, CT: Yale University Press.

Spiegelman, A. (1986). *MAUS: A survivor's tale; My father bleeds history.* New York: Random House.

Spiegelman, A. (1987). *MAUS II: A survivor's tale; And here my troubles began.* New York: Random House.

Weber, S., & Mitchell, C. (2002). Academic literacy performance, embodiment and self-study: When the shoe doesn't fit: Death of a salesman. Play written, directed & performed by S. J. Weber & C. Mitchell. *The fourth international conference on self-study of teacher education practices.* Herstmonceux Castle, East Sussex, England.

Weber, S., & Mitchell, C. (2004). Visual artistic modes of representation for self-study. In J. J. Loughran, M. L. Hamilton, V. K. LaBoskey, & T. Russell (Eds.), *International handbook of self-study of teaching and teacher education practices.* Dordrecht: Kluwer Academic Publishers.

STEFINEE PINNEGAR AND LYNNETTE B. ERICKSON

9. UNCOVERING SELF-STUDIES IN TEACHER EDUCATION ACCREDITATION REVIEW PROCESSES

INTRODUCTION

Institutions of teacher education committed to maintaining their reputation of preparing strong teachers for public schools have tended to seek external verification that the programs they offer and the practices their faculty engage in are of a high standard. Proof of their excellence may be found in the reputations of the teachers they prepare, the level at which these teachers perform on standardized tests of knowledge, the selection of graduates as award winning teachers, and/or the academic performance of students of the teachers who graduated from a particular institution. For example, superintendents may consistently seek out graduates from a particular program and give them preference in the hiring process. Another strategy for providing verification that a program is of the highest caliber could be an external review which determines how well courses and programs do in providing teacher candidates with state of the art, research-based teacher education. In such reviews, a strong program would be able to provide evidence that teacher candidates appropriately and effectively apply theory in real teaching settings. Official accreditation agencies offer institutions an avenue to document and assert their quality based on an external evaluation. Accreditation bodies review a program at every level (unit, department, courses, faculty, clinical placements, cooperating teachers, and teacher candidates) using established professional standards, thus providing assurance that the program has the capacity to educate highly qualified teachers. Across the United States it is almost de rigueur that teacher education programs be examined and approved by an accrediting agency, usually either National Council for Accreditation of Teacher Education (NCATE) or Teacher Education Accreditation Council (TEAC), in order for state offices of education to grant licensure to teacher candidates from an institution.

Doing an institutional accreditation review of a teacher education program involves everyone associated with the education of future teachers. Obviously this includes everyone in the college of education: the dean, department chairs, faculty, clinical faculty, teaching adjuncts, secretaries, advisors, support staff, and teacher candidates. Not as obvious are the large number of people and offices within the university beyond the college of education who are fundamental in the process: general education; all departments that offer teaching majors and minors or provide support coursework, such as upper-division courses in the arts, math, physical

C. A. Lassonde, S. Galman and C. Kosnik (eds.), Self-Study Research Methodologies for Teacher Educators, 151–168.

education, health, or English; advisement counselors in every department; deans, department chairs, and individual faculty. Not to be forgotten in the accreditation process are the public school personnel: Superintendents, curriculum specialists, principals, teachers, support staff and public school students. Being involved in the accreditation process requires time, it can create frustration, and it may hinder research and creative efforts of participants. As reports are constructed and evidence gathered, implicit assumptions, theoretical orientations, policies and procedures, resource allocation and use, are made evident, sometimes painfully so. Thus, institutional reviews produce knowledge about teacher education, but much of what is learned is not often included in the final accreditation report. While this suggests that accreditation reviews potentially produce knowledge about teacher education practices that would be of interest to teacher educators, there are actually few studies based on the personal learning gained through the accreditation review process that make this knowledge explicitly public and connected to the discourse of research on teacher education (Bullough, Clark & Patterson, 2003; Craig, 2008; Manke, 2004).

JUSTIFICATION OF SELF-STUDY THROUGH INSTITUTIONAL REVIEW

Accreditation and program reviews have long been referred to as "self-studies." Loughran argues: "This institutional use of the term self-study is one that has dominated the literature for a considerable period of time and although it is used across a range of disciplines and professional fields it has also consistently been linked to evaluating institutional approaches to teacher education" (2004, p. 9). Most researchers who conduct self-studies of teacher education practices would question the accuracy or value of identifying these institutional self-studies as utilizing self-study methodology. Indeed in the *International Handbook of Self-Study and Teaching Practices (2004)*, Loughran implies that these institutional self-studies are not exemplars of self-study of teaching practices research. Yet, he also acknowledges that they share fundamental commitments with self-study research: "The expectation that beliefs and practices should be closely aligned and the self (however, that might be described from the individual through to the institutional) carries a major responsibility in establishing this alignment" (p. 9). As we considered Loughran's delineation of what would count as self-study research, if we defined the self as institutional or individual, we found it difficult to rule out these institutional self-studies based on his definition. He says that self-study is about "researching practice in order to better understand: one's self, teaching, learning, and the development of knowledge about these" (Loughran, 2004, p. 9). Institutional reviews result in institutions having a better understanding of the institution, teaching and learning practices and programs in relationship to evaluative criteria. The self-study report, then, articulates the knowledge of the institution and its practices that were developed.

With this in mind, we reviewed LaBoskey's (2004) five characteristics of self-study methodology: self-initiated and focused, improvement-aimed, interactive, exemplar-based validation, and multiple methods. Our assessment of institutional self-studies is that they are self-initiated and focused, although they may be motivated by political considerations rather than a desire to simply understand how the program is working. However, they are improvement aimed, and involve interaction and collaboration across institutional boundaries and among large numbers of people. Validation of institutional self-studies is exemplar-based and the reader, in this case the external evaluation team, determines the validity of the study. While data are often reported numerically and may be entered into statistical analysis, a large portion of the data are words rather than numbers and typical qualitative methodologies are applied to their analysis to quantify them.

Thus, as we reviewed our participation in institutional reviews, we found that both LaBoskey's and Loughran's specifications accurately describe our experiences in the institutional self-study process. Yet, like Loughran, we do not think these institutional self-studies exhibit self-study methodology. We wondered what characteristics of institutional self-studies made them distinct from self-study research methodology. The criteria from Bullough and Pinnegar (2001) offer some indicators of what distinguishes these institutional self-studies from self-study research. They posit that self-study attends carefully to whole persons in contexts; fresh perspectives on established truths, an inside look at participant's thinking and feeling and interrogates relationships, contradictions and limits. In other words, makes private theory public.

This making of private theory public is one area in which we feel that institutional self-studies typically differ from self-study research methodology. The central function of an institutional self-study is to provide an argument accompanied by data that a teacher preparation program meets standards of practice external to itself. They are driven by political considerations, such as licensure, funding, and status. In fact, while self-study research makes the private public, institutional self-studies may be constructed in ways that conceal both. Institutional self-study reports are composed to communicate competence rather than develop insights from troubles and trials. Institutional self-studies articulate the conceptual framework of a teacher preparation program and provide evidence of where that program succeeds and falls short; however, the focus is not on understanding, but rather on accounting (TEAC, http://www.teac.org/accreditation/inquirybrief/claimsrationale/claimimportant.asp; NCATE, http://www.ncate.org/). While those who produce the document may emerge from an institutional self-study with intimate knowledge about factors that contribute to the success or failure of a teacher education program, the report itself may be limited in its distribution and obscure institutional self-understanding rather than increasing it.

Our argument here is not that the processes, understandings, collaboration, and interpretation faculty engage in when conducting institutional self-studies are drastically different from those of programmatic self-study methodology. Instead we argue that the institutional self-study report does not represent and make public the private understandings gleaned from engaging in the level of review and questioning required to produce that report and participants may not keep track of the personal reflections that could provide deeper insight. The process of accreditation examines teacher education in a particular context, at a particular place in time, and has the potential to produce knowledge about human and program relationships, fundamental and valued knowledge for preparing teachers in that place, as well as insight into the missing links (Hoban, 2005) in teacher education. Indeed if we utilize a functional definition of self-study as an individual's study of practice in order to improve it, self-study researchers could utilize their engagement in the processes of accreditation to conduct and produce self-studies of teacher education that have merit and value. Such studies could give us insight into the processes in teacher education generally, a more holistic view of teacher education as an enterprise, as well as a more complex perception about individual aspects of a teacher education program and the relationships among them.

Institutional self-studies become a context from which profound and ineffable knowledge of teacher education could be mined. Accreditation could become a process of self-study research if self-study researchers working individually or collectively explored the questions, dilemmas, paradoxes, and challenges that are uncovered in the process of institutional review. Such researchers would connect their wonderings about their teacher education programs and practices to the larger conversation of teacher education research, provide evidence supporting the understandings that emerged, and articulate the ways in which taking action could or did lead not only to self-improvement, but also to knowledge of teacher education. For example, studying the process by which a college develops a conceptual framework has the potential to provide insight into how knowledge grows collaboratively, how conflicting and competing assumptions about what constitutes good teaching and teacher education become harmonized, and how attending carefully to the conceptual framework of a program when designing individual courses impacts one's own teaching and understanding of teaching and teacher education. All of these examples are self-studies that a faculty could conduct while engaging in an institutional self-study.

SELF-STUDY METHODOLOGY

Other chapters in this book provide guidance to self-study researchers by presenting exemplars of their own self-study research and revealing the processes, designs, procedures, and standards for judging quality, as well as the analytic strengths and limitations of that methodology. Unlike others, this chapter will identify the ways in which teacher educators engaged in institutional self-studies might capitalize on the planning, observation, reflection, data collection and reporting central to such endeavors to conduct self-studies on their experiences.

Most teacher educators, at least in the United States, have engaged at some level in the institutional review process. Yet they do not appear to use these experiences as a site for self-study research. Perhaps these institutional reviews do not become self-study research because of the political nature of the task itself. Perhaps these institutional reviews do not become self-studies because they do not provide new insights or alternative ways of conceptualizing traditional experiences. Perhaps the process seems so routinized that the self-study researcher is at a loss to think of how other teacher educators could gain anything from an account of the process.

Perhaps the time commitment for conducting these reviews is so great that the teacher educators have little time to think about turning the process into self-study research. However, having conducted and participated in institutional reviews we think it is more likely that after the process is over and the report is submitted, the teacher educators begins to reflect on what they learned. At that moment they begin to wonder why they did not create a self-study. As insights from the review occur to them, they realize that they did not collect the data that would allow them to explore those insights more systematically and provide a basis from which to make assertions for practice or understanding. For example, during our last institutional study we were involved in requesting data from departments across the university as well as within the college. To our surprise, gaining that data turned out to be a monumental task requiring repeated phone messages, emails, office visits, requests from the dean of the college of education, and finally a mandate from the academic vice president. In retrospect, we realized how much this process taught us about the uneven status of teacher education in the university. But we had not written field notes documenting our experience in obtaining the reports, nor had we kept accurate records of messages, emails, office visits, nor a careful timeline of when reports were returned, after which intervention, and by whom. Thus, while we had insights into power relationships within the university, we did not have data or evidence to explore those relationships or the development of our understanding of them in ways that could legitimately contribute to research on teacher education policy and politics.

CREATING SELF-STUDIES WITHIN INSTITUTIONAL REVIEWS

Often when teacher education faculty are asked to participate in an accreditation review, the request comes in the midst of an already complex, demanding, professional life. Such teacher educators may be overwhelmed by, as well as conflicted about the competing obligations of teaching, scholarship, and service and their own personal commitment to the improvement of teaching and learning in public schools. The time demands of university requirements therefore exist in tension with personal foundational commitments to the education of children and youth, which not only require time, but also the development of intimate reciprocal ongoing relationships with the public schools. Given the complex positioning of their roles, teacher educators, when asked to engage in an institutional review, may focus narrowly on just completing the mandatory aspects of the task because they do not have the time or energy to do anything else. Frankly, we need to assert an aphorism used to explain a business orientation toward productivity—"work smarter not harder." Simultaneously conducting an institutional accreditation review and a self-study of teacher education practice research project allows teacher educators to work smarter and harmonize what may be considered to be competing or conflicting demands.

Being Pro-Active and Double-Visioned

The standardized nature of accreditation reviews demands that much of the task is specified and pre-determined, such as kinds of assessments, resource allocations, external review visits, and even the report itself. All elements in the process are clearly spelled out and are mandatory. It is also clearly understood that those directly responsible for the review spend inordinate amounts of time at national and local level meetings that focus simply on learning these requirements. Therefore, in order to do a self-study of practice in the midst of the mandates and time commitments required, teacher educators need to be proactive and double-visioned. By proactive we mean that teacher educators plan ahead and anticipate possibilities and opportunities for research. This calls for taking action prior to and during the accreditation process rather than reflecting in retrospect on the missed opportunities. By double-visioned we mean that teacher educators look at the dual possibilities of developing understandings, keeping records, collecting data, and engaging in processes, thus enabling them to uncover the self-study within the institutional review structure. When teacher educators participating in accreditation reviews decide to be double-visioned, they look at data both in terms of the institutional value and its role as evidence for a self-study. Teacher educators who are proactive and double-visioned look ahead for possible extensions of data being collected and have questions that increase understandings brought to light in the process. In other words, they consciously anticipate possibilities for extending understanding about teacher education and teacher education programs from their perspective.

Conceptual Tools

We provide two conceptual tools to guide researchers in simultaneously engaging in self-study of teacher education practices research project while participating in an institutional review. We will begin by introducing and then describing the Parallel Cycle of Self-Study. The cycle is essential for teacher educator researchers attempting to capitalize on an accreditation review and supports them in transforming any aspect of their practice into a self-study. In other words, if teacher educators embrace this cycle and utilize its phases they can continually conduct self-studies of their professional practices as teachers, advisors, supervisors, and administrators. In this chapter we invite readers to be proactive and double-visioned imagining the ways in which they can use these conceptual tools to exploit institutional reviews as sites for self-studies of teacher education practices research projects.

PARALLEL CYCLE OF SELF-STUDY

Introduction

This cycle (see Figure 1) provides practical and conceptual support to teacher educators who decide to conduct a self-study during an accreditation review.

Rather than being based on the accreditation review process, this tool serves teacher educators by identifying the on-going inquiry process that can underlie the accreditation review process if researchers are willing to be double-visioned and pro-active in the review process. As a whole, the cycle draws attention to the need for teacher educators to develop an awareness of the possibilities of doing self-study research during the review. It directs them to consider the development of nascent strategies for data collection that make personal record keeping an on-going and omnipresent aspect of their roles in the review process. It prompts them to continually seek out and identify questions. It reminds them whenever they are engaged in data collection for the accreditation review to also conceptualize those documents as data for a self-study. Finally, it invites them to explore the underlying elements and tensions they observe during the process and utilize the previous phases to support self-study researchers in being able to uncover the tensions and make their understandings public. This cycle therefore both holistically and simultaneously supports teacher educators in conducting self-study research during institutional reviews by helping them take advantage of the review process.

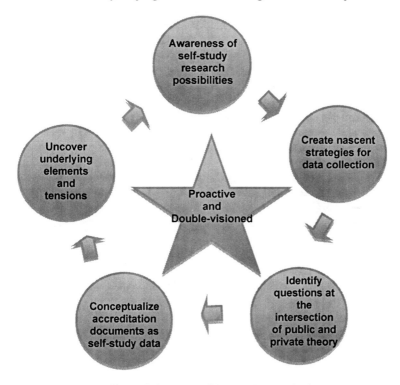

Figure 1. Institutional Review Inquiry Cycle

We have labeled this cycle "parallel" because of the way in which it always occurs alongside and in relationship to responsibilities and activities teacher educators regularly engage in as part of their practice, particularly when parti-cipating in accreditation reviews. In some situations self-study researchers experience themselves as a living contradiction or become intrigued about some aspect of their practice and decide to design and conduct a self-study research project targeting those specific queries (e.g. Manke, 2004). However, we know we do not typically engage in formal on-going self-studies. Yet, every semester through our interactions with our students and colleagues, our assignments, and in enacting our varied roles, we learn new things about ourselves, and our teacher education practices. Since this learning emerges in our day-to-day interactions within our context, usually without any formal record, opportunities for developing self-studies of practice escape us. Institutional reviews are the most visible example of this phenomenon.

Exploring the Cycle

Many looking at the cycle may think of the elements happening in no particular order; however, as we considered our own practice there seemed to be a natural progression and order for each of the phases. For example, researchers need to begin the process by being aware of the possibility of doing self-study research before conceptualizing strategies for data collection that become a regular part of academic life. As researchers journal, keep track of schedules, or track minutes from meetings they can begin to identify the tensions between public and private theory that lead to thinking about how formal documents are potential data sources for exploring those tensions and questions. This then leads researchers to uncover the elements and sources of tension that are embedded in that data or emerge from questions at the intersections of public and private theory. The beauty of this is that the cycle is recursive and as practices unfold and researchers engage in this Parallel Cycle of Self-Study they may revisit each phase of the process several times. We recommit to the data collection strategies we have developed or create new ones. We reconsider the questions at the intersection of public and private theory. We rethink the formal documents we collect and their potential as data. And, we revisit the underlying tensions and elements of our practice.

Activate Awareness of Self-Study Possibilities

As simple as it seems, making the decision to be double-visioned during the accreditation review and committing to it, as an opportunity for self-study research is the single most important element in being proactive, positioning the researcher to conduct and complete the study. Generally self-study research begins with wonderings about some aspect of practice or identifying a living contradiction. However, when invited to participate in the accreditation review, the teacher educator's attention may first go to the processes and requirements imposed by the review. Members of an accreditation team typically are so over- run with a torrent of requirements, processes, and documents they may not be able to think of anything other than planning and organizing their portion of the review. As they examine those requirements, they become aware that they are going to be attending meetings; observing interactions between the college, various departments, and public schools; considering faculty syllabi and assignments; and collecting information about various programs and practices related to teacher education. They realize that they will be analyzing and interpreting data from various assessments. In this moment teacher educators could become overwhelmed by the task of accreditation and the high stakes for their institution. In contrast, they might consider the opportunity the accreditation review provides for gaining new understandings about the practices of teacher education. In order to take advantage of the research potential that participation in an accreditation provides it is at this point that double-visioned, proactive teacher educators set in motion a research cycle that parallels the accreditation review process by activating their awareness that this is an excellent site for self-study. This means that in the first iteration they are cognizant that the experiences they'll have in an accreditation review will result in their learning new things about teacher education, particularly their own practices both personal and institutional. Activating this awareness then results in a commitment to use the accreditation review experience as a site for self-study.

Create Nascent Strategies for Data Collection

During our last accreditation review, we recall standing at the door of the evidence room and thinking, "How did we decide to arrange this room and the evidence the way we did?" "What does that say about our assumptions about demonstrating the quality of a teacher education program?" In that moment we realized that we had *thought* of how to design the room, we had *talked* about how to design the room, and even *drawn* diagrams of how to design the room prior to ever asking those questions out loud. All of these things would have counted as data that could be analyzed and thereby utilized to help us understand our assumptions about how to communicate quality in teacher education programs. Unfortunately we had not collected any of that data. Thus, while we could say some things about it, we had no evidence from which to speak. Therefore, as soon as teacher educator researchers commit to using a particular part of practice, like an accreditation review, as a site for self-study they need to proactively think about informal record-keeping and documentation. At this time, this may seem to be a simple record of their experience but it might later become valuable data.

An implicit requirement underlying the nascent strategies phase is the commitment of the teacher educator participating in the review to continually construct a potential record using identified strategies, even if there is not a question of deep concern apparent at the moment driving the data collection. Therefore, rather than curiosity or intellectual engagement motivating teacher educators to develop this documentation, it is their professional conviction that questions will emerge and those data collection strategies will provide the evidence needed to investigate the questions that will emerge.

This phase involves researchers who, having decided to use this situation as an opportunity for doing self-study, intentionally put in place strategies for collecting information about the experience that could subsequently serve as data. Because of the demands of the accreditation review process on teacher educators, these nascent strategies need to be simple and easily included as part of their day-to-day life. For example, teacher educators may commit to taking more detailed notes and minutes than they typically may have done. It might also involve writing more in their planners about the specifics, details, and accomplishments of meetings. We have labeled these data collection processes and procedures as nascent strategies to emphasize the fact that they should not be invasive. They should be unobtrusive, take minimal time, and be easily incorporated in regular duties.

Identify Questions at the Intersection of Public and Private Theory

One of the reasons to utilize the Parallel Cycle of Self-Study is that during the process of an institutional review researchers will eventually develop burning questions, deep insights, or experience themselves as living contradictions. The high stakes nature of institutional reviews guarantees that most of the questions to be answered are of a public nature. In the process of the review the researchers will be continually aware of the ways in which public questions call forth private understandings and deep concerns about teacher education and its institutional practices. Furthermore, institutional reviews—preparation meetings, assessments, reports, as well as the visit—are very public occasions. Within these public occasions the private beliefs and practices of teacher educators collide and, as a result, become more visible. Living contradictions abound. Within this space where the private and the public intersect there is great potential to develop new understandings that can inform teacher education. Teacher educators who are self-study researchers engaged in institutional reviews observe those points of intersection carefully and mine them for personally meaningful, practical questions then utilize the nascent data as well as the accreditation documents to develop assertions for action and understanding that can inform the research conversation.

Reconceptualize Accreditation Documents as Self-Study Data

From our own experience, researchers will not typically have a burning self-study question at the outset of the institutional review process. The reconceptualizing data phase refers to reconsidering data collected for the institutional review as evidence for exploring questions when they do emerge. In contrast, the nascent strategies phase refers to the researchers designing simple, non-invasive methods of capturing their experiences and representing them, as a result of an on-going commitment to collect data about the accreditation review process that could be used retrospectively as part of a self-study inquiry.

We recognize that these two phases are interchangeable and even simultaneous at times. While an effort to reconceptualize accreditation data can potentially direct researchers toward questions and help them identify or refine them, identifying self-study research questions can provide insights that lead researchers to reconsider the accreditation documents and use the data collected to respond to the self-study questions now being explored. In the first scenario above, the reconceptualization phase would precede the identifying questions phase. However, at the point in conducting accreditation reviews when teacher educators begin collecting and organizing evidence to support the claims made in or required by the review, they are usually not yet positioned to identify or focus on specific self-study questions. In fact, it is only after the teacher educator researchers identify a question, or even an ill-formed query, that they are positioned to seriously consider reconceptualizing the data they are collecting as evidence. Furthermore, in subsequent cycles refining of the question and making it more specific will guide researchers in considering wider possibilities for how the data from the accreditation review also serve as data for the self-study. For this reason, our cycle lists the identifying question phase prior to the reconceptualizing accreditation documents phase.

Accreditation reviews require units to collect evidence of teacher candidates' knowledge, skills, and dispositions (NCATE) or evidence to support the claims about how competent, caring, and qualified (TEAC) their teacher candidates are. Reports not only require data pertaining to the backgrounds of the candidates, but also the backgrounds of university faculty, including those in teacher education, as well as teachers and children in the public schools where candidates participate in field experiences. They also require reports about the relationship of individual departments within the school of education such as educational leadership, elementary education, early childhood education, language and speech pathology, instructional technology and psychology, and special education. Accreditation requires disclosure of a wide variety of resource data such as salary distribution, program costs, allocation of support funds, provisions for library and computing technology, compensation for public school mentors, and so on. Reviews require the unit being accredited to develop data management systems along with facilities for displaying and storing evidence, reports, and records. This results in a large body of facts, figures, text, diagrams, and documents that could be accessed to consider questions about teaching and teacher education not necessarily addressed in the accreditation review and even potentially tangential to the review. For example, a self-study might be focused on issues of the value and worth of a teacher educator. The researchers might use the economic data available, alumni surveys, or student exit interviews in relationship to other kinds of nascent data such as journaling, minutes from meetings, or personal reflections to explore this question and to trouble notions of value and value-added.

A necessary step in reconceptualizing accreditation documents as data is for self-study researchers to list and define the data and documents they will collect and produce as part of the review process. These lists should articulate how documents, reports, charts, and artifacts could act as data for refined questions posed for a self-study. This step allows the researchers to think strategically about the data to be collected, or in other words, to be intentional and systematic about how this data might be used to inform a self-study. One way to be double-visioned and proactive is to raise questions throughout the data collection process: what does the data mean, what does it say about the program, what does it obscure, and what does or does not it reveal about the place of the teacher educator in the program. Researchers should use nascent strategies to bring together the accreditation documents with the questions and puzzles that are at the edge of their consciousnesses: make notes about reports that intrigue, seek evidence in the data for insights from journaling, highlight data that surprises, investigate why documents are edited as they are, or question interpretations that seem off the mark. An example of a self-study that could emerge from the integration of nascent and accreditation data is one that looks carefully at the final 100-page accreditation report and its relationship to the 300-page document from which it was reduced. A series of reflective notes about the edits of the document raise awareness that certain kinds of details are consistently eliminated from, rather than condensed into the report. As the report is edited to align with the severe word count and page limit restrictions, a flattened story, more aligned with the standard script of teacher education programs, emerges. This self-study would explore what those eliminations reveal about what is and is not an acceptable story of teacher education within a specific program.

Uncover Underlying Elements and Tensions

Sometimes self-studies do not probe deeply enough into the intersections between public and private theory (Bullough and Pinnegar, 2001). As a result the researchers do not uncover underlying elements and tensions that provocatively answer the "so what" question that is vital if self-study of teacher educator practices research is to contribute significantly to the larger research conversation about teaching and teacher education. Being successful in producing strong self-studies, as part of the accreditation review process requires that the researchers push analysis of data to deeper and deeper levels. This kind of probing allows the self-study researchers to develop substantive research contributions. In the example above, we suggested that the researchers began to explore or question the relationship of the initial document to the final report during the accreditation process. This suggested, as we have implied elsewhere, that the researchers might cycle through phases of the Parallel Cycle of Self-Study more that one time. Embracing the recursive nature of the cycle would enable the researchers to reconsider data collection strategies, contrast between public and private theory, data produced for the report, and analysis that uncovers the underlying elements and tensions of teacher education more than just once. This should push the researchers' analysis to deeper levels allowing them to not only answer personal questions but also questions of importance to the teacher education enterprise as a whole. This process allows researchers to wrestle with tensions between that larger story of teacher education and their own particular story, as well as the implicit relationships between them.

STAGES OF SELF-STUDY INQUIRY PROCESSES CHART

Introduction

Utilizing the Parallel Cycle of Self-Study within the various stages of the accreditation can provide guidance and structure for researchers who want to attend to the opportunities for self-study research inherent in the accreditation review process.

Transforming Institutional Review Stages into Self-Study Inquiries

Our experience suggests that it may be difficult to be proactive and double-visioned at the very onset of a review process. We argue that this is a natural state of affairs. We further assert that researchers should not assume that if they did not begin a self-study at the very beginning of an accreditation that they forfeit their opportunity for doing self-study research on this particular accreditation review. Indeed, researchers do not have to feel that they have "missed the boat" if they do not begin at the beginning! The first phase of the Parallel Cycle of Self-Study calls attention to this very fact since the first phase is activating awareness of the possibility that the accreditation review, or some aspect of it, could become a self-study project. This suggests that teacher educators could, at any time, embrace the Parallel Cycle of Self-Study and begin a research project.

The specific requirements of accreditations may vary; yet, as we have considered the accreditation reviews we are aware of (e.g. NCATE, TEAC, Northwestern, and state teacher education accreditation), there appear to be similar requirements in all of them. To support readers in understanding the stages of accreditation review we turn at this point to definitions and descriptions of each of these stages.
- *Set the inquiry*—Establish the conceptual framework or determine the goals/claims for the teacher education program that will guide the review.
- *Defining evidence*—Identify the materials, facts, and details to be collected and determine how they provide verification for assertions.
- *Collecting evidence*—Create and utilize processes and structures for systematic collection and management of information from the assessments.
- *Transforming evidence*—Analyze data collected and transform it into actionable information.
- *Interpreting evidence*—Link evidence back to the conceptual framework, standards, and claims leading to data-driven decisions within the program.
- *Procedural display*—Create documents, presentations, and settings that positively represent the institution in terms of the program and goals.

Stages of Inquiry Process Framework

Often self-study researchers use an inquiry planner developed by Whitehead and McNiff (2003) to guide their construction of self-studies. The planner supports the researchers in imagining an issue to study and more completely articulating that issue. It helps them identify what would count as evidence and determine how to proceed in conducting the self-study. This Stages of Inquiry Process Framework (see table 1) can serve a similar function for those who want to use accreditation reviews as a site for self-study of teacher education practices. The framework lists and provides a description of the stages which reminds readers what occurs within each stage. Researchers are then positioned to identify topics or questions that might be particularly fruitful lines of study within the stage. In following the framework researchers are then pushed to link their private understandings of the questions and topics they have identified to public theory. In other words, researchers are asked to reconsider what they already know about the topic and what research in the field of teacher education or other areas of the social sciences have already suggested about it. Next, researchers are asked to contemplate both sources of nascent and accreditation data collection that could inform the study. This step in the framework reminds researchers of the need to utilize nascent data collection strategies during their participation in the review. It also prompts them to think more deeply about how accreditation reports can be reconceptualized to provide evidence for the topic under investigation. Finally, the framework not only encourages researchers to think strategically about the qualitative data analysis methods to be used to examine the data identified and collected, but also to push that analysis to deeper levels so that it reveals underlying themes and tensions in processes of teacher education.

Exploration of an Example of a Self-Study Based in Accreditation Review—Transforming the Evidence

While self-study of teacher education practices research is a simple idea (studying one's own practice in order to improve it), the conceptualization and execution of such studies is not always straightforward. In our own practice, illustrations and examples of work by others have helped us develop our own skills as self-study researchers. For this reason, guided by the Stages of Inquiry Process Framework, we turn to an exploration of an example of a possible self-study based in an accreditation review. In the table itself, we have provided an illustration of a potential study for each stage. We have listed a question under "possible studies" and filled in details in each of the other features. Because of space limitations we will unpack and articulate only one of the potential self-studies of teacher education practices research outlined in the table.

In the stage of inquiry identified as *Transforming the Evidence,* teacher educator researchers are engaged in analyzing the data formally collected for the accreditation review and transforming it into actionable information. In considering possible studies, we identified issues concerning how representing data impacts our personal understanding of teacher education in relation to the claims our own program makes about the education of teacher candidates. We also considered how raw data becomes actionable information that can inform our own practice. Further, we questioned how our engagement in transforming data into actionable information leads us to understand the role of assessment in guiding our teacher education practices. We realized that the very systems of data collection and representation of the data we chose to construct might reveal something about our engagement in the accreditation process and our understanding of judgment in relationship to those processes. We posed this question under *Possible Studies,* "What institutional values and ethics are implicit in the conceptual framework or claims, how is it revealed in the data, and what is my relationship to those?"

Table 1. Stages of Inquiry Process Framework

Stages of Inquiry Process	Description	Possible Studies	Linking of Private Practice to Public Theory	Evidence for the Study	Data Analysis for Deep Understandings
Set the Inquiry	Establish the conceptual framework or determine the goals and claims for the teacher education program that will guide the review.	What is the evolution of a teacher education program in relation to my beliefs and practices?	History of teacher education; teacher education practices; teacher effectiveness; teacher education programs	Past and current documents about your program; narratives (archived and personal); reflections on your practice	Shallow: Practices are now the same as in previous generations. Deep: The evolution of a teacher education idea in the history of teacher education and in your practice.
Defining Evidence	Identify the materials, facts, and details to be collected and determine how they provide verification for assertions.	What is the relationship between what is valued in a program, what is valued by accreditation bodies, and how do those match what I value?	Accreditation; moral and ethical aspects; quality teacher education; teacher preparation or training	Accreditation guidelines (NCATE, TEAC, etc.); personal reflections; journaling; conceptual framework/claims documents; field notes from formal and informal accreditation meetings	Shallow: Checklist comparing accreditation requirements, program requirements, and personal views. Deep: Examination of themes and patterns of tensions between accreditation, program values, and personal beliefs and values concerning teacher education.
Collecting Evidence	Create and utilize processes and structures for systematic collection and management of information from the assessments.	How does a program collectively negotiate what will count as evidence to support assertions put forth in the conceptual framework/claims in relationship to my own understanding of quality teacher education?	Quality teacher education; collaboration and negotiation; program outcomes; aims and objectives; educational quality	Artifacts (notes, posters, report outs, graphics, doodles, etc.) from committee or faculty meetings focused on developing or understanding the CF/claim; field notes from meetings; minutes; reflections and journal entries; conceptual framework or claims earlier and later document drafts	Shallow: Describe what ideas came from what persons and documents. Deep: Careful process tracing of how ideas started and were transformed through the course of the conversations and ideas emerged and which were purged as a result of the negotiations.

Table 1. Continued

Transforming Evidence	Analyze data collected and transform it into actionable information.	What institutional values and ethics are implicit in the CF or claims, how is it revealed in the data, and what is my relationship to those?	Quality teacher education; morals, values and ethics in teacher education	Journaling, logs, memoing, mtg. notes, final reports and your own response to them, narratives from self and others; CF, claims and goals, publicly distributed descriptions of the program or CF	Shallow: Document only the positive elements of the CF. OR Do an analysis of the program and the results are an un-nuanced CF. Deep: Careful interrogation of the CF themes, the themes underlying the actual practices of the department, and my own beliefs and practices.
Interpreting the Evidence	Link evidence back to the CF, standards, and claims leading to data-driven decisions within the program.	What does the data provide evidence of and how does that match the CF/claims and my own beliefs about quality teacher preparation?	Achievement measures; attitude measures; evaluation; teacher education; theories of learning to teach	Annotated list of data to be collected; conceptual framework/claims documents and artifacts; personal reflections & memos of my understanding of the CF/claims	Shallow: Chart overview showing match/mismatch between evidence, CF/claims, and personal theory. Deep: Analysis that shows what strengths and weaknesses/characteristics the evidence demonstrates and the tensions between that representation and the public and private theories of learning to teach represented by the teacher educator self and the program.
Procedural Display	Create documents, presentations, and settings that positively represent the institution in terms of the program and goals.	What is my understanding of the politics and power relationships in teacher education as revealed by the process of creating documents, presentations, and settings for procedural display?	Critical theory; teacher education policy; higher education; aims and objectives of education; program outcomes; accreditation	Journaling; field notes of meetings and interactions around accreditation; logs; memos; minutes; photographs; accreditation report documents	Shallow: A narrative plotline that presents the interactions and contributions of all participants involved in the accreditation process. Deep: Careful analysis using positioning theory to identify the assumptions and articulate the overlapping and contradictory plotlines concerning roles, rights, and responsibilities of the various participants in the preparation of teachers.

As we review qualitative teacher education research studies for publication, we are often dismayed at the shallowness of the data analysis. During our critique of studies, it is not unusual for us to identify deeper themes in the data than those the authors have arrived at. We feel this is particularly so when researchers fail to uncover the underlying themes and tensions. One of the features of the framework asserts data analysis for deep understandings. By recursively asking simple questions of their data, researchers can develop more conceptually meaningful assertions for action and understanding. Strategies of analysis that move to deeper understanding include multiple iterations in the analysis cycle, attention to the tensions between personal belief and public theory, and representations that are simultaneously parsimonious and complex. For example, a study of the institutional values and ethics implicit in the conceptual framework as supported by data and in relationship to our own values and ethics could lead to a shallow documentation of only the positive elements of the conceptual framework or a simple re-reporting of the aspects of the conceptual framework as findings of the self-study research project. In contrast, a deeper analysis would provide a careful interrogation of the conceptual framework themes in tension with the actual practices of a department evidenced in the data and in relationship to the researchers' personal beliefs and practices. This kind of analysis would produce a nuanced counter-balancing of the public and the private and the theoretical and the actual in relationship to the conceptual framework.

CONCLUSION

Whenever institutions engage in accreditation reviews, institutional and personal boundaries and plotlines bump up against each other in ways that make the hidden and covert, as well as the explicit and overt, highly visible. As a result institutional reviews are a critical site for reframing and reconceptualizing, as well as intensifying understanding of programs and practices in teacher education and our own personal theories and assumptions about our practices as teacher educators. Ironically, even though participating in and conducting reviews provide an amazing arena for developing new understandings and assertions for action that could transform, teacher education accreditation reviews are seldom used as sites for research by teacher educators. We believe this is so because participating in and conducting institutional accreditation reviews are fraught with constraining require-ments. They are politically sensitive, time-consuming, and usually personally taxing. Without strategic and practical guidance concerning the design and implementation of research studies in the midst of such a challenging and politically charged experience, this will probably continue to be the case. Our effort here has been to identify two conceptual tools that can guide self-study researchers. When teacher educators utilize them, they can simplify the process of simultaneously attending to both accreditation reviews and self-study research, and help overcome some of the crippling ambiguity inherent in such efforts.

REFERENCES

Bullough, R. V., Jr., Clark, D. C., & Patterson, R. S. (2003). Getting in step: Accountability, accreditation and the standardization of teacher education in the United States. *Journal of Education for Teaching, 29*(1), 35–51.

Bullough, R. V., Jr., & Pinnegar, S. (2001). Guidelines for quality in autobiographical forms of self-study research. *Educational Researcher, 30*(3), 13–21.

Craig, C. (2008). Change, changing, and being changed: A study of self in the throes of multiple accountability demands In M. L. Heston, D. L. Tidwell, K. K. East, L. M. Fitzgerald (Eds.). *Seventh International Conference on Self-Study of Teacher Education Practices. Pathways to Change in Teacher Education: Dialogue, Diversity and Self-Study* (pp. 87–90). Cedar Falls, Iowa: University of Northern Iowa.

G. Hoban (Ed.). 2005 The missing links in teacher education design: Developing a conceptual framework. Netherlands: Springer.

Beck, C. & Kosnik, C. (2002). Professors and the practicum: Involvement of university faculty in preservice practicum supervision. *Journal of Teacher Education, 53*(1), 6–19.

LaBoskey, V. (2004). The methodology of self-study and tis theoretical underpinnings (pp. 817–870). In J. Loughran, M. Hamilton, V. LaBoskey, & T. Russell (Eds.) *International Handbook of Self-Study of Teaching and Teacher Education Practices*. Dordrecht: The Netherlands, Kluwer Academic Publishers

Loughran, J. (2004). A history and context of self-study of teaching and teacher education practices (pp. 7–40). In J. Loughran, M. Hamilton, V. LaBoskey, & T. Russell (Eds.) *International Handbook of Self-Study of Teaching and Teacher Education Practices*. Dordrecht: The Netherlands, Kluwer Academic Publishers.

Manke, M. (2004). Maintaining personal values in the NCATE process. In *Reverberating self-study conversations: Seeing and re-seeing in the process of acting, knowing and informing*. Symposium at the annual meeting of the American Educational Research Meeting, San Diego, CA.

National Council for Accreditation of Teacher Education (NCATE) http://www.ncate.org/

Teacher Education Accreditation Council (TEAC) http://www.teac.org/accreditation/inquirybrief/claimsrationale/claimimportant.asp

McNiff, J. & Whitehead, J. (2003). You and your action research project. London: RoutledgeFalmer

10. CO/AUTOETHNOGRAPHY

Investigating Teachers in Relation

INTRODUCTION

March 28, 2008

My class was so different tonight. Usually it is filled with the banter of teachers sharing stories about their classroom, their families, and their lessons. Tonight the class was quiet as we discussed their proposals for their self-study/action research projects. My students (teacher leaders) are struggling to figure out which voice to use as they write. I encouraged them to stop writing from the voice of academics or Researchers with a capital R and start sharing their own stories- with strong knowledge and authority as teachers. We talked about how they feel they need to put on the academic impersonal voice because they are writing about research, and that's how researchers sound. They actually said "our own voices, our own stories could make us sound informal and dumb." I now realize that I have to help them release their teacher voices and hence their own real stories and struggles, not a canned version of what they think they should write. This is scary territory for them. One teacher remarked that she is scared because what I am asking is for her to reveal herself and be vulnerable. They were so quiet today. I think I am really pushing them. (Correspondence with Lesley)

March 28, 2008

I was sitting close to one of my student teachers at a presentation by an outside speaker last week. She arrived with a large stack of tests which she graded during the presentation. She was, to my mind, "playing" being a teacher - including the rolling of the eyes at the idiocy of her students and the use of a red pen. It made me think of my first year teaching and how I consciously donned the role of teacher, meaning all the while to keep it distant from the real me. Then I thought of one of our conversations years ago when we laughed as we remembered how we did actually become different people after teaching for a while: Both surprised at ourselves when, now unconsciously being teachers, we crossed the road to interact with teenagers we did not know. (Correspondence with Monica)

People are "story-telling animals" (MacIntyre, 1981; Bruner, 2002; Swift, 1985). Teachers tell stories about teaching in order to make sense of their experience.

C. A. Lassonde, S. Galman and C. Kosnik (eds.), *Self-Study Research Methodologies for Teacher Educators, 169–186.*

These stories are permissible in the teacher's lounge, the bathroom, or at the local happy hour. Teachers are comfortable telling each other stories when they are in their teacher roles. Storytelling, in their eyes, has its place. In the academy and within the research arena, however, stories are seen as anecdotal not "hard data." They are seen as informal and of lesser importance than impersonal theories and research. Co/autoethnography is a bridge between these two arenas: a method that prioritizes the stories of teachers as ways of making sense or theorizing about teaching, while not discounting the culture of teaching that includes the use of quantitative and so-called scientific research. Co/autoethnography places knowledge construction and theorizing in the thick of teaching and reflection, rather than seeing teaching and knowledge about teaching as separate entities. In accordance with the pedagogical nature of self study, it exists "at the intersection between theory and practice, research and pedagogy" (LaBoskey, 2007, p. 827). It interweaves multiple knowledges including teachers' stories and experiences, theories, and research (Zeichner, & Liston, 1996; Cochran-Smith & Lytle, 1993). Co/autoethnography exists at the intersection of these knowledges and this is where it gains its power. Our work starts with the privileging of teacher educators' own stories of their experience teaching, but with the understanding that these are not transparent or unmediated.

DESCRIPTION OF METHODOLOGY: WHAT IS CO/AUTOETHNOGRAPHY FOR TEACHER EDUCATION?

So what is our methodology? It is important, as van Manen (1990) reminds us, to think about the framework aligned with our method when considering methodology. A methodology is informed by fundamental philosophical positions on ontology, epistemology and metaphysics. Our methodology is an expression of fundamental philosophical orientations that ground our research method, tying the way we conduct research to our teaching. In this chapter we look at both our method and our methodology using concrete examples from some of our self-studies.

We started this chapter with short narratives written recently to foreground the importance of autobiographical narratives to our work, but also to illustrate aspects of our methodology. These extracts from our communication with each other are part of the larger story of what it means to each of us to be a teacher educator. We understand what teaching means, and therefore how we might go about our practice more effectively by the stories we tell to each other about our practice. What we mean by teacher educator is a teacher who teaches others about how to be teachers. Thus a fundamental concept is that of a teacher. By this we understand that a teacher is a person with a specific set of characteristics and attitudes. While it may seem banal or even pedantic to say that teachers are people it is nonetheless crucial. First and foremost teaching is an intentional act undertaken by people. While this does not exhaust the possibilities or come close to providing an adequate definition of teacher, by focusing on teaching as an intentional personal activity we keep in mind that it is people that teach. Fundamental to the way we approach self-study is the idea that a person is a persisting being, one who has a history, and whose identity is complex (Palmer, 1998). Thus, Monica is a teacher, a mother, a friend and so forth. When she is teaching, her understanding of herself as teacher is often foremost but she brings all her identities to the classroom with her. Our self-study method is rooted in a methodology which takes these understandings of what it means to be a teacher as a person as fundamental. This idea of the teacher as a person with complex identities that are grounded in and informed by past experiences raises questions about what makes each person the person she is, that is, what constitutes her personal identity. Here we focus on the idea that what makes us the particular people we are, and thus the particular teachers we are, is what we care about: those things with which we identify (Frankfurt, 1998).

TEACHER IN RELATION

Our teaching relies upon the relationships we nurture with our students. Our concept of person is essentially that of person-in-relation. As teachers, we care deeply about our students. Whether we are guiding, critiquing, or disagreeing with students, we strive to do so carefully with respect and thoughtfulness (Noddings, 1984). Our teaching involves being in practice with others. Who these others are will vary. They will include our students, our fellow teachers, our administrators, and our communities. The important point is that the concept of person implied by the idea that teaching is a relation between persons is that of a person who cannot be understood except in relation to others. Thus if we are to study ourselves, to engage in self-study for the improvement of our practice, we need to examine ourselves with others. The importance of others in our practice and therefore the study of our practice undergird our methodology.

An important corollary of the idea of teacher as person-in-relation is that teaching, being a teacher, is fundamentally different from other professional relationships. It is sometimes overlooked that our students come to us not as problems to be solved, but as people becoming. Teaching is more a question of being with, or engaging with than problem solving. Unlike clients or patients who go to lawyers or doctors to have their problems solved or to be cured, our students come with lives to share and we help or guide and learn with them. Our students are people with whom we work. In this sense we agree with those such as Donnelly (1999) who argue from a Heideggerian perspective that "teachers should acknowledge and celebrate that concernful Being-with which is at the basis of their practice, and look hard and critically at demands for an increased emphasis on instrumentality" (p. 947).

CULTURAL POSITION AS TEACHER EDUCATORS

Moreover, teaching takes place in human society. It is replete with cultural associations and meanings. Our understandings of ourselves as teacher educators in the United States is constrained and circumscribed by our local cultural situations and the understandings of others. The cultural meaning of teacher educator is in part reflective of the low status of teachers in general in our society, but we are also held in low esteem by many of our colleagues at the university, by national agencies, by the teachers we work with in schools, sometimes by our students who are less than impressed by the idea that one learns how to teach, and even by our colleagues in teacher education who often it seems, prefer to identify themselves with other disciplines. There are many reasons for this state of affairs of course, but the net effect is that our voices can be difficult to hear, and it can be hard for us to assert our own agency as teacher educators given that others have been quite successful in reducing our autonomy. Our cultural worth is similar to that of school teachers. We are more than familiar with cultural representations of teachers. They plague us in the media, when we respond to questions about our profession, when we enter schools, or when we engage with students. How can we find our voices when they are so often denied or denigrated? In trying to understand our own practice as teacher educators, who we are becoming as teachers, we are constantly aware of the ways in which teaching and teacher education are perceived by society, by the outside.

TEACHING CULTURE

There is, however, another more hopeful perspective of the teacher and teacher educator; one with which we are equally familiar. We exist as teacher educators within society, but we also belong to a culture of teaching. Our teaching culture does not always include all teachers: there is a clear distinction between technicians who follow recipe models to teach and teachers who accept an aesthetic or humanistic approach. Our teaching values our students as people. We understand the importance of the community that is intentionally formed in our classrooms (Wells, 1999; Vygotsky, 1978). Teaching and learning occur when there is a reciprocal relationship between teacher and student, when the teacher is teacher-student and the student is student-teacher, as Freire (1993) writes. This is our cultural domain: where sharing stories, trusting our instincts, observing and reflecting are second nature. This is a teaching culture where we are insiders but can also be outsiders at times. Our identities are complex: we move in and out of being "teachers." Teaching is a role that fits and doesn't fit depending on context. Often struggles in our other life roles can trigger a need to re-examine our teaching. Our identity as teachers requires investigation and we can problematize ourselves as teachers as insiders looking in but also from the outside in and the inside out. The interplay of being both insiders and outsiders to teaching and to one another as we dig deeper into our practice grounds our methodology. How can these subtleties be captured in a self-study? In what ways can we investigate our selves as teachers and people in relation to others?

DISCOVERING CO/AUTOETHNOGRAPHY

Fall, 2007

I have been reading Harold Rosen again and was reminded, not surprisingly of why I believe that, first and foremost language is a personal/political form of expression. Kids in London have the right to tell their stories in their language and be heard (well at least they did in the schools I was involved and at the time I was involved with them). This understanding of the rationale for teaching English is integral to the anti-racist and anti-sexist education at the core of what I do although today, reading Rosen, I am again aware of how my approach has changed over the years. It was so refreshing to read Rosen again and remember why teaching English was so great at the beginning of the 80s. We really worked with the students not only on helping them tell their stories but understanding the structures of society. A lot of that work had to do with showing students the political nature of language (who gets to speak; who gets to tell you who is right and who is wrong; who gets to tell you that your story is not worth telling). A lot of my work was helping students appreciate that they had a story to tell and that you have to tell it to understand other people's stories. I was so into the personal nature of this (rather than the genre or other lit theory bits of it). (Excerpt from Lesley's Personal Narrative)

Fall, 2007

I think language has always been an interest. When I became a teacher, I clearly understood, without formal training, that breaking the language barriers between my students and me would be essential to gain trust and to get to know them. I watched them intently to understand their expressions, culture, mannerisms, interests, and values. I began to dress like them, listen to their music, and sometimes speak like them. At the time I could easily have passed for being a kid. This interest and respect for them gave me a way in. My students respected me. We had a good rapport and it was the rapport that led to trust and eventually learning. They may not have learned a tremendous amount of Spanish and French, but I think they learned a lot about who they were and that their perspectives were important and valid. I helped them to find reasons to value themselves. (Excerpt from Monica's Personal Narrative)

We present this uncovering of an appropriate self-study methodology in a logical fashion in this chapter but we came to co/autoethnography organically, as we come to many understandings about our teaching. Our methodology was generated from our own experiences of trying to find meaningful methods to investigate our practice. Having studied English Education and Language, Literacy, and Culture, we have always been drawn to autobiography and personal narrative both for our own teaching reflections as well as those of our students. We have used these vehicles throughout our careers in teacher education in a variety of ways for a number of different purposes. For example, we invite our students to write about their own life histories of being learners and schooling through the analysis of artifacts; to construct narratives about critical incidents during their student teaching, and to develop literacy autobiographies. We have them write these for themselves primarily as the audience as a reflective tool but also for us and one another. Utilizing these methods in our classes raised issues of authenticity and power for us. In response, we created informal writing groups made up of teachers that met outside the university structures (Coia & Taylor, 2002). We also use these types of writing for ourselves as lifelong learners. We write narratives to better understand our struggles, decisions, and directions.

Although we invited the sharing of personal narratives because we knew inherently that it would be an important vehicle for meaning making, we had never deliberately examined the process. This became more apparent when we began to discuss our work in various professional settings. As we shifted our lens to think about this collaborative meaning making process among our students, our teacher groups, and even ourselves, we continually found the catalyst was in the dialogue, exchange and interweaving of the narratives and how these narratives moved between the present, past and future, and involved cultural understandings of our work as teachers. To examine this further, we attempted to record our exchanges, through audio-recording our dialogue and reflections, and writing narrative responses to the process. What were we doing?

Alongside the constant-comparative analysis of our collaborative exchanges, where a variety of characteristics emerged, we turned to the literature. Could we discover an existing methodology that matched what we were doing? Although we both came from English Education backgrounds where language, meaning-making, autobiography, and narrative are integral modes of thinking and analysis, we felt our process entailed something more. Additionally we were familiar with some qualitative research methodologies and valued the fundamentals of ethnography and the concern with being a participant observer as a means to understand the insider. This was part of our concern with issues of authority in the classroom and how these impacted work with personal narrative. We thought that participatory and feminist research might be a better fit for our process because of the emphasis on the voices of the participants. However the researcher still seemed to take some sort of a leadership role when working with participants. In our group, the participants are the researchers and the researchers are the participants. We fluctuate between being insiders and outsiders. Unsatisfied with our quest, we ventured to other fields of study, such as sociology, anthropology, and literary theory.

AUTOETHNOGRAPHY

Combining the interests of both autobiography and ethnography, we found that autoethnography shared some characteristics with our collaborative writing groups. We deliberately emphasize that we identify some autoethnographic characteristics that may be applied to our methodology rather than adopting the autoethnographic stance in totality. Additionally we are aware that there are multiple interpretations of the meaning of autoethnography (Ellis & Bochner, 2000) so we are intentionally specific about the shared characteristics and their origins. Reed-Danahay states,

> Autoethnography synthesizes both a postmodern ethnography, in which the realist conventions and objective observer position of standard ethnography have been called into question, and a postmodern autobiography, in which the notion of the coherent, individual self has been similarly called into question.

The term has a double sense- referring either to the ethnography of one's own group or to the autobiographical writing that has an ethnographic interest. ... When the dual nature of the meaning of autoethnography is apprehended, it is a useful term with which to question the binary conventions of a self/society split, as well as the boundary between the objective and the subjective. (p. 2)

This methodology addresses two important aspects of our process: the importance of blurring the researcher's role so that she is neither completely subjective, as an insider, nor completely objective, as an outsider; and the understanding of the self as multiple, dynamic, and always changing. If our writing, narrative sharing, and dialogue analysis is driven by the intention of capturing the complexity of the self as teacher, we needed a methodology that reflected that framework. Moreover, if the self is not coherent, then the role of the researcher will not automatically be solely subjective or solely objective. We needed a blurring vehicle to address the blurring process of the self. Autoethnography, much like our own process, "is a form of self-narrative that places the self within a social context. It is both a method and a text" (Reed-Danahay, 1997, p. 9). Our methodology mirrors similar tenets. As we compose our self-narratives, they are written both within the social context of our experiences as well as for the social context of our collaboration. The interweaving of our stories becomes the new, collaborative text that is formed through the process of sharing and discussing our individual narratives. In an important sense our use of self-narratives forms our lives as teachers.

Pratt (1996) describes autoethnography as "a text in which people undertake to describe themselves in ways that engage with representations others have made of them" (p. 531). Although there are aspects of Pratt's interpretation of autoethnography that do not resonate with our method, as we write about ourselves and our teaching we are constantly aware of the ways teachers are perceived by others and society. We want to ensure that our stories are always understood in a larger social context. Part of our own positioning as we write and share is a response to the ways in which we are viewed, treated, and described. Part of the idea of teacher as person-in-relation is the understanding that we are partially constructed and limited by the views of the larger society and culture. Autoethnography provides us with a vehicle to examine our pictures of our selves among the cultural portraits of "teacher" that are created by others. In this sense we draw on Reed-Danahay's (1997) under-standing of Strathern's description of auto-anthropology as "doing an ethnography of one's own culture" (p. 5). In a sense, we are doing an ethnography of our self as teacher within the context of what that means among teachers, as part of the inside culture of teaching, and within the greater cultural context of what that means from outside the world of teaching in society. We are insiders, investigating the culture of teaching. Those who collaborate with us are insiders because they are also teachers but at the same time outsiders because their experiences will be different and their identities complex. The interweaving of the narratives allows the insider to move from inside/out and the outsider to move from outside/in.

CO/AUTOETHNOGRAPHY

In co/autoethnography we take seriously the idea of complex identities and relationships with ourselves and others. As teacher educators researching our own practice together we are holding to the idea that we have a special perspective in virtue of being insiders, but we have been, and continue to be outsiders in that being teacher educators does not encompass our whole identities. The multiple perspective taking allows for autoethnography. If our self is multiple, fluid, changing and individual yet constructed by the relationships we have with others and the cultures of which we are a part, co/autoethnography becomes a perfect vehicle to honor these self characteristics. Co/autoethnography allows us to be reflective and do self-research in a way that mirrors how we engage with one another as teachers and people. We are always insider/outsiders. Our understanding of ourselves and others fluctuates according to context and setting. While no one can completely understand another, we do not completely understand ourselves. Our understandings of ourselves and others can, however, be enhanced by composing our autoethnographies together.

We are not claiming that persons somehow collapse into one through this process nor that the space between persons is absolute. Co/autoethnography complicates the space between persons. We are open to the perspective of others in a particular way: we look to these as we write and re-write our experiences in the attempt to gain greater understanding. We captured this idea in an early study when we spoke of "writing into each others' lives" (Coia & Taylor, 2002). We are most emphatically not saying that the co/autoethnographic experience collapses distinctions between persons, or between persons and their social, historical and cultural context. Rather, reflecting on the relation between persons and their context allows for greater personal and social understanding, and provides space for agency.

Co/autoethnography shares a variety of traits with autoethnography, but the process is slightly different. We insist on the role of the other or others in the research process including the analysis based on the concept of teacher as person-in-relation. Thus, while it is commonplace to say that autobiography is inherently social, it is also common for students as well as academics to fall into the individualist trap of thinking of autobiography as centered on either self-revelation or self-creation. There are good historical and cultural reasons why those engaged in autobiography give more credence to the powers of introspection than philosophers or anyone else is prepared to warrant, but we need to value both the individual's perspective on her life and to recognize that this can only be understood by moving betwixt and between the culture and the person. We need both and can downplay neither. Co/autoethnography provides a framework for this work. The very close work that co/autoethnography involves, where more than one is engaged in the same autobiographical project narrows while not collapsing the space between individuals, and introduces a perspective that runs alongside one's own. To reiterate: the "I" is always present and is distinct but it is not ultimately separate from others. This is because of the venture itself which is focused on the improvement of practice by bringing the self to fore, which brings us to an important final point in this section: Just as there are multiple perspectives on the definition of autoethnography and its use, we only claim to define co/autoethnography within the context of teaching and teacher education.

DATA PROCEDURES

The Essence of the Co/Autoethnographic Method

Conducting co/autoethnographic research involves the use of diverse data generating strategies. First and foremost, as we discuss in detail above, this research methodology necessitates multiple researchers. Co/autoethnography can only be conducted when there are at least two researchers involved. There are three other phases that are integral to co/autoethnography: the writing and re-writing of autobiographical narratives; the sharing of those narratives with one or more other person; and the discussions that emerge once those narratives are shared. These research phases do not necessarily follow a specific order: we move back and forth from one to another depending on both the theme of the writing as well as the context of our investingation. They have, however, become the pivotal ways we generate data for analysis.

Possible Data Collection Strategies

How these phases translate into data collection methods vary depending upon the location of the researchers/participants and the scope of the study. For example, of late, because we live in different parts of the United States, we rely heavily on the data generated through our communication via e-mail with attached narratives, our drafts on *google.docs* where we can write collaboratively, and our conversations on the telephone and the field notes from those conversations. No matter how much we can communicate via writing and the internet, we find our real-time dialogue on the phone is absolutely essential to process and discuss meaning. When we use co/autoethnography within our own communities, we tend to gather data by sharing written narratives and reflections, and audio-recording our dialogue sessions. Hence some of the researchers' possible data for co/autoethnography include: copies of written narratives and reflections on the process, transcribed audio-tapes of the sharing sessions, printed e-mail exchanges, drafts of collaborative writing on *google .docs*, and field notes from our phone call discussions.

Data Analysis

As the data are collected, they are analyzed simultaneously by all of the researchers. The mode of the analysis is collaborative, reflective, and participatory. The analysis involves the perspective of more than one person and is in search of deep insights about teaching. The analysis is participatory in that, as Anderson, Herr, & Nihlen (2007) write, "the dualisms of theory and practice, subject and object, and research and teaching are collapsed" (p. 25). We examine the data through the blurred lens of a researcher/participant, a subject/object or an insider/ outsider.

Together we analyze the data inductively by means of constant comparison (Glaser & Strauss, 1967; Strauss & Corbin, 1998). We attempt to continually break down, compare, and contrast the data in order to form "a spiral or dialectical pattern" (Anderson, Herr, & Nihlen, 2007, p. 223). We investigate the data searching for patterns or themes that emerge (Bogdan & Biklen, 1998). We triangulate one data source against another for trustworthiness to ensure validity (Gordon, 1980). As we find patterns, we develop codes so that we can categorize other data accordingly. Once we identify the patterns, we move back to the literature and research for further interpretation and explanation. Ultimately we strive to "build a theory for the work" (Anderson, Herr, & Nihlen, 2007, p. 223).

Trustworthiness

Because co/autoethnography relies so heavily on collaboration with others, the issue of the trustworthiness of this methodology is inherently of central concern. We use the term trustworthiness (Lyons & LaBoskey, 2002) rather than validity to reflect the qualitative nature of our research. We began to use co/autoethnography because we recognized the analytical power of our collaboration. No longer would we simply reflect on and analyze our own narratives alone but instead we would have others and their narratives in dialogue that would move us to new and deeper understandings of our teaching experiences (LaBoskey, 2007). Our research is trustworthy because it is conducted collaboratively with multiple researchers who share similar goals of better understanding and re-shaping their teaching (Loughran & Northfield, 1998). The new perspectives on our teaching through co/autoethnography could also indicate the trustworthiness of our methodology.

Representation of Findings

Our co/autoethnographies are cumbersome to present in traditional research report formats because these formats tend to be univocal and written from solely a scholarly perspective. We strive to find creative modes to share our research that highlight both our individual voices as well as the spaces within. Additionally we attempt to craft accounts of our research that combine our personal narratives, theoretical understandings, and data analysis and conclusions. We feel fortunate to have found the S-STEP SIG of AERA because it has provided us with a community that embraces the representative blending of our multiple selves as teacher educators. This support encourages us to continue to present and publish our research in the larger context of teacher education. Besides the academic community, we disseminate our method in our work as teacher educators. Although we have used this method as teacher educators to study our own practice, we believe it is similarly useful for the practicing teachers with whom we work. Monica, for example, is currently teaching a new graduate course on self-study and action research in teacher leadership. She has three students who are conducting their own self-studies using similar co/autoethnographic methods. As part of their preparation for this work they have read some of our work.

STRENGTHS AND LIMITATIONS OF CO/AUTOETHNOGRAPHY

Strengths

We hope one of the strengths of the methodology has already become apparent: It allows us to live and examine the complexities of teaching while not requiring an over simplification of the practice of teaching. As we shall show in the exemplar, the kinds of questions this method fosters and allows us to address are different from other types of research: we are, in an important sense, looking at the layering or interweaving of our selves-in-relation to uncover and better understand aspects of our teaching. This is not to say that in that process we are not concerned with or eschew the concrete but that these issues arise from an understanding of teaching as a complex messy practice at the center of which are people-in-relation. This method requires us to stay at that level of complexity and not fragment or reduce the practice to constituent parts. At this level, we are able to examine a continuum of conclusions that are neither all positive or all negative. We are able to discuss our struggles and challenges as well as new insights. This is not to say, of course, that the method is not suited to consideration of an aspect of teaching such as the choice of a teaching strategy. For example, in the discussion of the study that follows, the choice of certain strategies used to negotiate authority with students were shown to be effective but only after the data had been collected and analyzed.

It was only after months of work on the personal history of the researchers alongside the classroom dynamics of the classroom in social and political context that we could we come to this conclusion. In the final analysis it became clear that the classroom interactions could be understood in a different way that made sense of many of the participants' contributions. This suggested that certain strategies that had been used were successful.

This method of researching one's own practice is appealing to anyone interested in looking at teaching from the perspective that the teaching involves more than a narrow definition of either teaching or the teacher. It is appealing to those who see researching one's own practice as involving a multidimensional historical and social perspective that centrally involves more than the teaching self. It gives weight to the teacher educator's experience and voice. The telling of the experience by the person who had the experience is given epistemological weight and privilege, but it is recognized that each of us is not transparent to ourselves and that others can and do add to our understanding of ourselves. Moreover it does not see teaching as a practice occurring in a social vacuum. The personal understanding of our success, failure and the challenges we face in the classroom are to some extent socially constructed by the public understanding of teaching people to be teachers. This method affords importance to this perspective as well.

Limitations

In common with all research, co/autoethnography requires a great deal of the researcher. One of the methodological stances underpinning this approach is the idea of person-in-relation. This requires a trusting relationship between those conducting the research. Building and sustaining this relationship takes time, a willingness to be open to others and an interest in engaging in autobiographical work with one's self and others. It is important to stress that it involves more than researching together or admitting another to the research process: it is a project that involves working actively with the spaces between people to increase common understanding of issues around teaching. This can be seen as a limitation as well as a strength. We spoke above about using this method with our students. We have found that it does not always work with students given the relatively short time we are with them and that they have to build relationships with each other. This commitment to the relationship between the researchers seems necessary to us and so where it is not present, co/autoethnography would not be a good choice of research method.

Another limitation is that since the issues are complex, the analysis and reflection on the data takes a considerable amount of time. In a very real sense we have often had the problem of not knowing when the research started and when it is finished. Co/autoethnographic research could continue indefinitely. This is reflective of the nature of persons and the nature of the practice of teaching. Tolerance of ambiguity is a virtue in undertaking co/autoethnographic research.

It may be thought that we are missing the elephant in the room talking of these specific limitations. Surely, one could ask, isn't *the* limitation that co/autoethnographic research falls in the solipsistic trap of all self-referential work. As Roth (2005) says, "[I]nvestigating the Self, or rather, our actions, gives us access to the ways in which culture is concretely realized. At the same time, we are too close to ourselves, which gives rise to the possibility that we do not find the distance required for critically interrogating our own sense-making" (p. 19). Whereas Roth sees the only way out as the "constant interrogation of one's own presuppositions, and the interrogation of the presuppositions underlying the interrogation process" (p. 20), we find in co/autoethnography another route, one suggested, we contend, by our common histories in feminism. We started with and continue with the idea of collective dialogue that provides the basis upon which we identify aspects of our practice and work to understand them. While there are important and obvious differences between women working to understand and overcome their oppression and teacher educators working to understand and improve their practice, the collaborative working on our own histories to understand our current work draws from the former as we work with the latter.

AN EXEMPLAR STUDY: A CO/AUTOETHNOGRAPHIC STUDY OF AUTHORITY

Here we present an example of one of our co/autoethnographic studies on authority in the classroom (Coia & Taylor, 2004; Taylor & Coia, 2006) where we each conducted a study in our own classrooms but ended up focusing on issues of authority as they arose in one of Monica's graduate classes. We present this example through two lenses: we summarize and describe the actual study and then highlight characteristics of co/autoethnographic self-study research.

As we emphasized above in the methodology description, our research process is relatively organic and therefore not a cookie cutter model. Each time we conduct research our path varies depending on the topic and what transpires when we begin the study. Sometimes we begin with a question or focus and that is followed throughout the study. Other times we begin with a focus and diverge from it depending on the context of the research.

Background of the Study

In this particular example, we initiated the study with the intention of examining whether or not it is possible to teach democratically. This question shifted to "what does authority mean in the democratic classroom? In particular, what is our authority as teachers in relation to the authority of the students?" (Taylor & Coia, 2006, p. 54). We were interested in the ways that our teaching addressed authority in the classroom. We hoped to examine this topic from two perspectives: the abstract question of whether or not authority could be shared between teacher and students and the more practical question of determining which teaching strategies facilitate the sharing of authority. We recognized that we came from feminist and social justice orientations but we wondered if they were transparent to our students. We began the study hoping to examine these questions in two courses, in Monica's doctoral course at a large state university in the Northeast, and in Lesley's undergraduate course in a small liberal arts women's college in the South. As we began our data collection and discussion, we found ourselves gravitating towards the data generated from Monica's teaching, as this is where many of the issues of authority emerged.

We found ourselves slightly diverging from the original research plan because of necessity. Monica needed to focus on the challenges with which she was grappling in her course. As we tried to articulate our co/autoethnographic research process in looking at authority in her course, we began to examine our own collaborative process and through the lens and analysis of our own research process, we were better able to understand what occurred in her course. In other words, making sense of co/autoethnography gave us a new way to look at authority and teaching. As we concluded, "through our self-study research the research process became more center stage than the original intention of our study" (2006, p. 55).

Strategies to Negotiate Authority

Our self-study followed and built on co/autoethnographic research we had been conducting for two years prior to this study. The study of authority began in the fall of 2003. Monica hoped to focus on her teaching of a doctoral course "Race and Ethnicity in US Schools." Lesley was planning to use the study as a lens for a variety of education courses. Over the summer, we discussed ways to more explicitly practice our feminist beliefs about authority and teaching in our classes. Monica considered herself a democratic educator, but she wondered how her students' learning would be enhanced if she explicitly shared authority with her students.

She assumed, because her doctoral program is grounded on the principles of democratic teaching, that her students would be comfortable and familiar with democratic practices where decisions of curriculum, readings, and assignments are negotiated among the professor and the students rather than decided by the professor. Specifically, "she began the course with some selected readings and assignments but then invited the students to create the syllabus, select discussion topics, reading assignments, methods of assessment, and design the format of the class sessions" (2006, p. 55). She invited the students to negotiate with her about every aspect of the course (Boomer, Lester, Onore, & Cook, 1992; Short & Harste, 1996; Stock, 1995). She thought that this might be an effective way of transparently teaching democratically. Monica had taught this course before and it had evolved into a negotiated curriculum. She had previously begun with a set syllabus and readings and then when she met her students realized that their needs were different. She then adjusted her course and teaching to accommodate her students' needs and interests by negotiating the curriculum. She therefore thought that beginning the semester openly inviting students to participate in the negotiation of the curriculum would be beneficial for all.

What distinguished the first rendition of the course from the second was the decision making sequence. In the first course, Monica and her students made a decision to negotiate readings and assignments based on the needs of the students. As we reflected, "This re-negotiation was an authentic process that made sense to all parties involved" (2006, p. 56). In the second course, the need for shared authority did not emerge from the students, rather it was imposed by the professor. Monica started the course with an explanation of the democratic format which made most of her students quite uncomfortable. Used to a more traditional course format where the professor provides a syllabus and list of readings and assignments that are followed throughout the semester, the students were unsure of their roles in Monica's course. Wouldn't the professor impart knowledge? How would they know what to study or on what to focus? Some of the students seemed resistant.

Monica was surprised at the students' resistance. She found herself facilitating a lot of process discussion with the students, especially setting ground rules for discussion and class format. The students struggled to self-regulate their participation and some voices dominated others. Some students became frustrated with the continual reflection on the process. They wanted to get to the heart of the content of the course. Both Monica and the students felt uncomfortable with their new negotiated emerging roles and they struggled for most of the course to come to terms with their roles.

Data Methods and Analysis

Throughout Monica's course, we were engaged in co/autoethnographic self-study research. We generated data through a variety of methods. We spoke on the telephone for one to two hours each week after class to reflect upon the incidents in Monica's class. Lesley shared anecdotes about her own class which helped Monica to gain perspective about her own experiences. We wrote field notes and reflections after each conversation. We also communicated via e-mail, sending one another additional narratives. As we described, "we began to write over and through one another's narratives" (2006, p. 62).

These reflective sessions were invaluable but Monica still struggled to discern what was working in her class from what wasn't working. In typical teacher style, she focused on the negative aspects of her classroom, which really came from conflict with two of the students, and disregarded the positive aspects which emerged with the other five students. Monica was concerned with the ways in which the difficult students disrupted and dominated the discussions. One particular student made comments that offended and silenced others in the group. Monica felt as if she was at an impasse.

As we collected the data, we continued to read about feminist pedagogy and conceptions of authority both for our pedagogy as well as a way to better articulate our methodology. At this stage we noted that "[t]he texture of our narratives changed as we integrated the voices of scholars and teachers into our writing" (2006, p. 62). It was in the combination of reflection, discussion, analysis, and reading that led us to examine the issue of authority in our co/autoethnography methodology alongside the teaching in Monica's course. Investigating these alongside one another helped us to see Monica's course in a different light.

Reframing the Self-Study on Authority

Examining the collaborative nature of co/autoethnography more in depth helped us to think about the parallel characteristics of authority in our teaching. We realized that we shared authority as we worked collaboratively with one another in much the same way we negotiated authority with our students. We reflected:

> It is through opening ourselves to each other, allowing each other to write into each other's lives, that we learn from and about each other. It seems that for collaboration, as with good teaching, there has to be risk and trust. It is in essence a caring collaboration. . . In a caring relationship, based on shared authority, respect, trust, progress comes not primarily through critique but through increased understanding based on serious examination of self and other. Our collaboration is possible because it is based on the relational authority that is constructed through our caring relationship. We share authority and therefore we are both responsible to exchange knowledge, inspire, and influence. (2006, p. 63)

Using this new lens of collaboration and relational authority (Applebaum, 2000), we began to analyze the data differently. No longer focusing on the disruptive students and what was not working well in the class, we began to think about the ways that community was being built both despite and because of the disruptions. Monica realized that she initially had trouble recognizing these characteristics of sharing authority because she expected to see them manifest in ways that she was accustomed to in most of her courses, somewhat smoothly and without resistance and she was distracted with the challenging behaviors of a few students. By opening the space to accept a different rendition of sharing authority, she began to acknowledge that there had been instances of relational authority and community building. Several students took risks and shared personal narratives about race and ethnicity even though they were derided and put down by others. The students who were willing to take risks and participate in the community found ways to forge relationships with Monica and fellow students, even if that meant doing so after class or on the telephone. Parts of the class grew closer as they tried to together find ways to manage the disruptions.

Through this study, we realized that "caring and authority not only are complimentary but also need to be seen, as Applebaum (2000) argues, in relation with each other" (2006, p. 65). The teaching of this course was not in fact a failure but a complex learning experience that raised new questions for us to explore. We did not find specific answers or solutions but rather new ways to look at our teaching. This study reinforced for us that part of teaching is allowing ourselves to be vulnerable. We concluded, "[t]eachers who do not share of themselves with their students are isolated from the potential growth that can occur in relation to their students" (2006, p. 65).

HOW OUR PRACTICE HAS CHANGED IN LIGHT OF THE RESEARCH

It is commonplace that teaching is a complex activity. Using co/autoethnography to deepen our understanding of our own practice makes living with and appreciating this complexity easier as we have become used to working closely with others in a research environment that values the messiness not only of ourselves but of our situation. It also honors our past and takes the whole person seriously. As such it has led us to a better understanding of why we act as we do. It is commonly appreciated that as King and Ladson-Billings (1990) say it is crucial for us to understand our own beliefs and ideologies to help students "consciously re-experience their own subjectivity" (p. 26). The particular kind of autobiographical work we do has enabled us to focus on this vital aspect of reflective practice.

Co/autoethnography, with its emphasis on the embodied person, does not neglect the role of emotion in teaching and research on teaching. "Attending to the role of emotions in the conduct and analysis of fieldwork is an important and undertheorized aspect of reflective practice", as Naples (2003, p. 199) so rightly says. Indeed a fundamental characteristic of co/autoethnography is the way in which it embraces the whole person by the use of rich personal stories in the search for meaning.

While success is difficult to measure, we are aware of a deeper confidence in our practice through an increased understanding of ourselves in relation. This has allowed us to take greater risks in our teaching. We have also become more sophisticated users of autobiographical narratives with our students. We understand our practice more thoroughly because we live the idea that teaching is a complex personal and political activity.

REFERENCES

Anderson, G. L., Herr, K., & Nihlen, A. S. (2007). *Studying your own school: An educator's guide to practitioner action research* (2nd ed.). Thousand Oaks, CA: Corwin Press.

Applebaum, B. (2000). On good authority or is feminist authority an oxymoron? *Philosophy of Education*, 1999, (pp. 307–317). Urbana, IL: Philosophy of Education Society.

Bogdan, R., & Biklen, S. K. (1998). *Qualitative research for education: An introduction to theory and methods*. Boston: Allyn & Bacon.

Boomer, G., Lester, N., Onore, C., & Cook, J. (1992). *Negotiating the curriculum*. London: Falmer Press.

Bruner, J. (2002). *Making stories: Law, literature and life*. Cambridge, MA: Harvard University Press.

Cochran-Smith, M., & Lytle, S. L. (Eds.). (1993). *Inside/outside: Teacher research and knowledge*. New York: Teachers College Press.

Coia, L., & Taylor, M. (2002). Writing in the self: Teachers writing autobiographies as a social endeavor. In D. L. Schallert, C. M. Fairbanks, J. Worthy, B. Maloch, & J. V. Hoffman (Eds.), *The 51st yearbook of the National Reading conference* (pp. 142–153). Oak Creek, WI: National Reading Conference, Inc.

Coia, L., & Taylor, M. (2004). What is at risk here? Recasting feminist authority through the lens of the past. In D. L. Tidwell, L. M. Fitzgerald, & M. L. Heston (Eds.), *Journeys of hope: Risking self-study in a diverse world. Proceedings of the fifth international conference on self-study teacher education practices, Herstmonceaux, East Sussex, England* (pp. 59–62). Cedar Falls, IA: University of Northern Iowa.

Donnelly, J. F. (1999). Schooling Heidegger: On being in teaching. *Teaching and Teacher Education, 15*, 933–949.

Ellis, C., & Bochner, A. P. (2000). Autoethnography, personal narrative, reflexivity: Researcher as subject. In N. K. Denzin & Y. S. Lincoln (Eds.), *Handbook of qualitative research* (2nd ed., pp. 740–743). Thousand Oaks, CA: Sage Publications.

Frankfurt, H. G. (1998). *The importance of what we care about: Philosophical essays*. Cambridge: Cambridge University Press.

Freire, P. (1993). *Pedagogy of the oppressed*. New York: Continuum.

Glaser, B. G., & Strauss, A. L. (1967). *The discovery of grounded theory: Strategies for qualitative research*. Chicago: Aldine.

Gordon, R. L. (1980). *Interviewing: Strategies, techniques, and tactics*. Homewood, IL: Dorsey Press.

King, J., & Ladson-Billings, G. (1990). The teacher education challenge in elite university settings: Developing critical perspectives for teaching in a democratic and multicultural society. *European Journal of Intercultural Studies, 1*, 15–30.

LaBoskey, V. K. (2007). The methodology of self-study and its theoretical underpinnings. In J. J. Loughran, M. L. Hamilton, V. K. LaBoskey, & T. Russell (Eds.), *International handbook of self-study of teaching and teacher education practices* (pp. 817–869). Dordrecht, The Netherlands: Springer Press.

Loughran, J., & Northfield, J. (1998). A framework for the development of self-study practice. In M. L. Hamilton (Ed.), *Reconceptualizing teaching practice: Self-study in teacher education* (pp. 7–18). London: Falmer Press.

Lyons, N., & LaBoskey, V. K. (Eds.). (2002). *Narrative inquiry in practice: Advancing the knowledge of teaching*. New York: Teachers College Press.

MacIntyre, A. (1981). *After virtue: A study in moral theory*. London: Duckworth.

Naples, N. A. (2003). *Feminism and method: Ethnography, discourse analysis, and activist research*. New York: Routledge.

Noddings, N. (1984). *Caring: A feminine approach to ethics and moral education*. Berkeley, CA: University of California Press.

Palmer, P. J. (1998). *The courage to teach: Exploring the inner landscape of a teacher's life*. San Francisco: Jossey-Bass Publishers.

Pratt, M. L. (1996). Arts of the contact zone. In D. Bartholomae & A. Petrosky (Eds.), *Ways of reading: An anthology for writers* (4th ed., pp. 528–546). Boston: St. Martin's Press.

Reed-Danahay, D. (Ed.). (1997). *Autoethnography: Rewriting the self and the social.* Oxford, England: Berg.

Roth, A. M. (Ed.). (2005). *Auto/biography and auto/ethnography: Praxis of research method.* Rotterdam: SensePublishers.

Short, K. G., & Harste, J. C. (with Burke, C.) (Eds.). (1996). *Creating classrooms for authors and inquirers.* Portsmouth, NH: Heinemann.

Stock, P. L. (1995). *The dialogic curriculum: Teaching and learning in a multi-cultural society.* Portsmouth, NH: Heinemann.

Strauss, A., & Corbin, J. (1998). *Basics of qualitative research: Techniques and procedures for developing grounded theory* (2nd ed.). Thousand Oaks, CA: Corwin Press.

Swift, G. (1985). *Waterland.* New York: Washington Square Press.

Taylor, M., & Coia, L. (2006). Revisiting feminist authority through a co/autoethnographic lens. In D. Tidwell & L. Fitzgerald (Eds.), *Self-study and diversity* (pp. 51–70). Rotterdam: Sense Publishers.

Van Manen, M. (1990). *Researching lived experience: Human science for an action sensitive pedagogy.* Albany, NY: SUNY Press.

Vygotsky, L. S. (1978). *Mind in society: The development of higher psychological processes.* Cambridge, MA: Harvard University Press.

Wells, G. (1999). *Dialogic inquiry: Towards a socio-cultural practice and theory of education.* Cambridge, England: Cambridge University Press.

Zeichner, K. M., & Liston, D. P. (1996). *Reflective teaching: An introduction.* Mahwah, NJ: Lawrence Erlbaum.

RONNIE DAVEY AND VINCE HAM

11. COLLECTIVE WISDOM

Team-Based Approaches to Self-Study in Teacher Education

We know little about how effective learning communities develop, how they are sustained, and how teachers learn to work collaboratively throughout the enquiry process.

(Dooner, Mandzuk, & Clifton, 2008)

Many in the self-study, action research and practitioner research literatures highlight the importance of collaboration in the conduct of their various forms of self-study research, but relatively few make that collaboration the focus of the study itself. The literature is often long on the supposed value of doing self-study in collaboration with others, but short on the detailed description of the forms such collaborations took and shorter still on a specific analysis of the role of collaboration in improving either the process of the research or its impact on individual and collective practice.

This chapter looks at the forms, methods and impact of one model of 'collective' self-study, as implemented in a national programme of professional development for inservice teacher educators in New Zealand. The chapter outlines and analyses the contribution that incorporating a strong collective element in the self-study methodology made to the progress and impact of the various individual self-studies involved. It concludes that collective forms of self-study are particularly appropriate or useful when the purpose of the self-study goes beyond the improvement of individuals' professional practice, to include self-study for wider community, cultural or organizational change, and that, while individual-focused forms of self-study may improve a professional practice, collective forms of self-study may be needed to change a professional culture.

INTRODUCTION

The literature on reflection, critical reflection, and (self-) reflective practice in teaching and teacher education is significant and growing, but it is distinguished by only the broadest consensus around what critical reflection looks like, and offers little around what might be the most effective methods teacher educators can use to develop or promote it in themselves and in their colleagues. Compare and contrast, for example, Hatton & Smith's (1995) 'essential elements' in critical reflection with Brookfield's (1988) 'central activities'. Contrast Schon's (1983) separationist views on the division of labour between practitioner and researcher in self-research with the unitary perspective of Carr & Kemmis (1987) and other critical action

C. A. Lassonde, S. Galman and C. Kosnik (eds.), Self-Study Research Methodologies for Teacher Educators, 187–203.

researchers. Consider, too, the debate between those who see critically reflective methods as practical tools to improve teaching techniques or to solve individual's situated teaching problems or puzzles of practice (Robinson, 1993; Munby & Russell, 1989), and those for whom they are a tool for collective professional regeneration and the pursuit of social justice agendas (Gore & Zeichner, 1991; Lave & Wenger, 1991), and so on.

What the literature does have in common, however, is a recognition that 'reflective practice' and subsequent teacher or teacher educator professional learning is a complex process that involves more than just thinking about practice, and more than just a teacher self-improving themselves in isolation. In its ideal form, it involves a collaborative unpacking of assumptions and a willingness to challenge and have challenged deeply embedded beliefs and routines of practice. It involves a mentored gathering of evidence of one's own current practice and examining this in the light of new knowledge and emerging theories of effective pedagogical practice. It involves taking into account, and being responsive to, a range of contextual considerations, and it does not skirt the discomfort of cognitive dissonance that precedes any change in practice and action. By such accounts, professional learning through critical reflection is not achieved rapidly, it is not achieved comfortably, and it is not achieved alone. It involves and takes the form, in short, of collaborative and/or collective 'self-study'.

COLLABORATION AND COLLECTIVITY IN SELF-STUDY

Methodological collaboration in the self-study of teacher education practices comes in many forms and guises, ranging along various continuums of participation, purpose, and process from assistive support from another individual colleague at one end, to full blown cultural-collective studies undertaken by entire organizational and even national communities at the other.

At the 'assistive-individual' end of the spectrum of collaborative methodology in self-study, 'collaboration' may involve little more than a self-studier 'buddying' with one other trusted colleague, where that colleague acts as either an assistant or as a mentor to the self-studier, perhaps helping with co-coding data, perhaps helping with data collection on behalf of the self-studier, or perhaps acting as a sounding board for the self-studier's reflections. The aim of such assistive collaboration is principally to resolve situated puzzles of practice identified by the individual, for the individual. Thus, while such individual self-studies may well involve collaboration with a colleague or two as part of the process, they are focused on improving the practice of the individual self-studier and their purposes, questions and intended benefits vary from individual to individual. In other words: 'I will investigate my practice, and someone else will help me reflect on its significance to me'.[1]

In the middle of the spectrum might be co-formative collaborations, again usually involving 'buddying' with one or at most two other trusted colleagues, but this time in a process where both colleagues conduct their own individual self-studies but then share results and co-reflect on their respective processes and emerging findings on a more collegial and co-participant basis. These 'co-researcher' collaborations employ formal co-reflection methods of mutual sharing of findings, co-coding of data, co-interviewing, and so on, and still have the improvement of individual understanding or practice as their overarching purpose, but the content of the collaboration often has a stronger element of mutual critique than in purely assistive modes, and the role of the collaborating partner is more that of mutually critical friend, or fellow self-researcher, than either that of coach or assistant. Loughran and Northfield (1998) describe such co-formative collaborations as a "shared adventure ... [to] broaden the understanding of [both] the individual whose situation is the focus of the study *and* the significant 'other' with whom the sharing of the adventure occurs" (p. 15).[2]

At the 'cultural-collective' end of the spectrum, however, larger professional groups or communities are involved, and while each individual in such a group or community may still be involved in studying their own individual practice, the actual puzzles of practice or questions to be addressed are collectively determined and are seen to be of collective and not just individual significance. Individuals are actively engaged in the investigation of other group members' practices as well as their own, the group meets frequently and shares all aspects of data gathering, analysis, reflection and reporting, and, the collaboration of the group itself often becomes a part of the thing studied. In cultural-collective modes of self-study, in "the researchers are not just interacting around an external data set; the interactions are the data set, or at least part of it" (LaBoskey, 1998, p. 151), and the goal of the enterprise is felt to be to create or to critically transform the professional culture of the community or organization itself.

What we are choosing to call 'collective' self-study is thus differentiable from both assistive-individual and co-formative collaborations. It is closer to self-study by and for what Feldman, Paugh, & Mills (2004) refer to as 'the collective self'. It is different in that it is self-study consciously enacted by a community of practice, in which its purpose, questions and intended benefits are framed within common as much as individual interests, in which whole-team approaches are taken to data gathering, analysis, synthesis and reporting of findings, and in which the focus is on transforming aspects of the professional culture of the group or community itself. In other words: 'we will investigate our own and each other's practices and reflect on the significance for us'. In assistive and co-formative modes of self-study I consciously do my own individual self-study, with the help of others. Collective self-study is consciously done by a group, as a group, for the group.[3]

THE INSTEP 'MODEL' OF TEAM-BASED SELF-STUDY

Traditionally, those who provided professional development to teachers were considered to be trainers. Now, their roles have broadened immensely. ... they have to be facilitators, assessors, resource brokers, mediators of learning, designers, and coaches, in addition to being trainers when appropriate. (Loucks-Horlsey, 1996. np)

In New Zealand there has traditionally been a clear separation of roles and responsibilities between **preservice** teacher educators, who are responsible for the initial teacher education of student teachers and providing them with their formal qualification to practice, and **inservice** teacher educators, who are employed to provide the practicing teacher community with professional development during the course of their careers. As is the case in other countries, though, this latter group of inservice teacher educators these days is more often charged with assisting their professional peers by facilitating practitioner (self)-inquiries into their own practices, than they are with 'delivering' pedagogical skills or 'disseminating' the latest curriculum and policy information. Accordingly, the knowledge base of inservice teacher education is now to a substantial degree constituted as a knowledge not of curriculum or assessment (etc.) methods alone, but increasingly as a knowledge of the principles and practice of 'reflection' and 'reflective practice', and how these may empower teachers to improve their own practice.

Acknowledging this, the New Zealand Ministry of Education in 2006 established the InService Teacher Education Practices (INSTEP) project. This is a national research and development programme with the broad aims of exploring effective approaches for the professional learning of inservice teacher educators, and developing evidence-based forms for improving inservice teacher education practice. Across the country, twelve 'nests' of teacher educator collectives, each containing around 30 teacher educators working in self-study groups of six, were established and charged with investigating various aspects of effective teacher educator practice using a variety of self-study and action research methodologies (See Fig. 1). In our particular INSTEP group Ronnie worked as one of twelve National Facilitators (NFs), each of whom coordinated the collective self-studies of a group of five Regional Facilitator colleagues (RFs), who in their turn each worked with five other inservice teacher educators (ISTEs). Vince was one of the Regional Facilitators in Ronnie's 'nest', mentoring in his turn the self-study of a group of five Early Childhood teacher educator colleagues. Nationwide since 2006 around sixty of these collaborative groups of up to six teacher educators have conducted extended collective self-studies into their own teacher education practices.

The particular questions or issues about effective in-service teacher education practice addressed by each regional group were determined by the groups themselves, as were the methodologies and methods they would employ. The teacher educators in our particular group decided to experiment with collective approaches to self-study, and to investigate practices which were all in one way or another focused on 'learning conversations' and 'reflective practice' as key mediums in inservice teacher education activity.

In our particular self-study group we agreed to focus on facilitative techniques for having 'learning conversations that *matter*'. These we defined as conversations that were genuinely critically reflective. In the first round of the project (2006) our self-studies around this largely involved critically exploring the language we used in our work with teachers in order to bring about critical engagement and change. In the second round of self-studies (2006-2007), which is the focus this chapter, we agreed to concentrate on:

- exploring the practical application and value of some conceptual tools or frameworks for fostering reflection in professional learning conversations, and
- trialing ways of approaching the work of inservice teacher education together as
  a group.

The five Pod studies were thus all connected in some way to this common issue
of fostering critically reflective practice in our work with colleagues, through
severally and collectively investigating the practical application of a variety of
conceptual 'tools', frameworks', or theoretical 'models' for such reflection, in a
variety of quite different teacher education contexts. The specific study questions
or issues addressed by the six self-study groups within our research collective are
outlined in Figure 1. It should be noted that 'tools', in this context, were defined as
'any professional learning frameworks, models, processes, scaffolds, sets of
protocols, and so on, which could be used to enhance, enable or act as a catalyst for
critical reflection about practice or facilitate new professional learning'.

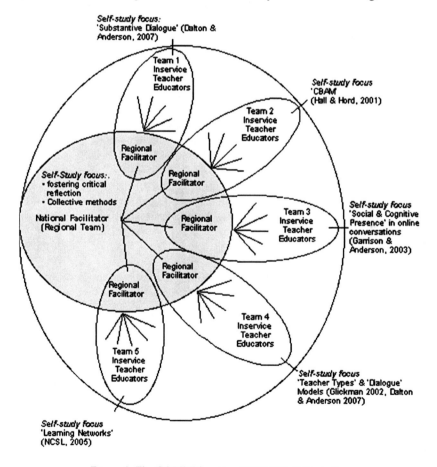

Figure 1. The CORE Education INSTEP Self-Study Groups

AN EXAMPLE OF CULTURAL-COLLECTIVE SELF-STUDY

In the collective self-study outlined below, an experienced inservice teacher educator coordinated a team of six novice Early Childhood (ECE) teacher educators in evaluating the usefulness of a Concerns Based Adoption Model (CBAM) in critically understanding their respective teacher education practices. The ISTEs were newly appointed facilitators in a national professional development programme on new technologies in pre-school education. The facilitators were all employed by a single organization, but they lived and worked from 'home offices' in different regions of the country. The facilitators provide a professional learning programme on new technologies to local Kindergartens and Early Childhood Centres over a three-year period. They conduct professional development workshops around the use of new technologies for teaching and learning in Early Childhood Centres, and mentor the Centre teachers in small-scale action research projects on their effective use of these technologies with pre-school children.

The ECE facilitators were all novices in the role of inservice teacher educator. All had some experience in conducting their own action research as teachers, but little or none in mentoring the action research and professional practice of their teacher colleagues. Vince worked as the professional learning mentor for the team, with responsibility for inducting them into their new 'facilitator' role, identifying what their particular needs as novice teacher educators were, and collaboratively working with them to meet those needs using collective self-study processes.

Over their first year 'on the job', the six novice ISTEs and their mentor tried out and evaluated a number of tools and models of facilitation. In this particular collective self-study we all investigated the usefulness of the CBAM in explaining and facilitating this initial induction period into the practice of inservice teacher educators. Vince used it as a framework for his mentoring of the facilitator group as novice teacher educators, and they in turn used it as a framework for their work mentoring teachers new to the use of new technologies with children.

THE THEORY

The Concerns-Based Adoption Model focuses on the concern or preoccupations that people have when adopting an innovation or undergoing professional change (Hall & Hord, 1987; Hord, Rutherford, Huling-Austin, & Hall, 1987; Loucks-Horsley & Stiegelbauer, 1991). The model proposes that that people experiencing such change, or adopting some new professional practice, 'shift' and 'evolve' over time in terms of what most concerns or preoccupies them about that change or practice.

For most of its advocates, CBAM is seen as a 'taxonomical stage theory' in that it suggests that early participant concerns are likely to be more self- or knowledge-oriented (What is it? and How will it affect me?), middle stage/level concerns are often procedural or task-oriented (How do I do it? Am I doing it right?), while later stage concerns are effect- or impact-focused (Is it working for 'them'? Could I do it better?). It is 'taxonomical' in that it also suggests that as a participant in adopting a new practice, one does not, or can not, proceed to later or higher level stages in this evolution until the questions and puzzles of the earlier or lower level ones are adequately resolved.

In its full form the model suggests that participants 'concerns' are often reflected in the kinds of questions they ask about something (Expressions of concern) and in the professional activities they engage in relation to it (Behaviours associated with concerns), and that there are particular mentoring activities (Interventions) and relationship management roles (Styles) that a facilitator of that change can usefully adopt related to each of the levels of mentee concern (See table below)

Table 1. Overview of Concerns-Based Adoption Model

Stage of Concern	Expression of Concern	Associated Behaviours (Levels of Use)	Interventions	Styles
6. Refocusing	I have some ideas about something that would work even better.	Renewal: Develops new and inventive ways of implementing the innovation	Respect and encourage experimentation; channel ideas and energies; sponsor dissemination	Responder
5. Collaboration	How can I relate what I am doing to what others are doing?	Integration: The teacher is making deliberate efforts to coordinate with others in using the innovation.	Provide opportunities for collaboration; network; arrange collaborative activities	
4. Consequence	How is my use affecting learners? How can I refine it to have more impact?	Refinement: The teacher is making changes to improve outcomes. OR Routine: Implements innovation 'as taught'; has an established pattern of use	Provide positive feedback and support; suggest evidence gathering strategies Provide 'sharing' opportunities and 'celebrations'	Manager
3. Management	I seem to be spending all my time getting materials ready.	Mechanical: Initial implementation of changes; organizing the change.	Answer specific 'how to' queries; provide useful resources; time management suggestions	

Table 1. Continued

2. Personal	How will using it affect me?	Preparation: Plans ways to implement change/innovation	Assist with action planning; provide time for resource collection; help teacher identify 'puzzles of practice to be changed	Initiator
1. Informational	I would like to know more about it.	Orientation: Begins to gather information.	Provide information, readings, references; relate changes to current practice	
0. Awareness	I am not concerned about it.	Non-use: No action taken; no interest	Involve teachers in discussion and decisions; give permission not to know	

It is important to note that in this model 'concerns' are not seen as synonymous with 'worries' or 'anxieties', or even 'problems', and are thus not necessarily associated with negative feelings on the part of the teacher or teacher educator. Rather, a 'concern' is essentially an expression of 'where someone is at' in relation to a given change in practice. Concerns are thus more analogous to the particular 'preoccupations', or what Munby & Russell (1994) call the 'puzzles of practice', that are uppermost in their mind at any given time, than they are to any angst or anxiety as such.

THE PRACTICE

There were two aspects of our collective teacher education practices that we subjected to analysis through the CBAM 'lens' in the study:
- practices in which we reflected on our own collective concerns as inservice teacher educators and mentors, and on how well the collective self-study process we were all engaged in was in addressing those concerns.
- practices in which the facilitators reflected on their *teachers'* concerns in relation to the use of new technologies in teaching and learning, and how they dealt with them as teacher mentors.
Data were gathered in the forms of:
- recordings of five extended learning conversations and workshops conducted by the RF with the facilitator group. These day-long research and mentoring workshops took place more or less monthly over the first six months of the year as part of a programme of professional learning and induction into the action research mentor role.

- archives of brainstorming and other reflective activities in which we discussed and analysed our preoccupations of practice and roles in terms of the CBAM.
- relevant sections of reflective journals, action research plans and other documentation kept by the facilitators about their ongoing work with teachers. For three of them, this included sessions in which they introduced teachers to the CBAM model or used it as a reflection-stimulus in teacher workshops.

These conversations, archives and journalled experiences were collectively analysed for 'fit' with the CBAM 'Concerns-Expressions-Behaviours-Interventions-Roles' elements during our three monthly professional learning 'workshop' times together. The CBAM model has its own self-questionnaire for teachers and others to complete to determine their 'place' on the continuum of concerns. However, this was felt to be too self-fulfilling when the question was to investigate the tool itself. As a consequence, a semi-grounded (closed coding) approach was taken whereby we all brought data to the table from a variety of sources and severally and jointly analysed it using constant comparison techniques and theme identification within the general framework of the seven 'stages' outlined above. This procedure was repeated on new data in several co-analysis workshops spread over the year. At the final workshop for the year we collated these various analyses in order to determine how comfortably the preoccupations identified in those discussions and reflections had 'fitted' with the CBAM continuum, and whether the balance of those preoccupations or concerns had changed over time in accordance with the theoretical model.

FINDINGS

Overall, we came to the conclusion that the CBAM tool was enabling for our respective teacher education practices in respect of:
- providing a framework for some of our own and some teachers' attitudes and actions in professional learning situations,
- providing a common language with which mentors and mentees might discuss and analyse those attitudes and actions, and
- providing some direction or guidelines for future action by both the mentor and mentees in their professional development programme.
  However, we found that the model was also:
- overly simplistic,
- much less useful as a stage theory than as descriptive categorisation of 'things to attend to' in the mentor-mentee relationship, and
- probably less useful in terms of defining our own development as mentors, than in terms of prompting timely strategies we could use with our teacher mentees.

Thus the most direct impact of the study has probably been to raise our conscious awareness of the need to scaffold the professional learning of our colleagues, just as we have been used to scaffolding the learning of children, and to use the framework as a touchstone for planning and critiquing practice rather than a formula for action. We realised that the CBAM theoretical model was going to be more useful as a list of ingredients to be considered in mentoring for reflection than as a recipe to be followed. Most useful of all, though, the study served as a constant reminder that a primary responsibility of the mentor starts with focusing the conversations and attention on the *mentee*, and continues as a conscious attempt to empower the mentee in moving from 'where *they* are at' to 'where *they* want to be'. For us, too, "the [real] strength of the concerns model is in its reminder to pay attention to individuals and their various needs for information, assistance, and moral support." (Loucks-Horsley, 1996. p.1).

It should be remembered that the aim of our self-study was not just to increase what we knew about teacher education, but to improve the way we all worked as teacher educators, both severally and together. We wanted to create a culture of critical collaboration within the team, and perhaps more widely within our organisation. Since the study we have been much more aware of 'paying attention' as a key part of our facilitation methods. We try to listen more, and to talk less. We use the language of 'concerns', 'levels', 'interventions' and 'styles' amongst ourselves when we come together to reflect and discuss what strategies and approaches we might adopt with the individuals in our groups in the future. We are also currently preparing a series of professional development workshops for our colleagues in the organization on this and other theoretical models tested during the INSTEP project.

WHAT WE FOUND OUT ABOUT COLLECTIVE APPROACHES TO SELF-STUDY IN TEACHER EDUCATION

There were two levels of self-study occurring during the project: the collective self-studies of the Pod members' professional practices, of which one is exemplified above, and an ongoing self-investigation of the team-based model itself. In the former we all investigated our own and each others' individual puzzles of practice in respect of our work with teachers and/or colleagues. In the latter, Ronnie coordinated an ongoing investigation of how effectively *we were working as a collective* in conducting those self-studies and that work.

Although each self-study group investigated a different framework or model for fostering reflective practice, and although each individual did so in their own unique teacher education context, all of the self-study teams used broadly the same methods and methodology illustrated in the example above. To summarise, the main 'collective' features of these self-studies were:
- pre-selection and investigation of a common overarching research question (that of how to foster critically reflection in professional learning conversations), and a common commitment to investigate the usefulness of a particular methodological model or tool in their practice of such conversations.
- the use of common or shared frameworks for the analysis and synthesis of data and evidence.
- shared research planning and execution, including helping each other with data collection at each other's sites and collective data analysis and critique of findings.
- frequent (monthly) meetings and workshops, sometimes as pairs or threesomes, but most often as a whole group.

- the common use of stimulated recall (mostly based on audio archives but occasionally video archives of practice) as an analytical technique.
- the co-writing of the final reports and joint presentation of the studies to the Ministry of Education.
- the gathering of cultural or organisational impact data in respect of the teacher educator colleagues with whom we were working.
- a commitment to reflexive data collection and analysis in relation to the collaborative aspects of the methodology itself as part of the process (all meetings, workshops, journals and report included the collection of reflections, conducting reciprocal interviews and other data gathering on the effectiveness of the team approach itself)

After an analysis of the record of this latter (reflexive) data we concluded that the specifically 'collective' elements of the model had contributed to the professional learning and self-study goals of the project in a number of ways. The most significant of these related to:

Making meaning and identifying significance. The negotiation of common elements in our study questions and addressing common puzzles of practice helped clarified the focus of our respective studies, and made easier the process of determining the essence of the 'puzzle of practice' to be investigated, especially for the novice action researchers among us. The joint development of our research plans was also felt to have been easier for this group. Having the group all investigate the same question, as Team 2 did, or grounding their slightly varying questions in a common literature, as Team 1 did, provided both common analytical frameworks and a common language for discussing the meaning and significance of the data.

Fostering internal and external validity. A constant shifting of attention to and from the individual 'me' to and from the collective 'us' was evident in our archived workshop conversations and journaled reflections. This helped constantly to remind us as individuals of what our own studies and findings might be 'a case of', and of what were and were not the common (and therefore potentially theorisable) aspects of our practices. Similarly, the extensive use of co-coding and cross-analysis of each other's data meant that several forms of validity checking were built in throughout the process. Qualitative case study research establishes much of its internal validity through the gradual accumulation of a body of published like and unlike cases, and much of its external validity by generalising to theory. Collective forms of self-study often consist of a body of already-compared like and unlike cases. In our case these consisted of the five separate 'team' studies and the 20 to 25 individual studies within those, as well as the meta-study that the five Regional Facilitators and the National Facilitator conducted together. There was therefore an inherent validity check in the extensive opportunity for cross-case comparison, as well as extensive opportunity for comparison across, and generalisation to, the various theoretical models being tested.

Making self-study logistically manageable. Many action researchers and practitioner-researchers find it logistically difficult to be both the actor and the researcher at the same time. It is common, and understandable, for self-studiers to ask questions such as 'how do I gather data on my actions at the same time as I am doing those actions?' or 'how do I analyse data on myself more objectively?' In our cases, this aspect of managing self-study was made much easier through the use of other members of the group to audio or video record a sample of our practice, to mentor a stimulated recall discussion on that archive after the event, to co-code transcripts of learning conversations, to conduct 'shadow interviews' with other members of the team about their practices, and so on.

Maintaining momentum. A self-study done alone is often a study done in fits and starts, or is one in which it is difficult to maintain impetus over an extended time period. Regular, timetabled, meetings and workshops helped keep the momentum of our studies. They provided deadlines for activity and simultaneously fostered and exploited a growing sense of responsibility to the group. One's individual study and practice was constantly being framed within the context of its contribution to the group study, and the growing awareness of this wider significance, the growing awareness of the 'collective self', was reported as a significant motivator by the groups.

Increased possibility of cultural change. Arguably the most broadly significant contributions of the collective elements of the methods used in the project was to embed a disposition to evidence-based self-inquiry as a preferred mode of professional learning among us as individuals or small collegial teams. But it also helped to embed a commitment to self-inquiry and critical reflection as part of the broader professional learning culture of some of the organizations involved. The extent of sustainability or spread of this commitment to a 'team' culture of professional learning beyond the time and scope of the project itself, has varied considerably from team to team. The team consisting of the regional facilitators and the national facilitator, for example, has met only twice in the nine months since the formal project ended, one of those times being at a joint conference of all the various INSTEP self-study 'nests' where we collaboratively presented our projects and findings to the rest of the national INSTEP community. On the other hand, while we have not continued as a study group ourselves, three of us have set up and are currently coordinating collective self-study teams of varying levels of formality with new groups of colleagues in our several institutions.

Of the other teams, members of Team 4 now tend to meet only as their daily work demands or allows and though as individuals they report continuing to be influenced by the findings of their collective study, they are not part of any formal grouping to continue team based professional learning. The same has been true of Team 1, except that the 'coordinator' of that team has now been given a time allowance to develop a programme of professional learning for her whole organization which includes the establishment of voluntary self-study teams where possible.

Team 3 was the most 'distributed' of the teams geographically and by employer and did not report any significant ongoing influence of the project on the general

culture of their respective organizations. However, they have remained a thriving community of practice amongst themselves, meeting several times face to face and ongoingly online as a semi-formal professional learning network.

Team 5 has not continued as a self-study team as such, but they have recombined with other colleagues in new professional learning teams within their institution. The members of this team were all based in the same 'college' within an even larger institution (a University), and all worked at the same location, even though they came from different disciplinary backgrounds. Their organisation had several teams taking part in the national INSTEP project and has since continued its commitment through time allowances and coordination of professional learning networks across the organisation.

The cultural-collective impact of the studies has perhaps been the greatest for Team 2, which is the group of ECE facilitators involved in our exemplary case above. Although the members of this self-study group are widely distributed geographically, working as we do all in different parts of the country, we are nevertheless all employed by the one organization, we all do essentially the same job of facilitating teachers' professional learning around the effective use of new technologies with children, and we work in the same (Early Childhood) sector. This was always the 'tightest' of the self-study teams in the project, and even after the resourcing from the Ministry ran out, this team has continued its commitment to continue collective self-study as a 'normal' part of its work together. Again, our organization is providing time and funding for this within its contract for the delivery of professional development to the Centres.

All of the teams involved were 'distributed' in one way or another. All but one comprised of teacher educators from different geographical locations; all but one contained members from a range of different employers; three drew their members from across both elementary and secondary school sectors, and two had members from a variety of disciplinary backgrounds. Looking at the teams which have and have not been the most sustainable in maintaining their collective activity and evidencing collective benefit beyond the group, it would seem that geographical distribution was the least influential of these variables. The table on the following page summarises the profile of distribution and similarity in the demographic composition of the teams, mapped against their impact on the wider culture of practice either within the group itself or in the members' respective institutions.

Considering these demographics in conjunction with the reflective data gathered on the INSTEP experience as a whole, we concluded that collective self-study is more likely to have wider community enculturation effects not so much when or because the groups may be geographically distributed across sites of work, but when the groups come from within a single organization and are composed of people from pre-existing, 'natural' communities of interest or practice, such as sharing the same disciplinary interests, or drawing membership from the same education sector.

Table 2. Study Group Membership and Impact

	Regional Team	Team 1	Team 2	Team 3	Team 4	Team 5
Geographical distribution	Regional (same city)	Regional (same city)	National	National	Regional (same city)	Same office
Employing organisation	Several different	Several different	All the same	All different	Several different	All the same
Disciplinary interest or background	Several different	All the same	All the same	All the same	All the same	All different
School sector background	Mixed	All the same	All but one the same	Mixed	All the same	Mixed
Impact on individual practice	High for all	High for all	High for all	High for all	High for all	High for all
Impact on collective practice	Low for study group; mixed for organisations	Low for study group; mixed for organisations	High for study group; high for organisation	High for study group; low for organisations	Low for study group; low for organisations	Low for study group; high for organisation

LIMITATIONS OF COLLECTIVE SELF-STUDY

From the many transcribed conversations relevant to the collective methodology employed in the project, there were four limitations of significance that emerged. Three of these relate to essentially practical and interrelated issues of time, timing and resourcing, and one, more substantive in nature, relates to authenticity and ownership of the central focus of the study.

It may be an inherent feature of all forms of practitioner self-research, self-study and action research to be time consuming. Gathering, analysing and synthesizing empirical research evidence about ones' own professional activity when that professional activity is itself a 'full time job', takes a lot of (extra) time. Being involved in gathering, analyzing, reflecting on and co-synthesising data with and for others in a collective form of such research takes even more time. We were fortunate in this respect during the first two years of the project in that the Ministry provided funding with which we could 'buy out' some of this extra time from our other professional commitments. However, all of the participants found that the time thus 'bought out' was still much less than the time actually taken for the project. Moreover, even in the two organizations where the enculturation effects have been greatest, this embeddedness has only been achieved by those organizations providing similar levels of funding support and time allocation from their own resources as were provided by the Ministry for the original project.

The other time-related limitation of collective forms of self-study relates to 'timing' rather than time itself. The fact that almost all of the groups were geographically and institutionally distributed, combined with the obvious difficulties of merging the diaries of up to seven individuals, and given the special importance of having frequent meetings in maintaining 'collectivity' in the studies, meant that it was often difficult to coordinate group sessions. This was especially true for the numerous half-day and whole-day sessions in which we collectively planned, analysed and reflected on our group data.

It is a commonplace of most action research and practitioner research models that the practitioner-researcher should determine research questions of genuine interest to themselves, rather than subscribe to those primarily of interest to outsider others. At the assistive-individual end of the collaborative self-study spectrum this is relatively unproblematic. The 'collaborating other' (assistant, coach, or critical friend) sublimates his/her own interests or preferred queries in favour of those of the self-studier. At the cultural-collective end of that spectrum, however, the injunction to study that which is *both* of interest to the individuals involved *and* of significance to the participant community, means a lot more 'front-end' negotiation of the puzzles of practice to be self-studied. In our INSTEP project we attempted to ameliorate this threat to ownership or authenticity in the research by having the members of the groups first conduct very small scale pilot studies in which we reviewed a particular recent practice or professional event and isolated any individual puzzles of practice of interest. We then discussed the common threads that emerged from all of these respective pilots and negotiated 'our common focus'. However, it is obvious that the potential will always exist in collective self-studies, and especially those intending to transform aspects of the professional culture of a group or organization, for individuals not to have their most pressing puzzles addressed and for the negotiation of common foci to result in a 'forced' or artificial consensus about the content of the study.

CONCLUSION

We have argued that collective self-study is not just the conduct of self-study by and for the individual 'me'; but also its conduct by and for the collective 'us'. For the teacher educators from various sites and organizations who took part in our INSTEP teams, their self-study was essentially praxis-oriented. It was about their own and their colleagues' professional learning, and about developing an experiential knowledge base to improve their individual and collective professional practices. It seems to have achieved high levels of enculturation for all of the individual 'selves' involved, and, for three of the five, broader team and organizational 'selves' involved. By its very nature, therefore, collective self-study has potential for impact not just on the practices of the individual teacher educators involved, but beyond that to an impact on the learning cultures of the various body-corporates and institutions to which teacher educators belong. We may improve as practitioners through assistive-individual forms of collaborative self-study; but we might improve as a profession through cultural-collective ones.

¹ See, for example, Loughran, & Northfield (1996)
² See, for example, Coia, & Taylor (2006) or Ham, & Davey (2006)
³ See, for example, Guilfoyle *et al* (The Arizona Group) (2000), or Fitzgerald, Farstad, & Deemer (2002)

REFERENCES

Brookfield, S. (1988). Developing critically reflective practitioners: A rationale for training educators of adults. In S. Brookfield (Ed.), *Training educators of adults: The theory and practice of graduate adult education*. New York: Routledge.
Brookfield, S. (1995). *Becoming a critically reflective teacher*. San Francisco: Jossey-Bass.
Carr, W., & Kemmis, S. (1986). *Becoming critical: Education, knowledge and action research*. Lewes: Falmer.
Coia, L., & Taylor, M. (2006). From the inside out, and the outside. Co/autoethnography as a means of Professional Renewal. In C. Kosnik, et al. (Eds.), *Making a difference in teacher education trough self-study*. Dortrecht: Springer.
Dalton, J., & Anderson, D. (2007). *PLOT: Professional Learning Online Tool*. Retrieved from http://www.plotpd.com.au
Dewey, J. (1933). *How we think: A restatement of the relation of reflective thinking to the educative process*. Boston: D.C. Heath.
Dooner, A., Mandzuk, D., & Clifton, R. (2008). Stages of collaboration and the realities of professional learning communities. *Teaching and Teacher Education, 24*, 564–574.
Feldman, A., Paugh, P., & Mills, G. (2004). Self-study through action research. In J. Loughran, et al. (Eds.), *International hanbook of teaching and teacher education practices* (pp. 943–978). Dortrecht: Kluwer Academic Publishers.
Fitzgerald, L., Farstad, J., & Deemer, D. (2002). What gets 'mythed' in student evaluations of their teacher education professors? In J. Loughran & T. Russell (Eds.), *Improving teacher education practices through self-study*. London: Routledge/Falmer.
Garrison, D. R., & Anderson, T. (2003). *E-learning in the 21st century: A framework for research and practice*. London: RoutledgeFalmer.
Glickman, C. (2002). *Leadership for learning: How to help teachers succeed*. Alexandria: ASCD.
Gore, J., & Zeichner, K. (1991). Action research and reflective teaching in preservice teacher education: A case study from the United States. *Teaching and Teacher Education, 7*(2), 119–136.
Guilfoyle, K., Hamilton, M. L., Pinnegar, S., & Placier, P. (The Arizona Group) (2000). Myths and legends of teacher education reform in the 1990s. A collaborative self-study of four programs. In J. Richards & T. Russell (Eds.), *Exploring myths and legends of teacher education. Proceedings of the third international conference on self-study of teacher education practices, Herstmonceux, Sussex, UK*. Kingston, ON: Queen's University.
Ham, V., & Davey, R. (2006). Is virtual teaching, real teaching? Learnings from two self-studies. In C. Kosnik, et al. (Eds.), *Making a difference in teacher education trough self-study* (pp. 101–116). Dortrecht: Springer.
Hall, G., & Hord, S. (2001). *Implementing change: Patterns, principles, and potholes*. Boston: Allen & Bacon.
Hatton, N., & Smith, D. (1995). *Reflection in teacher education: Towards definition and implementation*. The University of Sydney: School of Teaching and Curriculum Studies. Retrieved from http://www2.edfac.usyd.edu.au/LocalResource/Study1/hattonart.html
Hord, S., Rutherford, W., Huling-Austin, L., & Hall, E. (1987). Taking charge of change. *Association for Supervision and Curriculum Development, 703*, 549–9110.
LaBoskey, V. (1998). Introduction to Part IV: Case studies of collaborative self-study. In M. Hamilton, et al. (Eds.), *Reconceptualising teaching practice: Self-study in teacher education* (pp. 151–153). London: Falmer Press.

Lave, J., & Wenger, E. (1991). *Situated learning: Legitimate peripheral participation.* Cambridge: Cambridge University Press.

Liston, D., & Zeichner, K. (Eds.). (1996). *Reflective teaching: An introduction.* Mahwah, NJ: Lawrence Erlbaum Associates.

Loucks-Horsley, S. (1996). Professional development for science education: A critical and immediate challenge. In R. Bybee (Ed.), *National standards & the science curriculum.* Dubuque, IA: Kendall/Hunt Publishing Co. Retrieved April 20, 2007, from www.nas.edu/rise/backg4a.htm

Loucks-Horsley, S., & Stiegelbauer, S. (1991). Using knowledge to guide staff development. In A. Lieberman & L. Miller (Eds.), *Staff development for education in the 90's: New demands, new realities, new perspectives.* New York: Teachers College Press.

Loughran, J., & Northfield, J. (1996). *Opening the classroom door: Teacher, researcher, learner.* London: Falmer Press.

Loughran, J., & Northfield, J. (1998). A framework for the development of self-study practice. In Hamilton et al. (Eds.), *Reconceptualising teaching practice: Self-study in teacher education.* London: Falmer Press.

Munby, H., & Russell, R. (1994). The authority of experience in learning to teach: Messages from a physics methods class. *Journal of Teacher Education, 45*(2), 86–95.

National College of School Leadership (NCSL). (2005). *Understanding learning networks.* Retrieved February 20, 2007, from http://networkedlearning.ncsl.org.uk/collections/network-research-series/summaries/understanding-learning-networks.pdf

Robinson, V. (1993). *Problem-based methodology: Research for the improvement of practice.* Oxford: Pergamon.

Schon, D. (1983). *The reflective practitioner.* New York: Basic Books.

PART THREE: MOVING FORWARD

12. PROMOTING SELF-STUDY AS A HABIT OF MIND FOR PRESERVICE TEACHERS

The life which is unexamined is not worth living.
(Socrates, in *The Apology* by Plato, 399 BC)

When Socrates addressed a court of law in *The Apology* (Plato, 399 BC), he attempted to explain his need to examine himself and others not just to possess the appearance of happiness, but the reality of it. In this chapter, we propose that when preservice teachers are encouraged to participate in a study of themselves and their developing philosophies and pedagogy through rigorous reflection and systematic and critical examination of their context and actions (Samaras & Freese, 2006), they learn to seek the reality that makes teaching rewarding and effective and, on a larger scale, a profession and purpose that make life rewarding and meaningful.

Ultimately, teacher educators intend for preservice teachers to reflect on their practices and the context of those practices—including a close examination of themselves—for the purpose of improving their teaching and students' learning. Our objective is that their actions are consciously planned and driven rather than based on habit, whim, or what the teacher in the classroom next door is doing (Samaras, 2002). We invite them, in these days of high-stakes testing and top-down mandates, to take the remote out of the hands of policymakers (Yendol-Hoppey, 2006) and take charge of their learning and their classrooms. We want them to confront who they are as educators and people and examine how their identities interfere with or encourage learning within the context of their classroom. Our goal is for self-study to become a "habit of mind" for them—a way of thinking, acting, and becoming an effective teacher and a caring, fulfilled person (Lassonde, Ritchie, & Fox, 2008). As a result, they will recognize that life—as an educator—is meaningful.

Throughout the chapters in this book, it has been made consistently evident that self-study methodology parallels many of the qualities and dispositions teacher educators hope to instill in their preservice teachers (Mittapalli & Samaras, 2008). Galman writes of honesty and transparency as essential measures of quality and integrity. Kosnik, Cleovoulou, and Fletcher refer to educators being improvement-oriented. Kitchen and Ciuffetelli Parker describe the benefits of developing and sustaining an openness to reflect and collaborate with critical friends and colleagues.

Considering Kitchen and Ciuffetelli Parker's recommendations, it is significant that the co-authors of this chapter are a teacher educator and a preservice teacher.

C. A. Lassonde, S. Galman and C. Kosnik (eds.), Self-Study Research Methodologies for Teacher Educators, 207–224.

In our partnership, we have worked together in various capacities: teacher educator and undergraduate preservice teacher, teacher educator and teaching assistant (TA), co-presenters at educational conferences, co-researchers, and co-authors. We have created a respectful, professional relationship that allows us to learn from each other, study ourselves, and critically examine our professional and personal goals. Dusti clarifies the student perspective for Cindy and causes her to consider rationale, purpose, objectives, methods, what is important to know and experience, and what counts as knowing. Meanwhile, Cindy's reciprocal role has developed into one of a mentor for Dusti. Cindy provides her rationale behind her teaching strategies and methodologies from a teacher educator standpoint, causing Dusti to reflect upon her personal teaching philosophy, challenging her to consider the facets of her role and take into consideration the responsibilities of teaching. More about this partnership appears later in this chapter.

We hope to share with you an overview of possibilities and contexts for promoting self-study with preservice teachers. We begin with a description of the rationale based on current research by teacher educators studying their students and programs and a discussion of theories that ground this rationale. Next, we look at rich contexts and approaches disclosing findings others are discovering as well as our own experiences, trials, and thoughts. We highlight our work together as teacher educator and TA and end the chapter with a discussion of self-study as a habit of mind.

RATIONALE

There are a number of benefits to promoting self-study as a habit of mind for preservice teachers. Recent studies indicate self-study opportunities, when they encourage participants to move beyond just telling their story to producing new knowledge (Loughran, 2008), have been effective in helping preservice teachers understand their emerging identities and uncover personal beliefs and contradictions to these beliefs.

Freese (2006) studied the impact of self-study research on the professional and personal lives of preservice teachers. Results indicated that their self-studies allowed them to gain ownership of personal theories based on their prior experiences, recognize and come to terms with contradictions among their beliefs and the realities of teaching, and reveal fears and uncertainties they had about concerns such as classroom management.

Chryst, McKay, and Lassonde (2009) found that in preservice teachers' development of their statement-of-teaching philosophy, many attempted to sway or oscillate in their thinking as they contemplated what they perceived as their certainties and uncertainties in their understandings about teaching and learning. The researchers' impressions indicated preservice teachers held onto their image of an ideal teacher, perhaps a past mentor, and were resistant to changing this image based on course readings and discussions. Evidence of sway hinted at their emerging willingness to confront reality and consider their own forming identities. They began to create an authentic teacher image for themselves.

Richards (2006), using post-modern image-based research, assigned preservice teachers to create a series of self-portraits to illustrate their concerns and perceptions about going into the field to teach content reading. Their self-portraits with dialogue illuminated their fears and triumphs. Analysis of the portraits indicated arts-based techniques such as self-portraiture can potentially help preservice teachers explore and express their perceived realities and understandings in ways that written or verbal narratives alone might not reveal.

In their work with preservice teacher researchers, Lang, D'Annibale, Minzter, Peck, and Stein (2008) found that linking classroom practices to educational literature during self-study reflective writing was "crucial to the development of flexible, growth-oriented identities as teachers. This orientation [allowed] teachers to integrate research into practice rather than push it away" (p. 46).

Sowa and Schmidt (2008) scaffolded reflective practices for their student teachers to help them integrate theory, practice, and ethics as they reflected upon their practices and developed their philosophies. Themes emerging from their study included the use of metaphors, graphic organizers, and dialog as theories of practice emerged.

Finally, although Bass, Anderson-Patton, and Allender (2002) looked at graduate students' portfolios, they also noted shifts of awareness in thinking through self-study and reflective practices. We include this study here because Bass and colleagues' conception of reflexivity can help us think about preservice teachers' awareness. These researchers concluded that reflexivity, which they define as "worldviews clash[ing] from the input of critical friends and theory, can push reflection past defensiveness into transformative learning" (p. 67). Graduates documented reports of shifting that included transforming from a sense of self to one of teacher researcher and from a sense of being protective of independence to one of working with others. Their intensive work with colleagues is credited with moving beyond simply thinking about their teaching. We see how similar collaborations with colleagues, when made available to preservice teachers in field experiences, could open spaces for them to co-construct meanings for emerging personal and professional identities to help them negotiate authentic, cohesive relationships among these budding identities.

Figure 1 offers a list of potential opportunities self-study can offer to preservice teachers as reflected in the illustrative, exemplary studies cited.

THEORETICAL FOUNDATIONS

Teacher educators and preservice teachers, along with supervising and cooperating teachers and other associated colleagues and peers, work together to co-construct identities and negotiate meanings. Teacher educators empower preservice teachers when we provide the tools and knowledge for studying themselves within the context of their practice and lead them to generate new knowledge of the general from the particular (Loughran, 2008).

Self-study offers preservice teachers opportunities to

- Understand their emerging identities as teachers, researchers, professionals, colleagues, role models, lifelong learners, trusted confidantes, community leaders, and so on (Bass, Anderson-Patton, & Allender, 2002);
- Understand how their professional identities help shape and influence their personal identities and vice versa (Chryst, McKay, & Lassonde, 2009);
- Uncover personal beliefs, theories, and contradictions (Freese, 2006);
- Self-monitor with hopes of improving knowledge, classroom practices, and students' learning (Lang, D'Annibale, Minzter, Peck, & Stein, 2008);
- Inquire about issues that are important and relevant to them, their teaching, and their students (Lang, D'Annibale, Minzter, Peck, & Stein, 2008);
- Examine and create evidence-based practices (i.e., meaningfully linking theory to practice, becoming researchers) (Sowa and Schmidt, 2008); and
- Collaborate with colleagues (Bass, Anderson-Patton, & Allender, 2002; Woodcock, Lassonde, & Rutten, 2003).

Figure 1. Opportunities Self-Study Offers Preservice Teachers

This very important work cannot be done in isolation if it is to be highly effective and critical (Bass, Anderson-Patton, & Allender, 2002; Woodcock, Lassonde, & Rutten, 2003). Here, we define co-construction as the process of producing and shaping the content of discourse—which we broadly portray as including written, oral, and nonverbal forms of communication, such as self-talk, reflective writing, and the expressive arts—within situated contexts that relate to the social world (Lave, 1996; Mischler, 1999). Preservice teachers' development of identities is a result of forming relationships and participating in interactions with others. We propose that their ongoing self-study as novice teachers must include relationships and interactions in order to grow continually as educators. We refer to Lave's (1996) premise that

> People in activity are skillful at, and are more often than not engaged in, helping each other to participate in changing ways in a changing world.... [P]articipation in everyday life may be thought of as a process of changing understanding in practice, that is, as learning. (pp. 5–6)

We encourage and facilitate the development, or learning, of self-study tools in preservice teachers when we coordinate and produce opportunities for them to retrieve their prior knowledge; reflect on preconceptions they have formed about issues; share and discuss other's perspectives, including those represented in readings and discussions; and begin to take informed positions that carve out new personal and professional identities—all as they relate to their selves, knowledge, perceptions, beliefs, and values.

Positioning theory is a dynamic alternative to the static concept of taking on a role (van Langenhove & Harre, 1999). Positioning plays a major role in our quest to develop preservice teachers' habit of mind of using self-study practices. Positioning conceives of identities as fluid and malleable by the self and others. In our courses, we position preservice teachers to think critically about theory and pedagogy so they can determine who they are, what kind of teacher they want to be, and what positions they take on various issues in education based on introspection supported by the discourses made available to them.

Finally, we must consider here how reflection connects with self-study. Dewey (1933) defined reflection as "turning a subject over in the mind and giving it serious and consecutive consideration" (p. 3). He refers to it as a "better way of thinking" (p. 3). Egan (2007) proposes that we cannot actually teach reflective thinking. "We can only discuss ways to help preservice teachers cultivate a reflective attitude or way of life" (p. 3). Egan's proposition connects directly with our goals for self-study with preservice teachers: to develop it as a habit of mind so that life and teaching are worthwhile. Egan continues, saying.

> A teacher cannot thrive without a personal mission that enables him to be passionate about his teaching and student learning. To possess a personal mission, one must be able to go to the core of one's inner being, to the inner self that contains deep-rooted, core values, so to speak. Some of these core values could be identified as determination, courage, strength, compassion, flexibility, and so on. (pp. 7–8)

Therefore, theory supports that teacher educators can empower preservice teachers to, as Lave (1999) would say, *learn* to employ self-study methods. Let us now look at how educators are doing just that.

RICH, SITUATED CONTEXTS FOR PRESERVICE TEACHER SELF-STUDY

One context might be more or less conducive to self-study than another. As we analyzed our thoughts about this, we noted that many of the components we would consider favorable to self-study overlapped with what we thought made a context ripe for collaboration. The risks are similar (i.e., exposing one's vulnerabilities and scraping away one's conscious and underlying resistances); therefore, the prevention or antidote would be expected to be comparable. Figure 2 offers a list of conditions that would imply a situated context is ripe and appropriate for self-study.

Teacher education programs offer opportunities for preservice teachers to learn and participate in self-study through classroom and field experiences. Before we look more closely at specific approaches teacher educators have incorporated into their courses, let us first consider what boundaries might exist to their full implementation.

A context is conducive for self-study when **preservice teachers**
- Come to the conversation with an open mind ready to learn from others and break down barriers;
- Form trusting yet open and critical relationships with others;
- Feel safe to voice their vulnerabilities, confusions, questions, and doubts without being unconstructively criticized or denigrated and overly discomforted;
- Feel comfortable sharing their opinions, perspectives, and critiques even when they seemingly contradict or are in opposition to others;
- Expect they may feel a certain degree of discomfort if or when their positions are questioned, but look at such situations as learning opportunities to expand their knowledge and understandings;
- Are honest and forthright in a respectful manner;
- Seek to extend their self-knowledge through reflexive actions;
- Are willing to forgive and accept others and their opinions even if they are not their own;
- Look to the co-construction of discourse as an opportunity to grow and mature.

A context is conducive for self-study when **the teacher educator**
- Reaches out to show he or she takes an interest in them and cares about them and their education;
- Is flexible when possible to fit the needs of his or her students;
- Opens doors to communication through means that are commonplace and natural to today's student (i.e., email, instant or text messaging);
- Is a respectful listener;
- Explicitly models his or her own acceptance of new ideas (e.g., "I never thought of it that way!");
- Facilitates dialogue among students;
- Encourages students to generate new knowledge by looking beyond their story and moving from the particular to the general;
- Allows students to be the experts whenever possible; and
- Connects with students by sharing examples and anecdotes from his or her life.

Figure 2. Opportune Conditions for Preservice Teacher Self-Study

POTENTIAL BOUNDARIES TO CONSIDER

The approaches we found in our searches were what Samaras and Freese (2006) refer to as formal and informal self-study approaches. Informal approaches refer to

activities that provide practice in exploring one's teaching and learning using reflection as a critical dimension…(e.g., journaling, personal history papers, autobiographies) but does not necessarily involve formal data gathering, nor is it intended to be formally written up or made public…. Informal self-study may be incorporated in preservice and inservice programs to encourage teachers to gain practice using strategies to reflect on and inquire into their beliefs and theories in practice. (p. 62)

Formal self-study draws upon qualitative research methods; bases findings on a theoretical framework; and discusses methods, data sources, findings, and implications for the study. In our searches, we found both formal and informal approaches; however, reports of informal approaches teacher educators are using in preservice teacher courses seemed to be more common or at least more widely disseminated. We would also propose that informal approaches are less time-consuming and demanding than formal approaches and can more easily be integrated into a course assignment. However, we question whether or not informal approaches are also less rigorous.

That point leads to our first potential boundary. That is, preservice teachers have most likely not been trained to be qualitative researchers. Undergraduate programs typically do not include a course in qualitative research, nor do many have the time to do so. While educational psychology courses may touch upon research methods, preservice teachers' formal research knowledge may be limited to reading about research rather than practicing it.

Next, we must also consider the positions preservice teachers are in as undergraduates. Grades and impressions are very telling and visible indicators of one's ability and potential as a teacher, and teaching jobs are highly competitive in most areas. Undergraduates may not be willing to admit their vulnerabilities and doubts in front of their peers, their instructors (who are responsible for assigning a grade), and others in supervisory positions (i.e., supervising and cooperating teachers, administrators). In some cases, the student-teaching placement may lead to a hired position for the preservice teacher. Potentially, a preservice teacher who admits insecurities to a potential reference or employer, as a result of reflective thinking, may be passed over for an applicant who exudes confidence and presumably shows no vulnerabilities and self-doubt.

Furthermore, teacher educators cite their packed curriculum as a boundary to the luxury of teaching or providing spaces for their students to develop self-study methods. This concern is discussed further in the following section when we look at specific approaches.

APPROACHES TO PROMOTE SELF-STUDY WITH PRESERVICE TEACHERS

Teacher educators can offer opportunities for preservice teachers to participate in self-study through various approaches. Within the contexts of field experiences and on-campus classes, teacher educators are requiring preservice teachers to write reflective responses (i.e., reflective journals) and to analyze experiences through dialogue. In this section we describe several approaches that promote self-study.

Preservice teachers are frequently invited to study themselves and their developing teacher identities through written and narrative reflections in response to readings, discussions, or clinical practices of some kind. All too often, however, reflective practices are becoming commonplace—overassigned and underexplored—in teacher education, and packed programs allow little time to devote to them

(Kitchen, 2008). Furthermore, preservice teachers are expected to reflect without the needed explicit instruction of how to reflect effectively. Following a lesson, student teachers are typically assigned the task of reflecting on the lesson, their teaching, and student learning without being instructed in how to reflect or provided models of what reflection really looks like. Questions or prompts may be provided to guide reflections; however, the development of the reflective process and reflective thinking may remain mysteries to the student teacher and, in some cases, to the teacher educator as well. While it is not the purpose of this chapter to explore how to teach preservice teachers to reflect, we do provide some valuable citations the reader can investigate further to see how other teacher educators have approached this challenge.

Teacher educators are taking steps to teach reflection as a process. Egan (2007) offers an insightful account of how she attempts to foster in-depth, engaged reflection in a clinical experience. After careful evaluation of various reflection models, particularly Korthagen and Vasolos's model (2005) and Diltz's model (1990), she incorporated a cyclic model of reflection into her approach to supervising candidates and enabling their reflection processes. Candidates begin by focusing on problematic situations vs. ideal expectations, then work toward identifying limitations and what qualities are needed to overcome these limitations. Finally, candidates are asked to reflect on how to achieve the necessary qualities. Woodcock, Lassonde, and Rutten (2003), also looking at reflection in a self-study context, adapted Rodgers's (2002) conception of the reflective cycle based on Dewey's (1933) definition of reflection to include collaboration and meta-awareness. The researchers state that "collaboration was paramount, because...knowledge was constructed in relationships with one another" (p. 69). (Their diagram of what reflection looks like is found at http://www. und.nodak.edu/dept/ehd/journal/spring2004/woodcock.html.) Other educators are studying how reflection rubrics can guide preservice teachers through a systematic meta-analysis of readings and experiences (Lassonde, Black, Mi, Miller, & Jury, 2007). Preservice teachers practiced writing reflective responses to various types of texts and field experience prompts, such as

– Personal connection (text to self): Have you used a strong "I voice"?
– Growth and metacognition: Have you provided evidence that demonstrates a meta-awareness of personal or professional growth?
– Critical analysis: Have you questioned or considered others' perspectives?
– Other connections (text to text and text to world): Have you provided examples of how you have made connections to readings or other examples at a contextual and decontextual level?
– Comprehension: Have you clearly and logically expressed opinions, responses, arguments, and positions?

Following individual reflection based on these prompts, responses were pushed beyond reflection: Opportunities were provided for preservice teachers to share and discuss their responses with peers and the instructors. You will find the reflection rubric in Lassonde, Black, Miller, and Mi (2008).

While reflective writing is commonly assigned, teacher educators may be at a loss to know how to effectively respond to and evaluate preservice teachers' reflections. As Kitchen (2008) posits in his study of his own feedback responses to preservice teachers' reflective writing, "one way to enhance reflective practice among preservice teachers is to improve the quality of feedback provided by teacher educators" (p. 37). Kitchen begins by analyzing five years of his feedback responses. He then identifies and describes eight categories of responses: validating, echoing, questioning, analyzing, cautioning, exploring possibilities, sharing, and improving reflective practice. While Kitchen's study does not profess to provide evidence that his awareness and use of the categories enhanced reflective practice among his students, he says his findings do "serve as a prompt for reflection and dialogue about how to enhance written responses" (p. 43) and "attempt to make his practices explicit in order to grow professionally" (p. 45). His study pointed him toward increasing his use of systematic responses. For example, he notes he should make the questioning process more explicit before turning to analysis.

We suggest that to pursue a deep level of self-study teacher educators must push preservice teachers beyond simply reflecting into reflexivity as previously defined by Bass, Anderson-Patton, and Allender (2002). Approaches that provide opportunities for preservice teachers to interact with teachers in the field, their peers, and others as they shape their identities will allow them to engage authentically with the reflective process. Activities such as drafting, revising, and rewriting a statement of philosophy several times throughout the program, perhaps each academic year, allows preservice teachers to see who they are becoming as educators. Egan (2007) would want us to encourage preservice teachers to write about their values and beliefs to access and critique their core selves. Also, Kitchen (2008) believes that making personal connections with preservice teachers and sharing our experiences with them opens conversations about their goals, dreams, and concerns. In campus classrooms, teacher educators attempt to model approaches for reflective practice and self-study. And, how fortunate it is when preservice teachers are invited to collaborate with teacher educators in self-study and teacher research projects.

The final approach that we will discuss here is that of promoting preservice teachers' self-study through comprehensive work sample assignments. Having grown in popularity over the past few years mostly in response to political pressure to prove preservice teachers do improve student learning, Teacher Work Samples (Renaissance Partnership, 2002) and similarly Teaching Learning Projects (Maheady, Jabot, & Rey, 2008) are being implemented. These comprehensive work samples require preservice teachers to create complex instructional units and implement them in authentic contexts. They must use context to plan instruction, select learning goals, design lessons, assess, analyze students' learning, and reflect on the whole process. Maheady, Jabot, and Rey found in their study of Teaching Learning Projects that the projects were reported to improve preservice teachers' professional development, ability, and confidence to reflect upon the teaching and learning experience.

OUR EXPERIENCE

At this point, we would very much like to share what we have found to be a valuable experience in self-study. The co-authors, Cindy and Dusti, have been working together and studying our impressions as teacher educator and undergraduate TA. The following exemplar will help the reader see what a preservice teacher gained from this opportunity to develop in her practice of self-study methods. Following an introduction to our work, we will each narrate our perceptions about how our collaboration influenced our self-study.

Introduction

Cindy is in her sixth year as a full-time professor in the elementary education and reading department at a small teacher college in upstate New York. For most of her 20-year career, she was an elementary school teacher. Making the shift to teaching at the college level concerned her. Although she had worked with many student teachers in her elementary classrooms, she wanted to be sure that she could effectively relate to and meet the needs of adult learners. She also had some personal adjustments to make, finding the challenges of working with adults were very different from working with pre-adolescents and their families. Each semester she used self-study methodologies to examine her practice and her identities and positions as a novice college instructor.

In the Fall of 2007 she invited Dusti, an accelerated student in one of her sections of an undergraduate literacy course she regularly teaches each semester, to work with her as a TA the following semester in the same course. This came about mostly because faculty was offered the opportunity to enroll students in a new teaching assistantship course. Cindy thought it would be an excellent chance to mentor advanced preservice teachers, but she wasn't quite sure what to expect. In the following section, Dusti shares her journey as a result of this collaboration as a demonstration of what a preservice teacher can achieve from an opportunity to practice self-study.

From Dusti's Perspective as a Teaching Assistant

As a senior at Oneonta, I am majoring in childhood education to become certified to teach in grades one through six. When Cindy asked me to be a TA, a position that required aiding preservice teachers in their learning and communicating ideas effectively to adult learners—my college peers, I was initially intimidated. However, I soon found it to be an opportunity to broaden my experience with teaching in an authentic setting and a way to further develop my teaching philosophy. I reflected upon my experience on a weekly basis by conversing with Cindy and writing in a reflective journal.

I was Cindy's TA for her course EDUC 284 The Development of Language and Literacy during the spring 2008 semester. As a TA, I started my role in the classroom unsure of my responsibilities; but eventually I found myself continuously reflecting upon my emerging identities as a teacher and a professional. In this section, I will unravel my thoughts and reflections, conducting my personal self-study. Later, I will share my perspective of TAs and their potential value in the college classroom.

In the Beginning. My first assignment as Cindy's TA occurred during winter break of 2008 before the spring semester began. She emailed me her revised syllabus and asked me for my opinion on what to keep and change according to my past experiences as a student in the class. I thought to myself, "You want a student to help you with the syllabus, a document that for a college student you guard so dearly because it rules your life for the entire semester?" I was beginning to see that my role as a TA was not going to be Cindy's errand runner, nor her handout copier—in other words, her "gofer." I was going to play a more intimate role in the course.

Before the first day of classes began and I was officially going to be introduced to roughly sixty students as their new TA, I emailed Cindy asking her what I should be prepared to do and say on the first day. In response, she said to meet her an hour before classes started and we would discuss what we were going to say. I thought I would be observing for the first two weeks and slowly entering the teaching scene. I walked into her office anxious and excited. She immediately asked me, "So how do you feel about being up front with me today? I would like to have a dialogue with you. As I explain what to expect throughout the semester, I will look to you to give your insights from your perspective." I have an engrained memory of our first meeting. Observing for the first two weeks was out of the question. We were an instant mesh, a collaborative team. On the first day, we modeled to the students the beginning of a meaningful collaboration.

Within that first meeting we also discussed the parameters of my role as a TA. Cindy and I decided that it would be wise to express the boundaries of my role that first day of classes so everyone was clear with my position. We explained that I would not do any grading, nor have access to students' grades. I did not see test questions prior to the test. If a student wanted to know what Cindy expected, it would benefit them more to go directly to her. I did not want to set any expectations and have any student turn around and say, "But, Dusti said..." This was not my place. Most importantly, I was a helper to the students, giving them my insights from a student's perspective. Also, I was available as an ombudsperson to whom they could come to express their ideas about the course. In this way, they were anonymous to the professor and I could translate their concerns to Cindy. These parameters were shared on the first day of classes not to set strict limitations on my role but to help form a respectful relationship between the students and me, while enabling a more comfortable learning environment for students, professor, and TA.

This is only a glimpse into the beginning of the professional relationship Cindy and I strived to create. In my first journal entry, written before the semester had begun, I wrote, "As much as I will be there to help Dr. Lassonde and the students, I know *I* will learn a great deal on so many levels." I envisioned learning a great deal about teaching, but I never expected I would learn so much about myself and how I fit into my teaching. I am going to take the next few sections of this chapter to outline my personal self-study and how it became my "habit of mind" as a preservice teacher and TA.

Developing Categories of Self. Reflecting upon my experience, I found that my development can be categorized into three selves. These include Stepping Out of the Student Me, Budding into a Developing Professional, and Becoming a Colleague. Within these levels of development, I will discuss how each aspect helped to define me as a student, a person, and a future teacher.

Stepping Out of the Student Me. It was evident that I was able to work with Cindy on a professional level. I worried more about working with sixty college peers—sixty college-aged personalities. I can speak of my student self-development on two levels: recognizing the differences between my student self and my TA self and the influence on my growth as a student.

The first day after the syllabus had been presented, sometimes an overwhelming experience for college students, two female students approached me. They told me their names and immediately began to share their anxieties about the class, asking for advice on how to manage it. I smiled to myself knowing that I have these same questions after hearing the endless list of projects on the first day of classes. The difference here was that I never had anyone to go to for advice. I never wanted to have a professor's first impression of me be that of an insecure student. These two students needed the assurance the class was manageable and the peace of mind they could do it.

This interaction was the first to cause me to step out of my comfortable role as a student and into that of a TA. What may sound like an awkward comparison was the truth of my student-to-TA relationship: I became their exhorting cheerleader. I am not referring to the stereotypical view of the fake smile and heartless cheers one may assumingly associate with the admirable sport. I am speaking of cheerleading as an action taken to encourage a team to endure the challenge and complete the task. Teachers are expected to be encouraging and motivating. From my experience, I can say college students love to commiserate with peers who share the same misery: "Misery loves company." I am guilty of this as well, but as a TA this was not my role.

I can recall on several occasions during the semester I went around the classroom fielding what I thought were going to be questions about the assignment the students were currently working on. Instead, I received honest comments such as, "I can't do this" or "How are we expected to do all of this?" As a college student myself, I could understand their stresses. I knew the challenges each assignment presented. But, I decided I was not a TA who was going to help students wallow in their lack of confidence. I was there to encourage them to push forward. I stepped outside of my student identity and recognized my new identity as a TA was to encourage their optimal growth and learning. To do their best, they would need me to be more than a sympathetic peer who had similar experiences. They would need me to lead them on and show them effective strategies for success. As a TA I would need to be a leader, a confidante, a model, and a supportive friend.

A more specific example of my role as a "cheerleader" was during a creative assignment. As part of this literacy class, students were required to write and illustrate a predictable book. They were aware they were not going to be graded based upon their artistic abilities, yet a natural response to this assignment from a majority of the students was their expression of their inability to draw. The previous semester, I had the opportunity to watercolor my predictable book. Cindy had me model a read-aloud using my creation. I took my chances by giving a short motivational speech, cheering or nudging them to take a chance and be creative. They could use my book as a model. These were books the students could eventually use in their future classroom. These preservice teachers were given the opportunity to model their effort and creativity in their personal work for their future students, despite their initial hesitation. That semester, Cindy expressed her satisfaction in having received some of the most creative, well-constructed, and highest-quality predictable books ever. She attributed students' achievement to my having boosted their self-confidence and challenged them to take risks in creating books of which they would be proud. Students immediately started asking when the books were going to be handed back. They wanted to bring the books home to show their family over spring break. Their pride and new-found confidence was evident.

As a student, I was learning by defining my personal teaching philosophy: I was beginning to uncover my personal beliefs and theories. As a part of my developing teaching philosophy, I believe it is important to convey my personal enthusiasm as a teacher about the lesson or topic being taught, to lead and to nudge learning. This enthusiasm then becomes a model for students. I connected this experience to my readings of what Cambourne (2001) wrote about how crucial effective demonstrations and models are for students' learning. He described how expectations and self-esteem are linked. He explained,

> we usually achieve what we expect to achieve (or are expected to achieve by others); we fail when we expect to fail (or are expected by others to fail); we are more likely to engage with the demonstrations by those whom we regard as significant and who hold high expectations for us. (p. 785)

When I ask my future students to think creatively and they begin to doubt their ability, I want to be able to demonstrate with personal examples and to set expectations that, despite my ability, emphasize the effort I put into my work. After uncovering this personal belief, I was able to put theory into practice at the college level. I learned how to communicate my ideas to preservice teachers and witnessed their embracing acceptance, confirming my support of this personal theory. I found that when a teacher sets high expectations, most students will work to achieve them. As I continue to grow as a student and blossom into a teacher, I can attest to the fact that teachers are not "simply providers of knowledge," but they "direct the life of the classroom" (Tompkins, 2005, p. 76). They are not only facilitators, role models, instructors, and organizers. Teachers are cheerleaders, motivating students to put forth effort and find confidence in their abilities.

Budding into a Developing Professional. After looking more in depth at my role as a TA, I realized my position as an emergent professional making decisions, along with Cindy, were influential and directly affected the students. I had been empowered by my position to develop as a professional.

I felt empowered by the fact that my insights were valued. My ideas were not merely dismissed; they were discussed, considered, and frequently tried. I learned that part of being a professional included reflecting on my practice and making adjustments to fit students' needs. For example, one observation I made that was based on my value of authentic assignments and assessment involved the course's final assignment. Being a TA, I had endless opportunities to be in front of the classroom and to learn how to use and incorporate the available technology—the technology that is being seen more and more in elementary and high-school classrooms. Throughout the semester I would tell Cindy, "I know how much using this technology and being up front has helped me feel more comfortable and confident in integrating the technology in effective ways. We have to get these students doing what I am doing and teaching mini-lessons." I believed the opportunities I had were completely relevant to the course and would benefit the students. Many had expressed their lack of knowledge on how to use the new technology and their fear of presenting—two aspects a teacher will be expected to know. After much discussion and thought, Cindy and I decided we would restructure the final assignment into one in which our students would plan, write up, and demonstrate a literacy lesson that effectively incorporated at least one form of available technology.

With Cindy's support, I had the opportunity to draft a rubric for the grading of the presentations and lesson plans. We discussed what the important categories would be in the grading process based on our objectives for the task, and I drafted the language for each requirement. Through the process of drafting, I learned to construct the rubric so it would not only be a guide to facilitate students' preparation for the task but would be a clear tool for Cindy to use in her assessment of the demonstration and lesson plan. For me as a professional, the most meaningful aspect of the situation was that Cindy and I had made the decision to restructure the final assignment into an authentic learning experience for the students. This was who I wanted to be as a professional—someone who could directly touch and make a difference in people's lives. This feeling was an affirmation of the reason why I initially decided to become a teacher.

After reflecting upon the decisions I made along with Cindy's support, I was given a true foretaste of how influential teachers are as professionals. The latitude I was given to develop my professional identity by influencing the curriculum, creating authentic assessment tools, and being able to see the effects of my decisions and work encouraged my growth and confidence as a professional.

Becoming a Colleague. As a preservice teacher, I hear how essential collaboration is in the teaching profession. I have read about collaboration in textbooks, heard teacher educators speak on it, observed it in classrooms, and interviewed teachers and principals who have described it as one of the most crucial aspects in creating a successful classroom. As a TA, I had the opportunity to partake in meaningful collaboration with Cindy.

In a discussion in her office one morning before classes started, she explained to me how she wanted to use our collaboration to model to students how they can work along with their future colleagues in the field. For example, she went on to explain how, as teachers, we will have consultant teachers, aides, coaches, and family members in our classrooms. Often times they are on standby, when they actually could have a dynamic place in the classroom. This was a goal we set together as we worked side by side, creating dialogues and working as a team to produce an environment conducive to learning, lending as much support for the students as possible.

As a future teacher, I have this experience to bring into my future classroom. I will walk into my first elementary school position with an attitude geared towards ensuring meaningful collaboration, creating unanimity among my future colleagues and me. This is a facet I have incorporated into my teaching philosophy after reflecting upon this experience. I was part of a collaboration that combined two perspectives to construct effective ways of reaching the students and a way of ensuring open communication between teacher educator, student, and TA.

Cindy sent me drafts to review and edit, she sought my opinion on issues, and created strategies to aid her in presenting material. Doors have opened as I have been able to branch out by presenting at conferences and even co-authoring this very chapter. There was a respect between our teacher educator and student relationship that soon became collaboration between colleagues. I am still a student with many years ahead of me to learn, become more educated, and gain experience in the field. She is a professor with much more knowledge and years of experience than me. However, never once did I feel like a lowly student who was not able to communicate with her on a professional level. She understood my capabilities and meshed our talents in a way that banked upon our strengths. I plan to implement this respectful relationship among my future teaching colleagues. Despite a person's education and experience, each individual has a unique perspective or specialty to offer to the classroom.

A New Perspective. As I have tried to portray, this self-study has been an experience of growth, helping to define me as person, a student, and teacher. As for my personal outlook on the role of a TA, it has changed from my initial "gofer" preconception mentioned earlier in the chapter. A passage from my last journal entry says it best:

> As a child, I remember my teachers' aides as the people I was not afraid to approach. I knew their purpose was to help, so I could ask them questions. I could share with them my anxieties about an assignment and show them I was struggling. Not that a teacher shouldn't have this relationship with

students, but an aide presents another perspective to the classroom setting. There were times as a TA, many students shared their nerves or needed help from me, sometimes these being issues a college student does not want to admit or share with a professor. I could relate. In the beginning of the semester, I was concerned with how the students were going to like me. By the middle of the semester, many of the students viewed me as their friend. But by the end of the semester, I sincerely thought of myself as a teacher assistant *for* the students. I devoted my time to this role.

From Cindy's Perspective as a Teacher Educator

Although realistically not all preservice teachers can be given the occasion to act as a TA before they graduate as Dusti did, the contextual factors of this relationship can be replicated within teaching programs to provide similarly precious spaces for preservice teachers to move beyond their stories toward new knowledge to explore how their identities and selves influence their teaching and students' learning. Several approaches have been discussed previously in this chapter. Teacher educators should consider how they can frame their classes and curriculum so preservice teachers can place themselves within the context of their education and their teaching.

My interactions with Dusti allowed me to contemplate the perspective of a preservice teacher emerging as a preprofessional as I concurrently reflected on my position and influence as a teacher educator. For example, my belief that most college students were overstressed and often did assignments just to get them done came into question. I witnessed how Dusti's pride in her work and her encouragement to others to produce high-quality work of which they would be proud made a difference in student performance and engagement. As we observed our students over the semester, we noted that recognizing the importance of having pride in their work helped them determine their priorities and, thereby, seemed to alleviate the stress they expressed as a result of our course. Questioning my beliefs influenced a change in my willingness to empower students to become more active in their learning. Dusti and I, through reflexive teaching, altered assignments and activities in meaningful ways. I discovered that I had become somewhat disenchanted with teaching at the college level through several years of hearing students express their levels of stress. However, my work with Dusti proved that encouragement and authenticity were areas I was taking for granted.

At all levels, from completing readings and tasks to developing a teaching philosophy, teacher educators should consider ways they can encourage preservice teachers to come to know their identities and beliefs as they examine and create evidence-based practices. Sometimes, I found, this can mean our beliefs as teacher educators must come into focus and be re-evaluated first.

SELF-STUDY AS A HABIT OF MIND

Through self-study, preservice teachers can grow as caring, conscientious educators and people who continuously learn to become the best they can be. Self-study as a habit of mind is a great opportunity! "Excitement for teaching is what is involved in being interested, engaged, lively, hopeful, and everything else that a person associates with that makes life worth living" (Allender & Allender, 2008, p. 137). Developing the inner person, not just the external professional, "will help preservice teachers come closer to the core of their true professional personhood" (Egan, 2007, p. 11).

REFERENCES

Bass, L., Anderson-Patton, V., & Allender, J. (2002). Self-study as a way of teaching and learning: A research collaborative re-analysis of self-study teaching portfolios. In J. Loughran & T. Russell (Eds.), *Improving teacher education practices through self-study* (pp. 56–69). London: Routledge.

Cambourne, B. (2001). Conditions for literacy learning. *The Reading Teacher, 54,* 784–786.

Chryst, C., McKay, Z., & Lassonde, C. (2009). Evidence of sway: Teacher candidates' developing ideas about teaching and learning in a two-plus-two program. *The Language and Literacy Spectrum.* Retrieved from http://www.nysreading.org/Publications/newllsarchive.html

Dewey, J. (1933). *How we think.* Boston: D. C. Heath and Company.

Diltz, R. (1990). *Changing belief systems with NLP.* Cupertino: Meta Publications.

Egan, M. (2007). Reflective thinking: The essence of professional development. *Excelsior: Leadership in Teaching and Learning, 2*(1), 1–14.

Kitchen, J. (2008). The feedback loop in reflective practice: A teacher educator responds to reflective writing by preservice teachers. *Excelsior: Leadership in Teaching and Learning, 2*(2), 37–46.

Korthagen, F. A. J. (2001). *Linking practice and theory: The pedagogy of realistic teacher education.* Mahwah, NJ: Lawrence Erlbaum.

Korthagen, F. A. J., & Vasalos, A. (2005). Levels in reflection: Core reflection as a means to enhance professional growth. *Teachers and Teaching: Theory and Practice, 11*(1), 47–71.

Lang, D. E., D'Annibale, L. M., Minzter, L. M., Peck, S. L., & Stein, M. L. (2008). The significance of action research experiences for professional identity development in alternative teacher education programs. *Excelsior: Leadership in Teaching and Learning, 3*(1), 46–56.

Lassonde, C. A., Ritchie, G. V., & Fox, R. K. (2008). How teacher research can become your way of being. In C. A. Lassonde & S. E. Israel (Eds.), *Teachers taking action: A comprehensive guide to teacher research* (pp. 3–14). Newark, DE: International Reading Association.

Lassonde, C. A., Black, K., Mi, H., Miller, J., & Jury, M. (2007). *Developing the writing lives of preservice teachers. A symposium presented at the 97th annual conference of the national council of teachers of English, New York,* New York.

Lassonde, C. A., Black, K., Miller, J., & Mi, H. (under review). *Examining writing expectations through rubrics and scaffolded instruction: A collaborative model.* Unpublished paper currently under review.

Lave, J. (1996). The practice of learning. In S. Chaiklin & J. Lave (Eds.), *Understanding practice: Perspectives on activity and context* (pp. 3–32). Cambridge, England: Cambridge University Press.

Loughran, J. (2008). Seeking knowledge for teaching teaching: Moving beyond stories. In M. L. Heston, D. L. Tidwell, K. K. East, & L. M. Fitzgerald (Eds.), *Pathways to change in teacher education: Dialogue, diversity, and self-study. The seventh international conference on self-study of teacher education practices, Herstmonceux Castle, East Sussex, England* (pp. 218–221). Cedar Falls, IA: University of Northern Iowa.

Maheady, L., Jabot, M., & Rey, J. (2008). Using teaching learning projects to assess and impact candidate practice and pupil learning. *Excelsior: Leadership in Teaching and Learning, 3*(1), 72–81.

223

Mischler, E. G. (1999). *Storylines: Craftartists' narratives of identity.* Cambridge, MA: Harvard University Press.

Mittapalli, K., & Samaras, A. P. (2008). Madhubani art: A journey of an education researcher seeking self-development answers through art and self-study. *The Qualitative Report, 13*(2), 244–261. Retrieved from http://www.nova.edu/ssss/QR/QR13-2/mittapalli.pdf

Plato. *The Apology, Phædo and Crito* (B. Jowett, Trans., Vol. II, Part 1. The Harvard Classics). New York: Collier & Son. Retrieved June 2, 2008, from www.bartleby.com/2/1/

Renaissance Partnership for Improving Teacher Quality. (2002, June). *Teacher work sample: Performance prompts, teaching process standards, and scoring rubrics.* Western Kentucky University. Retrieved from http://fp.uni.edu/itq

Richards, J. C. (2006). Post modern image-based research: An innovative data collection method for illuminating preservice teachers' developing perceptions in field-based courses. *The Qualitative Report, 11*(1), 37–54. Retrieved November 7, 2008, from http://www.nova.edu/ssss/QR/QR11-1/Richards.pdf

Samaras, A. P. (2002). *Self-study for teacher educators: Reflections on teacher education.* London: Falmer Press.

Samaras, A. P., & Freese, A. R. (2006). *Self-study of teaching practices primer.* New York: Peter Lang.

Sowa, P., & Schmidt, C. (2008). The professional working theory: A self-study of scaffolding reflective practice. *Excelsior: Leadership in Teaching and Learning, 3*(1), 57–71.

Tompkins, G. E. (2005). *Language arts: Patterns of practice* (6th ed.). Upper Saddle River, NJ: Pearson Education, Inc.

Van Langenhove, L., & Harre, R. (1999). Introducing positioning theory. In R. Harre & L. vanLangenhove (Eds.), *Positioning theory* (pp. 14–31). Oxford: Blackwell Publishers, Ltd.

Woodcock, C. A., Lassonde, C. A., & Rutten, I. R. (2003). How does collaborative reflection play a role in a teacher researcher's beliefs about herself and her teaching? Discovering the power of relationships. *Teaching and Learning: The Journal of Natural Inquiry and Reflective Practice, 18*(1), 57–76.

Yendol-Hoppey, D. (2006, Summer). Understanding the complexity of teacher learning. *Teaching and Teacher Education, Division K Newsletter.* American Educational Research Association, pp. 9–11.

CLARE KOSNIK, CINDY LASSONDE, AND SALLY GALMAN

13. WHAT DOES SELF-STUDY RESEARCH OFFER TEACHER EDUCATORS?

Self-study research is a powerful process that has grown in sophistication and influence the past two decades. S-STEP, having actively supported many teacher educators, teachers, doctoral students, and administrators, has become a thriving community. The self-study community offers teacher educators a professional identity, support for improving their practice, and opportunities to develop both professionally and personally–all of which we believe are helping to advance the field of teacher education.

In this chapter, we consider what self-study research offers teacher educators through the lenses of identity, support, and possibility. We look at the diverse nature of the work of teacher educators and provide information on conferences and resources to help others develop as educators and self-study scholars. Interestingly, many of these support collaboration and reflection, two hallmarks of self-study research. We conclude *Self-Study Research Methodologies for Teacher Educators* by looking beyond the stories-one of John Loughran's favourite expressions. To do this, we present a Readers' Theatre script that both seriously and playfully considers the implications for collaborative self-study research.

IDENTITY

As simplistic as it sounds, teacher educators are teachers who teach teachers, and self-study teacher educators are those who study their practice in the process. Our S-STEP members, like many other teacher educators around the world, do not aim simply to train teachers; our goal is to prepare a new generation of highly capable teachers.

In these turbulent times, we need teachers who can confidently and effectively organize learning opportunities for a diverse student body. And teacher educators are key to the complex process of becoming a teacher. Cochran-Smith (2003) refers to teacher educators as the "linchpins in education reforms of all kinds" (p. 10); although this sets the bar very high, she acknowledges the diverse nature of the work of teacher educators – teaching, writing, providing professional development, mentoring, supervising, and leading. We believe that studying each one of these roles will provide clarity and coherence to our work.

We recognize that as a profession we will always be in a state of becoming, never completely satisfied with our work or believing that we have finally found "the answer." Since schools are very dynamic places, we teacher educators need to

C. A. Lassonde, S. Galman and C. Kosnik (eds.), Self-Study Research Methodologies for Teacher Educators, 225–239.

be constantly studying our work and modifying our activities; however, we must also take the time to celebrate our accomplishments. In the S-STEP community, there are regular updates on the achievements of our members (e.g. a text published, tenure granted) and definitely support when a member experiences a set-back (e.g. failure to be granted tenure). Teacher education is demanding; in order to continue our work (or "soldier on"), we need others. Although our members hail from many countries around the world, electronic communication and easily accessible modes of transportation have allowed us to become a community. We believe that together as a community, we are improving teacher education and each of us is a better teacher educator because of our participation in S-STEP. Each of the editors of this text and, we suspect, most of the contributors to it are proud to identify themselves as self-study researchers. We are confident that our community will continue to flourish and play a key role in the development of teacher education programs and research.

SUPPORT

The self-study community provides a wide-range of support for its members: conferences to study/present our work as teacher educators and scholars; gatherings to identify potential colleagues; "space" to work with collaborators; and even permission to raise difficult questions. For Cindy, Sally, and Clare, the editors of *Self-Study Research Methodologies for Teacher Educators,* S-STEP has helped us grow both personally and professionally. We have found S-STEP to be a community where teacher educators and researchers strive to be the best they can be and continue to look for ways to support their students in becoming the best they can be. This effort to improve is infectious – when we gather at an S-STEP event, we feel invigorated and energized; this renewal sustains us through the day-in-day-out work of teacher education.

As we reflect on our work with preservice students and practicing teachers, we can see how our self-study way of being provides a model for our students that we hope informs their emerging philosophies about teaching and learning. By studying our interactions with preservice teachers, we learn what methods, strategies, and practices support the development of their identity, expand their repertoire of teaching practices, and help them acquire a solid approach to teaching. We model for them, but we also learn from them. We believe that it is essential to tell our students about our self-study research. In this way, when we encourage them to reflect on their practice, they know that we too are inquiring into our work. We are walking the talk.

Self-study can help us develop professionally as scholars also. A growing number of journals, publishers, professional organizations, and conferences have a space for us and welcome self-study research. Tables 1 through 3 provide the names and contact information for such groups.

Table 1. Journals Receptive to Publishing Self-Studies

Studying Teacher Education: A Journal of Self-Study of Teacher Education Practices
    http://www.informaworld.com/smpp/title~content=t713727674
European Journal of Teacher Education
    http://www.tandf.co.uk/journals/titles/02619768.asp
Excelsior: Leadership in Teaching and Learning
    http://www.nyacte.org/journal/journal.html
Journal of Teacher Education
    http://jte.sagepub.com/
The Qualitative Report
    http://www.nova.edu/ssss/QR/
Reflective Practice
    http://www.tandf.co.uk/journals/titles/14623943.asp
Teacher Education Quarterly
    http://www.teqjournal.org/
Teaching and Teacher Education
    http://www.elsevier.com/wps/find/journaldescription.cws_home/224/description
#description

Table 2. Book Publishers Receptive to Self-Study Books

Peter Lang
    http://www.peterlang.net/Index.cfm?vUR=5&vLang=E or
    http://www.peterlang.net/Home.cfm?vLang=E&vScreenWidth=1680
RoutledgeFalmer
    http://www.routledgeeducation.com/
Sense Publishers
    https://www.sensepublishers.com
Springer
    http://www.springerpub.com/default.aspx?pid=27 or
    http://www.springer.com/?SGWID=0-102-0-0-0
Taylor and Francis
    http://www.taylorandfrancisgroup.com/

Colleagues who collaborate with us in self-study research challenge us to look at ourselves with a "slight edge" as Allender and Allender (2008) explain. Self-study allows us to identify compatible colleagues and to position ourselves among others. Professional organizations, such as the American Educational Research Association previously described in the Introduction and Chapter One of this book, provide venues to network and share our work. During the 2008 Castle Conference, Chryst, Lassonde, and McKay shared the Readers' Theater script that appears at the end of this chapter to describe their growth as researchers, scholars, and writers through their collaboration. Collaboration acts as a mirror so we can reflect on our positions among colleagues.

Table 3. Conferences Receptive to Self-Studies

American Educational Research Association
  http://www.aera.net/
Self-study of teacher education practices (S-STEP) SIG
  http://web.ku.edu/sstep/ and http://sstep.soe.ku.edu/
Action research SIG
  http://www.aera.net/Default.aspx?menu_id=368&id=4718
Lives of Teachers SIG
  http://galileo.stmarys-ca.edu/jbrunett/livestch/
Association of Teacher Education
  http://www.ate1.org/pubs/home.cfm
Association for Teacher Education in Europe
  http://www.atee.org/
Canadian Society for the Study of Education
  http://www.csse.ca/home.html
International S-STEP Conference (Castle Conference)
  http://sstep.soe.ku.edu/conferences/

POSSIBILITY

Finally, self-study offers teacher education the opportunity to look beyond the stories in rigorous ways. This book shows the rigor self-study methodology encompasses.

APPENDIX

Readers' Theater Script on Collaboration

THE INVISIBLE RESEARCHER: NEW INSIGHTS INTO THE ROLE OF
COLLABORATION IN SELF-STUDY

A PLAY IN FIVE ACTS

By
Carolyn F. Chryst
Cynthia A. Lassonde
Zanna McKay
SUNY College at Oneonta
Oneonta, New York, USA

Act I Who Are We as Colleagues?

Scene 1: Logistics of Location and Time

Narrator: During the Fall 2006 and Spring 2007 semesters, we found time to meet on campus to analyze data and work on our initial study. During the summer months that followed, however, when we thought we'd have more time to write and get a manuscript out, the logistics of where and when to meet became problematic. Although we did much of our drafting through emails, there were some conversations we needed to have face to face to move the work along.

We live approximately 50 miles in opposite directions from each other. So, what was "fair" regarding time, travel, and hosting during the Summer of 2007 became an issue. Whose space would best facilitate the writing/research process was another important factor. Equity was never established but was always on the table. While the need for publication outweighed the concerns of cost in both time and travel for Zanna and Carolyn, it did not for Cindy who had other priorities as seen in this email exchange.

Carolyn: We should get together. Where do you want to meet? We can meet here but my house is in chaos and I don't have the energy to fix it up.

Cindy: Kind of distracted right now. Just got some news and may have to fly out to help my daughter, but if you want to come out here this week we can get something done.

Zanna: Hope everything's all right. Do you really want to meet?

Carolyn: Everything all right? If possible, it'd be great if we can finish this manuscript and get it out for review by end of summer.

Cindy: I'll be honest. This isn't a priority for me right now, but it'd be nice to spend some time with you guys even if it is to work. Let's meet Thursday at 10. I'll make lunch. Lots going on here.

Scene 2: The March for Tenure

Narrator: The "March for Tenure" seemed to drive many aspects of our work. Tenure pursuit pressure allowed for compromises in quality. Individuals were silenced for the sake of expediency. This exchange took play during the Fall 2007 semester.

Cindy: Where are we with the manuscript? Let's get it out there and get some feedback on it.

Carolyn: I still don't think the pieces flow together well.

Zanna: Whatever you guys want to do with it is fine with me.

Cindy: We've tossed it back and forth a lot. I think someone besides us has to look at it. Let's get it out to a journal and see what the reviewers have to say. I need to hear an outsider's opinion on it to know what to work on.

Narrator: Almost a year after the manuscript was rejected by the first journal, the manuscript was still unpublished. The original respect for mutual agreement and open discussion evolved into assumptive actions that others would not mind being lead. As life circumstances changed in each researcher's household, openness declined and work stalled. Each member was silenced, and in that silence each member developed unchecked theories as to "what was happening" with the other regarding the work and the desire to continue. The project more or less was just sitting there until in the Spring 2008 semester Cindy emailed this message to Zanna and Carolyn. By that time, Zanna was teaching in Vietnam.

Cindy: I reworked the sections according to the reviewers' comments. See attached. What do you think? I want to send it out to another journal I've found that I think will fit. This project has been sitting, and we've all put so much effort and time into it. You took me on to help get this published, so I'm going to push forward to do that. I'm sending it out to *The Language and Literacy Spectrum,* a peer-reviewed literacy journal. Hope you're both okay with that.

Scene 3: The Invisible Researcher Born of Conversations Around an Oak Table

Narrator: The Invisible Researcher, not yet named or recognized as such by any of us, was born as an entity who embodied our personal caring for each other within the context of real-life circumstances and logistics that became problematic. Out of consideration for each other, with guidance from the Invisible Researcher, we attempted self-organization and, later, self-reorganization. We had this discussion sitting around Carolyn's kitchen table in the Summer of 2008 as we reflected about our collaboration:

Zanna: The Invisible Researcher began as the essence of our collaboration.

Carolyn: We were helping each other professionally…

Cindy: But it was also an opportunity for us to get to know each other socially.

Zanna: The research gave us personal permission to socialize…

Carolyn: So even when we had tons of stuff going on, we could justify getting together to work on this.

Cindy: We each had hectic schedules and we were moving in different directions. But this project gave us a chance to spend time together and become friends.

Zanna: We empowered each other through that growing friendship and trust. So when it all began, the Invisible Researcher was a togetherness of community building.

Carolyn: For academic and social purposes. Trust and confidence in each other became the foundation for our community.

Cindy: I think because I felt like you guys trusted me and had confidence in me that I could help you get published, I felt like I had to make a drastic move and get the manuscript out there…maybe before it was ready the first time, and maybe without getting your okay the second time…but I felt like I had to move forward. When I write, I keep things moving forward. I wasn't comfortable with the manuscript sitting around for so long. Yes, I did feel empowered by your trust in me. That's why I felt I could send it out and you'd both be all right with that.

Narrator: The scary thing is we really talk like this—very academic…hmmmmm.

What does that mean for communicating to our undergrads not steeped in a deeply ingrained academic mind set?

EPILOGUE

Consider these questions as you close this Readers Theater and this book:
- How does the March for Tenure affect collaboration and self-study? How do we stay true to our personal goals and still make tenure? Is there a human component to achieving tenure at your institution or are policies strictly expressed and adhered to? Where does self-study fit in to your institution's tenure and/or promotion policies?
- In a collaborative self-study how do we recognize when someone is being silenced? Is it always detrimental to be silenced, isn't there the potential of a positive outcome, as there was in this study? Is it always detrimental to silence others?

Act II Who Are We as Researchers and Instructors?

Scene 1: Negotiating Rigor (Is It Negotiable?)

Narrator: Meeting notes and emails reveal that the concept of what constitutes rigor is a powerful and unresolved issue in this self-study and in the original study. The divergent theoretical backgrounds that form the narratives and academic identities of each individual are not congruent in regards to rigor.

Zanna: I still believe we "mined" for data supporting our pre-existing notions about the students involved in the study.

Carolyn: I disagree--The search for disconfirming data was as essential to the analysis as establishing the categories of like-responses.

Cindy: I have some articles in my office on qualitative research and rigor—I can run and get them (exit stage left).

Narrator: Our understandings of rigor seemed to drive each of us to learn from the others' perspectives. Carolyn went back and looked for places she might have "mined" given she had a continuing relationship with the cohort of students in the original study. Zanna stuck to her guns—distrusting or discounting her objectivity. Cindy, very excited by this difference in approach to data sets, was eager to explore the ethics of research and rigor.

Scene 2: Armed with References

(CC, ZM, CL enter Center stage, stage right and stage left each carrying more books and papers and bags than they can hold.)

Narrator: Each researcher seemed certain about her perspective on ethics and literally brought to the table a shield of literature (journals, papers, internet sites, and books) to protect her positions. This strategy, which was not on the day's work agenda, did not sway any of the researchers from their original opinions. Our inability to sway caused us to wonder if we were having any impact on our students by having them read the same literature we held up as seminal in the field. We were expecting our students to sway; yet in our collaboration, we were resistant to change.

Carolyn: (unloading a bag from each shoulder, overstuffed purse and laptop with internet bookmarks of references) If we are resistant to change, or what we are calling "sway," then it only makes sense that our students would be, too. Think about how they react to and process the reams of information we provide them.

Cindy: (setting neatly stacked folders and books to her left) What factors have ever changed us from our strongly held beliefs?

Zanna: (plops an overwhelming stack of books on the table and floor, out of breath from having hauled them up in her arms from the library across campus) What causes us to explore more carefully the consequences for our students who do not conform or sway toward our particular belief system within the timeframe of a semester?

Narrator: Leading the examined life, AKA--Self-study! (Narrator takes a bow)

Scene 3: Making Meaning Through the Invisible Researcher

Narrator: Recognizing our resistance to swaying or changing gave rise to the Invisible Researcher as a tool to give voice and shape our concerns for ethics and professionalism. The Invisible Researcher took on the voice of "the other." It wasn't *us* questioning each other, it was the potential questions from others or what a colleague might question. Through deeply intense discourse, we were energized to resolve our tensions through meaning-making. The Invisible Researcher, at that point, embodied the true scholar, who breathes life into understanding through debate and discussion. Here are three separate examples of intense discourse with which we challenged each other: Cindy's from early in the process, Zanna's in the middle, and Carolyn's just prior to the original study's first conference presentation.

Cindy: I had this great vision for a metaphor watching the trees in my back yard sway in the breeze—the students are swaying back and forth like the trees between what they believed to be true about teaching and what we (the breeze) are telling them is true!

Zanna: Hey guys—I'm uncertain about our methodology. Do you think it is possible that we are pulling what we want out of our data to support our agenda? Are we just looking for evidence that the students are "swaying"?

Carolyn: I'm no better than our students! I can't sway! Cindy, I'm not understanding this "foregrounding" and how it fits into our work. I know what it is in theater terms—but not getting it here. I'm not comfortable answering questions that might come up at the conference.

INTERMISSION

- How do we use self-study to transform from resistant professionals into the "true scholar" who is able to synthesize ideas through debate and discussion?
- In collaborative self-study, do we always synthesize our beliefs or are there times when they stand separate?

Act III Who Are We as Academic Writers?

Scene 1: A New Voice = The Blending of Our Individual Voices

Narrator: As the data set took on character and the drafting process wiped out idiosyncratic phrasing, a new voice emerged in the writing. The narrative was no longer recognizable as any one of us—each researcher's contribution, cognition, and character merged and emerged as a clear new voice.

Zanna: (reading from a manuscript draft) We say here that "we define *sway* as candidates' oscillation in thinking as they contemplate what they perceive as their certainties and uncertainties in their understandings about teaching and learning."

Cindy: Wow! That's really good! It's exactly what we want.

Carolyn: That's brilliant! Who wrote that?

All: (looking at each other) I don't know!

Scene 2: Three Heads Are Better Than One—Or Even Two

Narrator: This new voice would not have been as powerful if any of the players were missing or if the administrative choices along the way had been made differently. It was through our writing that we recognized the birth of a new voice. We began to call this new voice, The Invisible Researcher. This entity, who we have come to envision as a superhero, embodied our combined theoretical underpinnings, our thoughts, our sense of humor, and our hearts. This conversation defines our superhero further:

Carolyn: The work became our work, not her part and my part.

Cindy: Our understanding of the value of a democratic group process and the writing process transformed our voices. We wrote together, but we also each took turns "possessing" the manuscript and rewriting/revising/re-visioning parts.

Carolyn: Then we'd pass the manuscript on with comments and track changes for each other to clarify, question, debate, and so on. We encouraged and used the writing process to help us think. Our manuscript drafts became a tool for our original study of preservice teachers and for our self-study research.

Zanna: As we made choices along the way through these processes, a new voice was born representing each of our backgrounds, beliefs, thoughts, and passions. We each choose to develop this relationship with each other, perhaps because of our divergent goals.

Scene 3: The Invisible Researcher Is Invited to the Table

Narrator: Recognizing the existence of the Invisible Researcher seemed to give him (more on that later) additional superpowers. We began to imagine ourselves with lasers set, not on stun, but WAKE-UP in front of our morning or after-lunch classes. We began to carry on conversations in our heads with others on the Starship, trying to "Go where no one has gone before" AND bring our students with us! We invited the Invisible Researcher into our research, our writing, our teaching, and our daily interactions with colleagues and candidates.

Here is an example of how our superhero helped us clarify his (we'll deal with this pronoun shortly) possible nemesis, the Ghost Teacher, an entity we were beginning to discuss as our candidates' ideal past teacher. Here is how it went:

Cindy: It just seems like our students rustle around. We think they are swaying and reframing new identities for themselves as educators, but they are not. There is something that keeps them root bound and stagnant.

Carolyn: Yes, they just never seem to be willing to change their basic schemata. They think they know what good teaching is because they remember their favorite teacher as perfect and attempt to emulate her.

Zanna: Yeah, it is like the opposite of our hero, the Invisible Researcher, who is more than each of us and more even than the sum of our parts. They have a superhero, and it is that memory of the "perfect teacher." The Ghost Teacher! We need to make a graphic novel about this!

Cindy: The Invisible Researcher takes on the Ghost Teacher!!

Carolyn: Yeah, they can't even reach disequilibrium about what it means to teach, because they can't see anything wrong with the way they were taught. They see no need for a new schemata. Their Ghost Teacher is always perfect, always right, and we "academics" just don't have a grip on reality!

Zanna: Wouldn't it be great somehow if we could get them to come to ways of developing a group voice like we have? They could build from each others' experiences and clarify how their Ghost Teacher fits within the world of readings and ideas we offer them.

Carolyn: The group process is far more complex than I knew. I've been expecting my students to do seamless presentations where you couldn't tell who produced what. I didn't truly understand just how that happens until our project—I didn't realize how much effort and patience it actually requires to write so that the reader or audience cannot tell who produced what part.

Cindy: Yes, it really is like there is another, more powerful voice that has come into being when we write, the Invisible Researcher almost seems real.

Zanna: It's the coming together of ideas in a voice that represents a synthesis of the ideas of the group. We each don't recognize it as our own voice; and, therefore, don't recognize who wrote what.

Narrator: In the Summer of 2008, as we gathered to prepare for this conference, this conversation took place.

Cindy: Do you see the Invisible Researcher as a being?

Zanna & Carolyn: (look at each other and hesitate) Yeah.

Cindy: Male or female? I see it as male.

Zanna & Carolyn: (hesitating) Yeah, I guess, male.

Cindy: Doesn't that bother you? We're all female, yet we've created a superhero that supposedly represents us and we've each, without even talking about it, imagined it as a male. What does that mean?

Zanna: It means we've given the power to the typical prototype gender for power...the male.

Cindy: We've bought into the Good Ole Boys Club vision of power.
Carolyn: So from now on, the Invisible Researcher for us is female.
Cindy & Zanna: Agreed!

INTERMISSION

- How does the writing process act as a tool for your research?
- What has to happen in a collaborative self-study to allow the Invisible Researcher to erase the dividing lines between participants? In particular what should the writing process and the group process look like? Is it always democratic?

Act IV Who Are We as Colleagues?

Scene 1 Stop Talking—I Can't Type That Fast

Narrator: Collaboration silenced or gave voice to each participant. The sheer volume of ideas emerging through prior knowledge overwhelms the process. The first instance of silencing was quite literal: we were using overlapping speech and stream of consciousness in a group writing session. Cindy, the self-appointed typist, literally could not keep up with the flow of ideas. This technical/mechanical issue, however, dramatically changed the process and ultimately the product. How many shifts in thinking opportunities to sway were lost in only offering well-healed, thought-through arguments formulated while the typist caught up? One researcher would forget her brilliant argument moments after it was offered. This silenced another researcher who became the self-appointed historian for the group conversations—again, in an effort to produce a piece of writing for publishing purposes—and less and less a contributor within that context.

Zanna: Bahktin tells us that this process of meaning making is as constant as the wind. Our current understandings are shaped by our codified past responses, which in turn position, define, and/or limit our future responses.

Carolyn: These theorists ought to get out more and talk to each other. That is no different from the constructivist approach.

Cindy: Stop talking—I can't type that fast! (Silence as the sound of typing fills the air)

Zanna: Now, what did I say?

Scene 2 Voices Are Silenced

Narrator: Much later in the process, voices are silenced by the need to get the paper out of an "inbox" or working papers folder. Others' opinions are not solicited perhaps in fear of yet another stall in the process. Alternatively, it could be a deep trust evolved among the players that individual decisions would be made only with the others' best interests in mind.

Cindy: Should we ask Zanna to work on this?

Carolyn: Naw, she's trying to get organized for her move to Vietnam. She won't mind.

Narrator: Later in the year...

Cindy: Look over this draft. Let's get this out.

Carolyn: Okay, but I don't think it's ready yet.

Narrator: Article is rejected.

Carolyn: I knew it wasn't ready. At least I now know I can trust my instinct on scholarly writing.

Cindy: I don't think rejection is a bad thing. It's just feedback. Because we had different thoughts about where the manuscript was going, we needed outsiders' input. Collaborative writing can be piece meal. It's hard to see where to start when you're required to start in the middle. Reviewers offer a fresh perspective that we can't see anymore because we're so engrained in it.

Scene 3 Learning to Share

Narrator: Our interaction leads each to "dig deeply" into personal understandings. Though we each learned to share in many respects, we believe we have yet to sway in our approach and understanding of the collaborative research process. Communications between researchers give evidence indicating that each researcher failed to be swayed in her certainties or misgivings about the analysis and reporting of the data. However, personal growth is clear and evident as indicated in the next act.

Carolyn: I adapted instruction to more gently unveil the realities of education, honoring the reverence that students come with for their Ghost Teacher.

Cindy: I adapted to the tempos of my colleagues non-linear lives, and grew to greatly appreciate how their minds wondered from great idea to great idea without clear bridges and pathways.

Zanna: I find there is honor in taking on more of a leadership role and not viewing administrative responsibilities as trivial or unimportant.

Narrator: The Invisible Researcher became a means of transforming our self-perspectives as we reflected on where "We" stood in position to our individual and colleagues' perceptions. Individually, Carolyn, Cindy and Zanna oscillated between their certainties and uncertainties as the new voice of "We" evolved in the writing with each re-visioning of the research, analysis, and manner in which we wanted to present what we had learned from the collaborative process.

INTERMISSION

– As instructors, how many shifts in thinking opportunities--sway--are lost in only offering well-healed, thought-through lectures? How do we genuinely respect

our students' positions when they are counter to or foreign from our own point-of-view?
- How do we get the Invisible Self-reflective Researcher within our students to counter-balance that iconic Ghost Teacher?

Act V Who Am I Now?

Scene 1 Personal Growth

Narrator: We conclude our drama with insights into our personal growth from this experience.
Cindy: One of us learns to be more respectful of others' sense of time.
Carolyn & Zanna (spoken together): Two of us learn to take on responsibilities we'd rather abdicate.
Cindy, Carolyn, & Zanna (spoken together): All of us learn to recognize the stranger within each of us, who is perhaps inflexible and resists negotiating or even networking with The Invisible Researcher.
Cindy: We discovered within ourselves a stranger.

Scene 2 The Stranger Within

Narrator: Coming to know this stranger's strengths, leadership qualities, gaps of understanding, ambitions, and goals, reshaped who we were and wanted to become. In every relationship the individuals must either assimilate or accommodate the other's world view or the relationship will fall apart—such is the case here.
Carolyn: Why am I the only one who cares about this project? (turn away from group)
Cindy: What, am I the only one working on this project? (turn away from group)
Zanna: Remind me. What is it we're working on here? Sorry, I was on the other side of the world. (unaware others have turned away)

Scene 3 March Forward

Narrator: The opportunity to fall apart and just walk away presented itself on numerous occasions. However, the choice was always to march forward, interestingly not merely for the pursuit of tenure. Each took a leadership role at some point, each questioned other's ambitions and drive, each explored more fully their understanding of their own beliefs, and each attempted to understand better the other's theoretical underpinnings.
Carolyn: Guys, I sent this off to the Castle Conference. Hope you don't mind.
Cindy: Guys, we are accepted in *Spectrum,* with revisions. Hope you don't mind.
Zanna: Guys, I just love that you value my input and are keeping me on track while I pursue Vietnam. Hope you don't mind.

Narrator: The synergistic energy created by the manifestation of the Invisible Researcher became the driving force. Our collaborative process only wobbled when we retreated to our caves and worked alone. As individuals each player had strengths; however, it was through working as a team that our weaknesses were forged and we were made stronger.

The Invisible Researcher came to the party and helped to reshape each individual's perspective and understanding. The Invisible Researcher ensured the collaborative process remained democratic, progressive, and meaningful. The Invisible Researcher was, after all, *US*. And, those are the values we collectively and respectfully brought to the oak tables that scaffolded our work.

EPILOGUE

Consider these questions as you close this Readers' Theater and this book:
- How do we avoid defaulting to old habits and familiar caves? How do we help our students see the caves they are hiding in? How do we forge in our students a desire to be true scholars?
- How did self-study give birth to the Invisible Researcher? What merit does the Invisible Researcher have in self-study research? Can recognition of the Invisible Researcher add rigor to self-study methodology?

CURTAIN CALL

Inspired by self-study, this is who we are today:

Empowered voices in our fields. One researcher finds her strength in collaborative processes on a grand scale. She has found a powerful voice in academe through becoming an editor for a scholarly journal and an author and editor of several books in the field of education. Another researcher discovers her voice has value through writing and presentation of plays, poetry, and academic articles on an international scale. One researcher literally learns to speak in a new voice, as she learns to share and negotiate her professional understandings and certainties in an Asian culture.

More empathic practitioners. Each of us became far more cognizant of the impact of assignments on her students. One becomes much more explicit as to learning objectives and helps students conduct their own self-study of group process activities. Another actively explores less traditional read/lecture/lab instructional choices hoping to find more effective means of promoting sway in her students.

Involved professionals. Through the process of reframing this self-study from a presentation piece into a work intended to be read, it became clear that each researcher in her own way became a brave spirit embarking on a new professional path. For each individual, this self-study helped to illuminate the need to change career focus. The paths we chose are very different, but each equally empowering to our selves. We recognize our collaborative self-study and the Invisible Researcher's supportive guidance as instrumental in making this empowerment possible.

THE END

Notes

In the writing of this play we have each "put words in each other's mouths" as Bahktin would have it to make meaning of the discourse. We have to consider the meaning the audience would make. Therefore, the dialogue is often paraphrased for emphasis and distilled for clarity.

Conclusions/Interpretations

The adage "the whole is greater than the sum of its parts" is manifest in this collaboration. The parts: one is a natural at the big picture, one is brilliant with critical inquiry; one is skilled at administrative detail; two are Shakespearen in turn of phrase; two are associative thinkers; two are addicted to writing; three are exhausted by the march to tenure. When we add all the parts, energy is created, creativity restored, and the will to keep marching is revived. As the collaboration takes on more elements of community, it becomes stronger, more powerful, and efficient. The project reduces much of the isolation of professing and living in a world populated by words and worried undergraduates. Given that these undergraduates are one of the *parts* to consider—what does this revelation mean for them?

As instructors, preparing future teachers for a workforce that demands ever more collaborative projects, we need to scaffold the skills and mindset needed to be successful. We learned from this self-study that
- the combination of individuals is not as important as helping them capitalize on each other's strengths;
- each individual's strengths need to be valued equally;
- a collective plan of action needs to be established;
- members need individual and overlapping tasks to keep the project moving; and
- a sense of *Our Work* verses *My Work* has to be established so the magic, creativity, and insights occur.

This is where The Invisible Researcher comes to the party and helps to reshape each individual's perspective and understanding. The Invisible Researcher ensured the collaborative process remained democratic, progressive, and meaningful. The Invisible Researcher was, after all, *US*. And, those are the values we collectively and respectfully brought to the table.

REFERENCES

Allender, J. S., & Allender, D. S. (2008). *The humanistic teacher: First the child, then curriculum.* Boulder, CO: Paradigm Publishers.

Cochran-Smith, M. (2003). *Teaching and teacher education.*

ABOUT THE EDITORS

Cindy Lassonde, Ph.D., is Associate Professor in the Elementary Education and Reading Department of the Division of Education at the State University of New York College at Oneonta in the United States. Cindy teaches undergraduate and graduate courses in literacy. Her research interests include positional identities, writing, and, of course, self-study of teacher education practices. She is editor of the New York Association of Colleges for Teacher Education's journal *Excelsior: Leadership in Teaching and Learning* and co-editor with Susan Israel of *Teachers Taking Action: A Comprehensive Guide to Teacher Research* (IRA, 2008) and *The Ethical Education* (Peter Lang, 2008). Email: Lassonc@oneonta.edu

Sally A. C. Galman, Ph.D., is Assistant Professor in the departments Teacher Education and Curriculum Studies and Child and Family Studies in the School of Education at the University of Massachusetts at Amherst in the United States. An award-winning cartoonist and visual artist as well as coordinator of the Collaborative Teacher Education Program at U-Mass, Sally is interested in bringing the transformative power of the image to bear on her work in teacher education. Her current research focuses on preservice teachers, gender, and identity development. She is the author of *Shane, the Lone Ethnographer*, a comic book guide to ethnography for novice researchers. Email: sally@educ.umass.edu

Clare Kosnik is Associate Professor and Head of the Centre for Teacher Development in the Department of Curriculum, Teaching and Learning at the Ontario Institute for Studies in Education, University of Toronto (OISE/UT). She was recently the Executive Director of the Teachers for a New Era project at Stanford University. Previously, she was the Director of the Elementary Preservice Program at OISE/UT. She also taught and supervised in the Midtown preservice program at OISE/UT. She has recently co-authored the text, *Innovations in teacher education: A social constructivist approach* for SUNY Press and co-edited the Springer text, *Making a difference in teacher education through self-study: Studies of personal, professional, and program renewal.* She is currently co-editing another text for Springer on learning communities. Professor Kosnik recently completed a term as Chair of the Self-Study of Teacher Education Practices Special Interest Group of the American Education Research Association. She was Co-Chair of the Program Committee for the Fourth International Conference of the Self-Study of Teacher Education Practices SIG in 2002. She continues to use her research on her program to inform practice and policy. Email: ckosnik@oise.utoronto.ca

ABOUT THE CONTRIBUTORS

Carolyn Chryst is Assistant Professor in the Elementary Education and Reading Department at SUNY College at Oneonta in upstate New York. She has a varied career path (actress/director, zoo curator, exhibit designer, college educator), which has lead her to focus on education reform efforts that improve teaching practices (kindergarten through college) and that support the learner's curiosity and innate love of learning. She has presented a workshop on "Infusing Theater Across the Curriculum" and co-authored a play for science discovery centers. She has also published several articles on constructivist approaches in teacher education. Email: chrystc@oneonta.edu

Darlene Ciuffetelli Parker, Ph.D., is Assistant Professor of Education at Brock University in Hamilton, Ontario, Canada. Her research focuses on narrative inquiry and self-study which includes interest in: literacy teacher development; initial teacher education, and; school and educational communities. Dr. Ciuffetelli Parker currently is a principal investigator of a funded province-wide research project exploring success stories of school communities affected by poverty. The research grant is supported by the Elementary Teachers Federation of Ontario, Canada. She is co-editor of Brock Education Journal with Dr. Julian Kitchen. Email: dciuffetelli-parker@brocku.ca

Yiola Cleovoulou is a doctoral student in Curriculum, Teaching and Learning at the Ontario Institute for Studies in Education. Her major research interests are in the areas of social inclusive pedagogy and urban schooling, elementary school teacher practices, and the study of teacher education. Her recent publications include: A Practicum Experience in Teacher Education (VDM Verlag Dr. Muller, 2008; A whole-school approach to urban educational renewal: Community, collaboration, and leadership, In A. Samaras, C. Beck, C. Kosnik, & A. Freese. (Eds.) Learning communities in practice , with Beck and Kosnik (Dordetcht: Springer Academic Publishers, 2008); Socially inclusive pedagogy in literacy education: Fostering inclusion in the inner city, Journal of Urban Learning, Teaching and Research, 2008. Email: ycleovoulou@oise.utoronto.ca

Lesley Coia, Ph.D., is Associate Professor and chair of the education department at Agnes Scott College, Georgia, USA. Her research focuses on the use of co/ autoethnographic methods in the self-study of teacher education practices. She is the co-author with Monica Taylor of numerous papers including: From the inside out, and the outside in: Co/autoethnography as a means of professional renewal (2006), Revisiting feminist authority through a co/autoethnographic lens (2006), and Complicating our identities as urban teachers: A co/autoethnography (2006). Email: lcoia@agnesscott.edu

Cheryl J. Craig, Ph.D., is a Professor in the Department of Curriculum and Instruction at the University of Houston where she serves as the Director of Elementary Education and the Coordinator of Teaching and Teacher Education. Craig serves on the Editorial Boards of Reflective Practice, Teachers and Teaching: Theory and Practice, and the International Journal of Education and the Arts. She also is the Co-Editor of the ATE Yearbook. Craig is the author of many handbook chapters and several articles that have been published in the field's most esteemed journals. Email: ccraig@uh.edu

Ronnie Davey is Principal Lecturer, English Education at the University of Canterbury College of Education, Christchurch, New Zealand. Ronnie taught English in Secondary Schools before becoming a teacher educator 15 years ago. Her research interests are in English education, literacy, critical literacy, teacher education and new technologies in education. Ronnie's doctoral study is an investigation of preservice teacher educators' professional identity in a time of structural change. Email: ronnie.davey@canterbury.ac.nz

Lynnette Erickson is a teacher educator in the McKay School of Education at Brigham Young University. After teaching elementary school for seven years, she received her MA from Brigham Young University and later her PhD from Arizona State University. Lynnette served in the Department of Teacher Education as associate chair for over seven years. During that time many of her responsibilities pertained to the ongoing issues of accreditation. Lynnette's professional interests and research focus on understanding the roles of teachers and teacher educators and teaching social studies in elementary classrooms, particularly the implementation of democratic characteristics and practices in the public schools. She has recently become involved in self-study and narrative research methodologies to explore and reflect upon her own practices as a teacher educator. Lynnette has published in the areas of teacher education, social studies education, and self-study research. Email: Lynnette_Erickson@byu.edu

Allan Feldman, Ph.D. is a Professor in the Teacher Education and Curriculum Studies Department of the School of Education at the University of Massachusetts at Amherst in the United States. His research focuses on the nature of self-study, action research, and how people learn to do research. He has written numerous papers on self-study and action research, as well as on science teacher education. He is a co-author of the book, "Teachers Investigate Their Work: An Introduction to Action Research Across the Professions." He has been PI and co-PI of numerous NSF projects, most of which have incorporated action research. Before receiving his doctorate he taught middle and high school science for 17 years in public and private schools in New York, New Jersey and Pennsylvania. Email: afeldman@educ.umass.edu

Tim Fletcher is a doctoral student at the Ontario Institute for Studies in Education of the University of Toronto, whose current work focuses on physical education teacher education in Canada. He has published and presented several papers at the national and international level, including a monograph on student attitudes and grouping strategies in physical education. Prior to starting his PhD, Tim taught in schools in Ontario for six years, as well as a period in the pre-service teacher education program at the University of New England in Australia. Email: tfletcher@oise.utoronto.ca

Anne R. Freese, Ph.D., teaches at the University of Hawai'i in the Department of Curriculum Studies. She received the University of Hawai'i President's Award for Excellence in Teaching in 2000 and the Board of Regent's Medal for Excellence in Teaching in 2006. Her recent publications include *Self-Study of Teaching Practices*, co-authored with Anastasia P. Samaras, 2006, *Learning Communities In Practice* (co-editor, 2008), *Making a Difference in Teacher Education through Self Study* (co-editor, 2006) and a chapter in *The Missing Links in Teacher Education Design* (Gary Hoban, Ed., 2005). Email: freese@hawaii.edu

Vince Ham is Director of Research at CORE Education, an independent not-for-profit research and development centre specializing in teacher professional development and new technologies in education. Vince has been involved in teacher education in various guises for the last twenty years. His research interests are in teacher mentoring and professional learning, new technologies in education and research methods, especially action research and self-study. Email: vince@core-ed.net

Julian Kitchen, Ph.D., is Assistant Professor of Education at Brock University in Hamilton, Ontario, Canada. In his research, Dr. Kitchen uses self-study, narrative inquiry and mixed qualitative methodologies to study on teacher education, induction and development. He is currently engaged in Social Sciences and Humanities Research Council of Canada funded research projects on teacher induction and Aboriginal education. Dr. Kitchen is President of the S-STEP Special Interest Group of the Canadian Association of Teacher Educators and a member of the Internatinal Advisory Board of Studying Teacher Education. He is co-editor of *Brock Education Journal* with Dr. Darlene Ciuffetelli Parker. Email: jkitchen@brocku.ca

John Loughran is the Foundation Chair in Curriculum and Pedagogy in the Faculty of Education, Monash University. His research has spanned both science education and the related fields of professional knowledge, reflective practice and teacher research. John is the co-editor of Studying Teacher Education and his recent books include Developing a pedagogy of teacher education: Understanding teaching and learning about teaching (2006) with Routledge; Understanding and developing science teachers' pedagogical content knowledge (Loughran, Berry & Mulhall,

2006) with Sense Publishers; and The international handbook of self-study of teaching and teacher education practices (Loughran et al., 2004) with Kluwer.

Zanna D. McKay, Ph.D., is Assistant Professor in the Department of Elementary Education and Reading at the State University of New York College at Oneonta, where she teaches Diversity in Education and History and Philosophy of Education. McKay has taught in Africa and is currently completing a two-year sabbatical teaching in Vietnam. She has had articles published in the fields esteemed journals. Email: mckayz@oneonta.edu

Patricia Paugh, Ph.D., is Assistant Professor in the Curriculum and Instruction Department at the University of Massachusetts Boston. Her research interests include school-university research partnerships, equitable access to academic literacy for students in high poverty, linguistically and culturally diverse communities, critical literacy, and the value of practitioner research in teachers' professional development. She is co-author of A Classroom Teacher's Guide to Struggling Readers with Curt Dudley-Marling. She has also published several articles based on collaborative research projects with classroom teachers in urban public schools. Email: patricia.paugh@umb.edu

Stefinee Pinnegar, a teacher educator in the McKay School of Education at Brigham Young University began her teaching career working on the Navajo Reservation in Arizona. She received her Ph D from the University of Arizona. She and a group of her fellow graduate students (the Arizona Group) were founders of the Self-Study in Teacher Education Practices research movement. As acting dean of the Invisible College for Research on Teaching, she is concerned with developing conversations about research on teaching and teacher education. She is most interested in what and how teachers know as teachers and the research methodologies such as self-study and narrative that allow investigation in tacit memory and practical knowledge. She has published in the areas of teacher education, narrative, and self-study research and research methodology. Email: Stefinee.pinnegar@byu.edu

Elizabeth Robinson is a doctoral student in the Language Literacy and Culture Program at the University of Massachusetts, Amherst. Her research focuses on ESL teachers and the impact of research on their teaching practices within current high-stakes, neoliberal US public school environments. Elizabeth is an instructor and the coordinator of student teaching in the Education Studies Program at Suffolk University. Email: earobins@educ.umass.edu

Tom Russell is a Professor in the Faculty of Education at Queen's University, where he also holds the 2007 Chair in Teaching and Learning. He is an editor of Studying Teacher Education: A journal of self-study of teacher education practices. Recently edited books (with John Loughran) include Enacting a Pedagogy of Teacher Education (Routledge, 2007) and Improving Teacher Education Practices through Self-Study (RoutledgeFalmer, 2002). He is also a co-editor of the International Handbook of Self-Study of Teaching and Teacher Education Practices (Kluwer, 2004). Tom is particularly interested in action research for the improvement of teaching. His teaching includes preservice courses in physics methods and practicum supervision. Email: russellt@queensu.ca

Anastasia P. Samaras, Ph.D., is Associate Professor in the Graduate School of Education at George Mason University and has served as director of several teacher education programs. Anastasia's research and teaching include self-study research, Neo-Vygotskian curricula applications, and arts-based self-study pedagogies. She is author of *Self-Study for Teacher Educators* (2002), co-author with Anne R. Freese of *Self-Study of Teaching Practices* (2006), and co-editor with Clare Kosnik, Clive Beck, and Anne R. Freese of *Making a Difference in Teacher Education through Self-Study* (2006), and *Learning Communities In Practice* (2008). Email: asamaras@gmu.edu

Dusti Strub is a senior attending the State University of New York College at Oneonta. Her major is Childhood Education certifying in grades one through six with a concentration in Liberal Arts. She has worked as a teacher assistant for an undergraduate literacy course. Dusti also works at an elementary after-school program during the school year and at an elementary daycare program during the summer. She enjoys creating children's books by writing and illustrating stories she hopes to publish in the future. Email: strudr12@oneonta.edu

Monica Taylor, Ph.D., is Associate Professor in the Department of Curriculum and Teaching at Montclair State University in New Jersey, USA. Her research focuses on the use of co/autoethnographic methods in the self-study of teacher education practices. She is the co-author with Lesley Coia of numerous papers including: From the inside out, and the outside in: Co/autoethnography as a means of professional renewal (2006), Revisiting feminist authority through a co/autoethnographic lens (2006), and Complicating our identities as urban teachers: A co/autoethnography (2006). She recently edited a book titled Whole Language Teaching, Whole Hearted Practice: Looking Back, Looking Forward (2007). Email: taylorm@mail. montclair.edu.

INDEX

LaVergne, TN USA
05 November 2009
163229LV00002B/7/P